More Praise for *Simple Fun for Busy People*

"An ingenious solution for parents, especially those feeling overwhelmed with scheduling constraints, who not only want to get closer to their kids and to each other, but have more fun in the own lives as well."

—Jerry D. Pollard, Vice President, Discovery Toys

"Chock-full of refreshing pastimes that will energize your family, shed new light on misunderstandings, and turn the daily grind into joyful together-ness."

**—Judy Ford, author of *Wonderful Ways to Love a Child*
and *Wonderful Ways to Love a Teen***

"Our own experience, as well as research, tells us that one of the most important things we can do to help families cohere is to make it easier for them to play together ... And most families badly want this themselves, but have given up for lack of time and/or, in the case of the more than 12 million families in America below the poverty line, for lack of money. *Simple Fun for Busy People* provides an enormously creative solution to both of these problems—time and money."

**—Kathy Baxter, Executive Director, San Francisco Child
Abuse Council**

"Being a busy mother and a teacher who's tried out a lot of activity books, I was delighted to see this one. It's wonderful. Its ideas are more useful, edu-cational, and entertaining than any book I know."

**—Arena Sagranichne, special-education and fourth-grade
teacher and mother of two girls**

"There are several other good activity books out there. But this is the first one I can actually use almost anytime of the day or night, no matter what I am doing with my kids or spouse, whether it's cooking, eating dinner, shopping, doing chores. . . really anything, even arguing. And simple, clear directions make these games and activities some of the easiest to use of the family activity books I've seen."

**—Diane Brodkey, third- to fifth-grade schoolteacher
and mother of a six-year-old daughter and an eight-
year-old son**

"As both a teacher and a single mom, Simple Fun for Busy People is the first book I've ever found that meets my needs to have fun with my child without having to find extra time, to have fun that I enjoy, too and, last but not least, that offers terrific basic skill development for my kid."

　　　—**Lois Glass, third grade elementary school teacher**

"I never knew my husband could be so playful!"

　　　　　—**Pat Cambanes, wife and mother of five (Brooklyn Park, Minnesota), after playing a *Simple Fun for Busy People* dinner game**

"I love *Simple Fun for Busy People* because it gives me permission to be silly with my wife and kids! I used to keep my crazy ideas in. Now I let them out and we all have a ball!"

　　　　　—**Ben Elliott (Washington, D.C.) attorney, husband, and father of two seventeen year olds (boy and girl) and a seven-year-old boy**

Simple Fun

for

Busy People

• • • •

333 Free Ways to Enjoy
Your Loved Ones
More in the Time You Have

GARY KRANE PH.D.

Foreword by John Bradshaw

MJF BOOKS

NEW YORK

All the author's post-tax net proceeds from this book and related products go to organizations that help prevent child abuse, increase democracy, and protect our environment.

Published by MJF Books
Fine Communications
Two Lincoln Square
60 West 66th Street
New York, NY 10023

Simple Fun for Busy People
ISBN 1-56731-342-6

Disclaimer: The author, publisher, and distributors of this book disclaim any liability of loss directly or indirectly in connection with the physical and psychological exercises, games, and advice herein. Please consult your physician before beginning any of the physical games herein. People with serious emotional stress or disturbance should avoid any of the role-playing or dramatic games in this book, particularly those in Chapters 10 and 15.

Cover photo: Courtesy of SuperStock
Figure on page 21 is courtesy of M. Csikszentmihalyi
Book design: Suzanne Albertson

This edition published by arrangement with Conari Press.

Manufactured in the United States of America on acid-free paper

MJF Books and the MJF colophon are trademarks of Fine Creative Media, Inc.

10   9   8   7   6   5   4   3   2   1

This book is dedicated to

my mother and father,
Rhea B. and David I. Krane,

to the poetic genius in all of us,

and

to all those fellow activists
who struggle to help others
less fortunate
have an equal opportunity to
create their own lives.

Simple Fun for Busy People

The Games:

Foreword

Having spent so many years focused on helping people heal their wounds caused from childhood, I am always delighted to see a visionary effort to encourage the kind of parent/child interaction that fosters, rather than stifles, the "inner child." I applaud this book for its marvelous achievement toward that goal. *Simple Fun for Busy People* promotes humor, playfulness, spontaneity, and creativity. It shows us how to make our lives poetic by transforming daily events into hilarious and often even sublime moments—moment by moment.

The best way to cure an ill is to prevent it from happening in the first place. The vicious cycle must be broken before our multi-generational ills can stop robbing children of their childhood—which is their birthright.

One of the most important things we know about children is that they have an inherent need to play. Play is to children what work is to an adult. In my book *Homecoming* I talk about reclaiming your "wonder child." Your wonder child's natural state is creativity and play fosters creativity. Getting in touch with creativity is more than a homecoming. It is the discovery of your essence, your deepest self.

Many traditions say that we are created in the image of God. And what is God-like? It's being creative. Creativity is the glory of being human. It is what distinguishes us from all other created beings. Our human destiny is to create our own unique lifestyle. You may do it as a parent by challenging the "old order" or by refusing to play a designated cultural role. Some of the childlike qualities that I talk about in *Homecoming* that foster creativity are: playfulness, spontaneity, the ability to live in the now, the ability to experience wonder, to concentrate, the capacity to be one's own focus of evaluation, and a sense of satisfaction with oneself.

Creating your own life takes the courage to risk new ways of being. So creativity is closely related to success, which I see as doing what you want with your one and only life—finding your bliss. This takes creativity and courage. Each of us must find our own style. We are our own work of art.

Most folks aren't aware of their creative power because they stay congealed in the frozen grief of their wounded child. "The mass of mankind live lives of quiet desperation," says Thoreau. They will never get in touch with their uniqueness because their awe, wonder, and ability to be creative have been lost in childhood. It's a tragedy that many will go to their death, having never lived, and do not know who they are. Cardinal John Henry Newman said, "I don't fear that I will die. I fear that I may never have begun to live."

The tremendous loss that many of us must grieve is the loss of our childhood. And yet we compound the problem by continuing to deprive ourselves of play. We have a false dichotomy that says, "Okay, you're an adult now, so buckle down, get serious, and be responsible." And that's our problem—we're far too serious. It's impossible to live in the moment, another childlike quality, when we're so serious.

I was looking at some pictures one day of my family vacation at Snowmass. I was on the trip, but I totally missed it! Why? Well, I was so busy planning and worrying the whole time that I was absolutely not in the moment—I was somewhere else. And so I decided that as long as I live, this will never happen to me again. We must live life in the moment, while we have it. Because this moment is all we have.

I was brought up to believe that life was a sort of gloom. Isn't that terrible? Religion has, unfortunately, conveyed to us that this life is a "Valley of Tears" and that happiness doesn't come until we die. What a crock! I was taught that to be holy meant you had to be a conformist. You had to walk, talk, and act a certain narrow way in order to be acceptable to God. There was a lady in church who my mother said was holy. But to me, as a child, she just looked like she had gas!

One of my favorite people, Nietzsche, said, "I can only believe in a God who dances. And if they want me to believe in their God, they have to sing me better songs."

T. S. Elliot said, "Do I dare disturb the Universe? Every new creation disturbs the Universe a little bit, and brings something new and novel." Each of us is uniquely

qualified and endowed by our creator to impact the Universe. It, too, is our birthright.

I believe, in fact, that doing something new, or being creative, is the answer to violence. Parents and politicians would do well to find ways to stimulate creativity as a solution to teenage violence. When kids are being creative, they are getting in touch with something far deeper than their socio-cultural adaptations. I've been involved in teaching photography to boys in the ghetto, who get totally absorbed in the creative process. Being creative and being destructive are mutually exclusive of each other—they cannot coexist.

Kids need to be encouraged to be themselves, which means being playful, spontaneous, curious, creative, and resilient. Had they been encouraged to be themselves as children, they would not be involved in violence and destruction, but rather in celebration and creation.

Beyond the pressures and stresses of being parents, breadwinners, chief cooks, and bottle washers, we can find a way to temper the seriousness of it all with humor. We are the only species who knows how to laugh. Isn't that wonderful? We can be dedicated, totally committed, seriously involved—and still laugh at ourselves! We need to adopt the attitude of laughter. We'll definitely live longer and be a whole lot happier.

We learn from Ashley Montague, in *Growing Young,* that civilizations surviving the longest maintained the qualities of childhood. As a species, we must experience a reconnection to our inner child or we will self-destruct. And this is why I am recommending *Simple Fun for Busy People* to you. It is a big step in the right direction, a "wonder-filled" homage to creativity in everyday life.

The beauty of the *Simple Fun for Busy People* is that most of the activities don't require extra planning. And it doesn't require money—you already have what it takes in your home and in your hearts and minds. The activities fit into your daily routines, from getting up in the morning to eating dinner to going to bed at night, and unlike other activity books I've seen, most of the games are as much fun for parents as they are for kids, some even more so!

"We shall not cease from exploration, and the end of all our exploring will be to arrive where we started and know the place for the first time."

—*T.S. Eliot*

The objective is simple—this book helps you spend more interactive time with your children. And remember, there are chronological children and there are grown-up children. There is an inner child in everyone and this book invites it out to play. Use it often and send in your own inventions. It has been said that inside everyone there is at least one novel. So, I'm sure as you and your family do the activities in this giant of a book, you will even invent some of your own.

Here's to play!
John Bradshaw

CHAPTER 1

How This Workaholic Discovered Having Fun

Life is a daring adventure, or it is nothing at all.
—*Helen Keller*

If you're reading this, chances are you're like millions of other Americans who are feeling they just aren't having enough fun in life. That certainly was true for me and my friends when I set out to write this book. I was a workaholic. Life had lost its zing as I made the daily rounds of office, car, and home. When I looked around me, everyone else seemed to be in the same rut—nothing but work, work, work. Yechhh! Those most stressed were my friends with kids, especially single parents. I heard essentially the same complaint over and over: "I can't seem to find the time or money to have enough fun with my family." I met mothers, for example, who told me they had bought books of wonderful games and arts and crafts projects to do with their kids, but never had the time to do them. For some, enrolling their kids in endless activities cost a fortune, and all they seemed to do as a parent was to chauffeur their child from place to place.

Now that was almost ten years ago, when people had on average significantly more leisure time than most of us have today. As the pace of life has quickened, because of technology and increasing corporate control over our lives, the situation has definitely become worse. More and more of us are strapped for time, many of us are strapped for money, and almost all of us are strapped for fun. There's just a whole lotta strappin' goin' on.

So I, being an eternal optimist and lover of fun, decided to see if I could come up with a way to help people have more fun in their lives without necessarily having to schedule extra time or spend any extra money. Child and family interaction weren't new to me. I had been a psychologist and teacher for many years, working with many kinds of kids and their parents. I even started one of the first alternative schools of the '60s and helped others do the same. I then became an investigative documentary journalist, and I figured what I didn't know, I could find out. But after more than a year of trial-and-error researching, brainstorming, and writing, I still had no answer.

Then, one fateful evening, I was having dinner with a wonderful woman, Pinky Zalkin, and her children, thirteen-year-old Heather and nine-year-old Philip. I was extremely close to Pinky and like an uncle to the kids. But that night there was a cloud of doom over the table. Pinky and Heather were having one of those mother/teenage daughter arguments and weren't even speaking to each other. Philip was also very angry and silent about something. And I was wracking my brain about what I could do to make this dinner happy, more fun.

Suddenly I got an inspiration and said to the kids, "How would you like to eat dinner in a different way?" Their eyes immediately opened with curiosity—the beginning of all creativity. Just the question—*How can we do whatever we're now doing in a different way?*—visibly changed their mood. (That question has since become like a magic, abracadabra-type incantation for me. I consider it the primary question behind any creative act.)

The kids immediately responded with something like, "What do you mean?"

"Well, how about you two kids pretend to be your mom and me and we will pretend we're you two. Heather, you and Mom can be each other, and Philip and I will be each other. Okay?"

They said something like "sure," in a tentative tone. Then I, remembering how Philip used vast quantities of salad dressing on his salad, grabbed the salad dressing bottle and poured a third of the bottle's contents on my salad. Well, from that point on we all were in hysterics.

Philip began laughing so hard that he fell off his chair twice. Pinky and Heather's angry exteriors vanished in seconds as they spoke and laughed together. That experience was the most hilariously fun experience we ever had together. And it didn't cost anything but a little imagination, which is in infinite supply if you can just tap into it.

That's when I had an epiphany that was to change my life forever and give me a passion that has consumed most of my life since that fateful dinner: I realized that if this one single, minor, and absolutely free variation in how we ate dinner could lead to such a wonderful experience, why couldn't there be other easy ways to make dinner an extraordinary experience? Maybe lots of others. *And since this new and free way to make one ordinary situation extraordinary came from my imagination, and imagination is unlimited, then there should be an unlimited number of new and free ways to*

make any ordinary situation extraordinary! I was ecstatic with this realization.

Let me add quickly that I am not advocating that parents stop setting aside "quality time" with their kids or with each other. That will always be essential. In fact there are some ways of getting close as a family that can only be done by setting aside special, sacred time, like going on an overnight camping trip, or attending religious services together, or doing good works together (see Chapter 19). All I'm saying is that playing together is the *quickest* way to create connection, and certainly the most fun, and that we don't need to always schedule *extra* time for that fun and playfulness to happen—we can make it happen almost anywhere, at any time.

Having spent the previous twenty years helping the underdog, I was also motivated to create something that would be so popular, and make so much money, that I could help support my favorite causes, like preventing the abuse of children, the planet, and our democracy. After all, it's hard to have fun if you're being abused, downsized, oppressed, or getting cancer from environmental carcinogens. Realizing my dream, which now includes a Simple Fun TV series and internet web site as well, has turned out to be much harder than I thought—in fact, it's the hardest thing I've ever done in my life. Like many entrepreneurs, I went through my life savings and even had to sell my home in 1994. But several things have kept me going.

First, I remember how that alienated dinner scene was transformed by a simple suggestion that took no extra time in preparation or extra money. Secondly, I think of the reaction I get from people who have tried out the ideas in this book. For example, as I was leaving the home of a couple one evening where I had just tested one of my games, the woman said, "You know, I never knew my husband could be so playful!" Third, I have a vision of perhaps millions of people every morning waking up in hilarious or otherwise extraordinary ways and eating dinner together every evening in extraordinarily joyful ways, all because of this book and its offshoots.

Fourth is the vision I have of creating an organization to make a major difference in healing the planet and fighting injustice. All of the profits from Simple Fun ventures—including books, videos, the Web site, and, some day soon, a TV series—go to these causes. In other words, after fifteen years of trying to wake up people through investigative documentaries, I realized that if I couldn't get people off their butts to save their jobs, their kids, and maybe the planet, for the right reasons, maybe I could get them to do it for the fun of it.

Finally, what motivates me is something told to me by Mathew Mitchel, who at the time was head of the board of directors of the Center for Attitudinal Healing in Tiburon, California. Mathew had talked to hundreds of people on their deathbed, and asked me to guess what those people regretted most. Being obsessed with my fun project, I of course answered "that they

didn't play enough in life?" And he said, "No, but that's probably number two. More than 90 percent regretted most that they hadn't gotten close enough to the people in their life!"

Since play can also be a powerful tool for creating intimacy, it thrills me to realize that this book and other Simple Fun materials will help you and your family gain perhaps the two most important things in life: intimacy and fun. Because I believe the thing that prevents people from playing enough is the same thing that prevents them from getting close enough to those around them—fear, usually imagined, rather than real. In other words, a lack of courage. So the quote I would like to leave you with (and have on my gravestone) is this one from author Anaïs Nin: "Life shrinks or expands in proportion to one's courage." Don't be afraid to have fun! And remember what Emily Dickinson said: "That it will never come again is what makes life so sweet."

CHAPTER 2

How to Play with This Book

We do not stop playing because we grow old,
we grow old because we stop playing.

—*Anonymous*

his book is for busy couples without kids, two-parent families with two or more kids, and single parents. (This book is not specifically for single folks, although I think it would liven up most dates. In fact I'm working on the dating version, which should be coming out soon after this one.)

The games in this book are, in fact, carefully designed by our team of Harvard-trained engineers (just kidding) to be able to be done by as few as *two people*. That's right. I wanted to make sure that couples or a single parent with one child can do these games as easily as two-parent families with three, four, or more kids. After all, partners and single parents probably need the fun more than anyone else today. The only games that would require more than two players would be just a few games in Chapter 14 (popular sports), which are for teams.

Whatever you do with this book (which I think also makes good coffee-table art), I hope you'll try to read at least the next two chapters before plunging into the games. I realize I may be asking a lot here. But trust me on this. We're not talking about a lot of pages here. And if you have a mate, the two of you will get the most out of this book if you can, somehow, in your busy lives, manage to read Chapters 2 through 5 *together*, like in bed or at the dinner table after the kids leave, or in the car, or someplace. I mean, there must be some time you're still together. Or is this book reaching you too late? Gee, I hope not.

I know you're anxious to try out many or at least some of these games, or maybe just the "going to bed" games. Maybe not; I don't know you. But unless you play a game with a playful attitude, it won't be fun, no matter how great a game it is. So forgive me, but I need to get a little serious about fun in this chapter and the three that follow. This is because simply "playing a game," no matter how great a game it is, won't guarantee that you have fun. Having fun is much more than just knowing *what* to do. *Play is an attitude*; it's the *how* you do anything. Almost anything can be playful and fun. It's *all in how you do it.*

So Chapter 3 ("Are We Having Fun Yet? Why Americans Don't Play Much & What's the Cure") will tell you about this attitude and how to best play these games, so you won't screw it up, so you'll get the most out of the game, and out of the game of life itself, or at least you'll get some darn good clues. Chapter 3 will also talk about the lack of fun in America and give you some perspective on that, which you definitely won't hear from the mainstream media.

Chapter 4 ("If You Play with Me, I'll Be Your Friend: Why Play is So Important and How It Strengthens Relationships") will tell you what's in it for you, your spouse, and your kids, besides all the fun. Play benefits us in so many other ways, like making a so-so relationship good, and a good relationship great. It can increase your own and your kids' creativity, problem-solving ability, mental and physical health, and so much more. "What about wealthier?" you might ask. Yes and no. It will probably save you lots of money on things you've been buying to have fun, since all the ideas in this book are free and I bet lots more fun. But I don't claim this book will make you a millionaire. In fact, after reading this chapter, you might realize you don't really need to be richer to be happier, assuming you have your basic needs covered. After all, my company's motto is "The best things in life aren't things."

Chapter 5 will help you at least identify some barriers to play, one of the more significant ones being the possibility that your spouse or your children are significantly less playful than you.

Chapters 6 through 19 are simply organized around eighteen of the most common situations of everyday life, which are listed in the table of contents, and contain all the 333+ games in the book. Each game is explained using between five and eight different sections (see below). Some of the distribution of games is arbitrary; for example, many of the games I suggest for mealtimes also work well while riding in the car, for example. Feel free to play these games wherever you feel like it.

In fact, if you take one game intended for one situation and try applying it to another, you might just invent a whole new game, which brings us to perhaps the most important chapter, Chapter 20, where I try to help you to make up your own games. If you have the patience, games you invent can be even more exciting than playing the ones in this book. I'll tell how you can send your own games to us, so that

you can share them with others via the Internet and maybe a weekly or daily TV show, and in turn discover what new games others have invented. Chapter 20 also explains how you can be rewarded for your own game discovery or invention, and how your fun creations can help those less fortunate than us and save the world all at the same time, and even get you lots of people thanking you every day and telling you what a wonderful person you are.

Finally I have four appendices, including a list of possible rewards you can draw upon to give winners of games, poor losers to shut them up, or just to be nice; a list of interesting things to discuss over dinner or in the car; a list of many of the best organizations working to help others; and a resource guide listing books that address different topics raised by this book.

How I Explain Each Game

The write-up on each game is usually divided into anywhere from five to eight sections:

1. *Thank You,* where I thank whoever first suggested the game to me. When this section is missing, it's because I came up with the game myself or lost a slip of paper at some time or another over the past ten years collecting these ideas. For those of you affected, my apologies in advance; I will remedy the situation in future editions. I might occasionally share a humorous anecdote of how the game was invented or discovered.

2. *Benefits,* which explains the particular value of playing this particular game. (At the beginning of each chapter, I describe the general benefits to playing all the games in this section.)

3. *Equipment Needed (if any):* Most of these games do not require anything but imagination. A few require common household materials.

4. *How to Play,* which details the rules or steps for playing the game or activity. Here I also provide special suggestions when the manner of playing for a pair (partners or a parent and one child) might be different than that for a family of three or more.

In this section I will often mention the use of a reward to add more excitement to competitive games. Since I strongly believe we could use a lot more imagination in how we reward adults as well as children, I've included in Appendix A a long list of potential rewards that should keep you going for years to come. I think we all could be more imaginative—playful—in our rewards, hence this list.

5. *Warning,* which describes potential physical or emotional dangers, if any, and suggestions as to how to prevent them. (Note: None of these games require you to seriously rethink your medical or life insurance plan. But if you're accident prone or have serious physical problems, I recommend you leave the physical games alone.) One more note: Even drinking a glass of water or eating a sandwich can be danger-

ous. But living life fully is much less risky than not living it at all. Just be forewarned and don't blame us.

6. *Helpful Hints.* These are important suggestions for getting the most out of the activity. In this section, I also give suggestions for what to do for a child too young to play the game (or for a culturally disadvantaged spouse), so he won't feel unduly challenged and freak out or tune out.

7. *Handicaps,* which I will suggest occasionally, especially for competitive games. These are ways to handicap the better player(s) so as to better equalize everyone's chances to win, and thereby make the game more fun for everyone. Gee, if only our parents had this concept when we grew up, huh?

8. *More Fun Ideas,* which offers variations to the primary game. This is, in a way my favorite section, because here you can discover some new games that you might like even more than the original game. The more you try out some of the variations, or just think about them, the better able you will be to make up your own variations and new games.

My Use of Pronouns

I've tried my best to avoid sexism in my writing, usually by using the words "they", "their", or "them", rather than "he", "his", or "him", or "she"and "her", even though I may only be referring to a single person. Occasionally, if you find a male reference pronoun, you'll soon find I balance it out later with a female reference pronoun.

Quotes from Famous and Not So Famous People

Over the years, I have interviewed a variety of celebrities such as Dr. Benjamin Spock, Jack Lemmon, Martin Sheen, and Dr. Bernie Siegel, about easy ways to have fun. (I tried Bill Gates, but he was too busy counting his billions, and I'm still waiting to hear from the president. Or maybe Bill Gates was waiting to hear from the president. Oh, now I'm getting all mixed up.) In any case, few of them know anything more about play than most of the rest of us. Big surprise. And I think many parents and kids know much more than celebrities about such matters.

But since many adults, unfortunately, still need "permission" to be silly, I thought it might be of some value to sprinkle some of these celebrity comments about their own playful experiences and wishes throughout the book. In addition to these celebrity quotes, I have added my own favorite quotes—about play, creativity, courage, imagination, and life itself—from some of the most influential and inspiring people who have ever lived, from Plato to Blake to Chief Justice Earl Warren. I hope their comments will be yet another element to inspire you to live your life more fully through play, by making the ordinary situations of everyday life extraordinary and by helping others do the same.

CHAPTER 3

Are We Having Fun Yet?:
What We Need to Know
About Playfulness

P-L-A-Y says PLAY

Children may play; adults must work.
American, Russian, Israeli, or Turk.
We preach this creed from day to day:
Adults must work; children may play.

But do we believe it? Not on your life!
Show me the husband or show me the wife,
Whose kids are encouraged to dawdle and diddle,
Forbidden to study and practice the fiddle—

Show me the woman or show me the man
Who dream not of lazily getting a tan,
And stuffing themselves from the cupboard and fridge
And playing at tennis, golf, poker, or bridge—

Show me the guy who denies the desire
For leisure, and I will show you a liar.
A creature like that one has never been found.
Even a square likes to play around.

Why then don't we do what we all wish we could?
Run happy and carefree through meadow and wood.
Fly kites and throw baseballs and shout, laugh and sing,
As joyful and silly as anything?

The problem is so unbelievably subtle,
That, to solve it without any risk or rebuttal,
Takes genius—and therefore I've managed to do it:
So listen, and don't say, "Who needs it?", or "Screw it."

I'll tell you the answer, I'll tell you the truth.
Why do old-timers yearn to return to their youth,
Yet labor and slave in a way that's absurd?
Because play, to adults, is a four-letter word.

—*Harvey Mindess*

• • • •

The most common regret of the terminally ill is,
I made a living, but I never really lived.
—*Elizabeth Kübler Ross*

I assume you bought or are considering buying this book for any or all of the following reasons:

1) You want to play more in your own life.

2) You want to play more and have more fun with your partner and/or kids.

3) You want to get closer to your partner and/or kids.

4) You want to give the perfect gift to all your employees, a colleague, your boss, a friend, or your workaholic son or daughter to save their marriages.

5) Your spouse made you buy it.

6) It jumped off the shelf into your hands and won't let go.

Whatever your reasons, this is the only book I know of that can help you play more and get closer to your mate or kids through play *in spite of your lack of time or money.* The following pages are filled with over 333 games and activities that are wonderful "vehicles" to help bring you and your partner, or your kids, almost instantly to the magic land of playfulness, *without the time hassle of having to schedule a special trip,* and all for *free.*

But before you jump into these games, please wait a minute. We must first get serious about play. (Isn't life full of paradoxes.) Ask yourself and what, *besides time,* prevents "fun," from happening in your life?

Sure, half the reason you're not playing enough is about time, maybe even more, but another big reason, truth be told, I bet, is about you. Fun can be scary, especially to workaholics. Working and working is "safe," though you're in fact playing fast and loose with your own life. But now we're getting into the subject of another book. I just want to at least put the danger on the table in this chapter, rather than sweep it under the rug.

In any case, should you accept this mission to play and have more fun, and begin to play more and "live your life out loud," as the writer Emil Zola put it, you'll be taking the "road less traveled." You'll be leaving the pack of your fellow workaholic Americans and their lives of quiet desperation, you'll become (dare I say it?) a *nonconformist,* and it could get scary. But if you remember only one from quote from this book, remember the one I used to end Chapter 1: "Life shrinks or expands in proportion to one's courage."

Yes, to live a truly playful life, as an adult, takes *guts,* a lot more guts than most of those sports stars everyone talks about. Yes, even though the ideas in this book won't take any significant extra time from you, they will take courage. If you really start getting as playful as this book will enable you to be, getting up in the morning, on the job, coming home, at dinner, going to bed, etc., people might start wondering about you, and you might even start wondering about yourself. If you have a teenager or an uptight mate, they might start wondering about you as well, and tell you to act more "grown up." It could be embarrassing or otherwise very annoying, even depressing, to say the least.

Worry no more. The following facts and perspectives about fun in America, and the twelve values of play mentioned in the next chapter, will give you a strong enough "grownup-proof" shield to protect you from their slings and arrows. Read this chapter well, or better yet, read and talk about this chapter and the next with your partner and kids, and they might just start realizing that you might be right, and even join in the fun with you. You will need each other's permission and reassurance to really maximize this book's value.

So now, please forgive me, but in this chapter I need to continue being serious with you about fun and play. After all, your relationships and your life might depend upon it.

Why We're Overworked and Underplayed

It's an expression nearly as old as time itself: "Family comes first." Or if you're a couple without kids, "We come first." Okay, it sounds good, and we've all probably said it more than a hundred times in our lives . . . but how often have we meant it? Adhered to it?

The truth about America is we aren't having much fun. On our deathbeds, it's our biggest regret—that we didn't live our life fully enough, and after that, that we didn't get close enough to those around us. It's never that we didn't work enough.

Family time or couple time should be precious. So why don't we have enough time for one another?

The reasons are always the same: we've got too much work to do, too many other responsibilities, too little time. And this is probably at least partly true. According to a 1995 Harris survey, the leisure time enjoyed by the average American has shrunk 37 percent since 1973, which of course has paralleled the concentration of corporate wealth and power in America and the decline of the labor movement. It reminds me of the phenomenon of boiling frogs without them knowing it by raising the water temperature very slowly, degree by degree. Pay has gone down for huge sectors of the economy, and those who didn't get downsized out of a job have had to work more and more. Work weeks have lengthened, while vacations have shortened.

Many, if not most Europeans, and certainly most Scandinavians, look at Americans as "workaholic maniacs." In many European countries, the work week is thirty-five hours. There are societies such as Italy, Greece, and even Germany, that have much more vacation time, too. In Italy and Germany, for example, everyone takes off on vacation for the entire month of August, and they aren't made to feel guilty by their peers for "indulging" themselves in such a long vacation. None of this should be a surprise. Play and leisure time are no different from anything else in a society. The rules of the political-economic "game," determines the amount of leisure time, just like they determine just about everything else in a society. For example, one out of three Europeans will go on strike at least once in his or her lifetime, while only one out of 500 Americans will do so. All European democracies have more than two parties as well, one of which truly represents labor.

Americans also usually see work and play in much more black-and-white terms. We draw deep divisions between the two, saying, "eight to twelve hours a day, five to six days a week is when I work. After that, I can enjoy leisure time." People in other cultures don't differentiate play and work as much as Americans do. In Greece, for example, a work day begins at 9 a.m. with reading the newspaper and discussing politics. Then at about 10 a.m., it's time for a break of baklava and coffee. The day ends about 2:30 p.m., when the entire city shuts down for siesta until 5 p.m. And though folks may work again in the evening, there is not that sharp demarcation between work and play that there is in the United States. In tribal societies, play was, and in some cases still is, actually intertwined with work. For example, people will often sing continuously while farming or washing their clothes.

I hope, for the sake of our health, our relationships, and our families, that the American attitudes toward leisure time, and our understanding of play and work, will change. Some things are already changing. In the chapter on office games, for example, I mention some examples of American corporations where some very fun things happen in the workplace. Changes like this, of course, depend on people banding together with fellow programmers, salespeople, professionals, etc. They also depend on your imagination. This book can release the power of your imagination. It's up to you to get together and start talking with your colleagues.

> "'If I had more time, I'd have more fun,' we like to tell ourselves, but this is seldom the truth. To test the validity of this assertion, ask yourself how much time you allot each week to fun: pure, unadulterated, nonproductive fun? For most blocked creatives, fun is something they avoid almost as assiduously as their creativity. Why? Fun leads to creativity. It leads to rebellion. It leads to feeling our own power, and that is scary. 'I may have a small problem with overwork,' we like to tell ourselves, 'but I am not really a workaholic.'"
>
> —*Julia Cameron*
> *from* The Artist's Way

We're Afraid of Fun

On top of all the pressures we have on us by our corporate bosses, too many of us really have ourselves to blame as well. Let's admit it, many, if not most, of us are workaholics. We almost always put everything that smacks of success and achievement before closeness and play. People will often claim that leisure is more important than work to them. But what they say and what they do are two different things.

It's not a coincidence that we have one of the highest rates of heart attacks in the world. And psychiatrists are reporting an epidemic of hidden depression among men, who are more adept than women at hiding their depression from themselves and everyone else by using work-activity.

Even when Americans do take time off, we don't seem to know how to relax. We pursue leisure with the same intensity as we do work, as John Bradshaw painfully pointed out in his ski vacation story in the foreword. As a society we are good at teaching most people how to work, but seriously underdeveloped when it comes to teaching people how to play.

Whether it's corporate life, American culture's obsession with work, or our own workaholism, we feel we just don't have enough time (or if single parents, enough money) to have fun in our lives. Well, if I may say so, we're wrong. The good news is that we can have a lot more fun in our lives—all we could ever want—without scheduling extra time or spending any extra money. We can do this by simply putting the attitude of play, meaning playfulness, into the situations we already are in every day—whatever we do, wherever

> We are most human when we are at play.
>
> —*Frederich Schiller*

we are, at home or at work. And this book will give you many easy ways to do this, and help in coming up with your strategies as well. So, what is this "attitude of play?"

What is Play

There's a very important reason to really understand what play is, and the difference between play (or fun) and games, before taking your trip with Easy Fun's games: If you don't know what play really is (and worse, if you think you do), you might enter into these games with a compulsive, anal, or overly competitive, win-at-all-costs attitude, or with some other negative attitude that isn't much fun. And if you do that, you might be playing a game, but you won't be playing, You won't have fun, and neither will your spouse or family. Worse, they will be less likely to want to play with you in the future.

So what is playfulness? We call someone playful when we see that person (usually a child) consumed with the free spirit of exploration. Playfulness, when it continues into adulthood, is also the feature that makes us human. Adults from other species cannot play as we can, in such an infinite number of ways, in so many different situations. After all, we're the only species that laughs.

The core of this attitude is always being curious, exploratory, consciously or unconsciously always asking, "What will happen if . . . ?" Notice that this attitude has nothing to do with needing to win. It is an attitude that mostly has to do with being curious enough to explore and test one's abilities and the world around us. Part and parcel of *curiosity* is being *flexible* and *receptive* to new ideas.

Attention

The other extremely essential element to playfulness is *attention,* or intense focus on the activity at hand. Again, all you have to do is remember how intent a child is when he is playing, or how intent you are the last time you truly were playing. For those of you who meditate, you can see an obvious parallel between play and meditation in this respect, both often leading to a temporary "loss of one's ego." By the way, this is not to imply that competition and play can't go together. In fact, competition can under certain circumstances be a delightful example of another necessary ingredient to play: obstacles.

Obstacles are Necessary for Play to Occur

The other ingredient for play to occur, besides curiosity, flexibility, receptivity, and attention is to have or create at least one or more obstacles. It might surprise some of you to hear that obstacles or dangers are necessary to play. To explain this truth, anthropologists point to "galumphing," one of the prime behaviors displayed by higher life forms such as dolphins, mon-

keys and apes. According to Stephen Nachmanovitch, author of *Free Play,* "Galumphing is the immaculately rambunctious and seemingly inexhaustible play-energy apparent in baby baboons, chimps, gorillas, dolphins, children—and also in young communities and civilizations. Galumphing is the *seemingly useless elaboration and ornamentation of activity* [author's emphasis]. . . . We galumph when we hop instead of walk, when we take the scenic route instead of the efficient one, when we play a game whose rules demand that we handicap our powers, when we are interested in means rather than ends."

In other words, says Nachmanovitch, "Galumphing is when *we voluntarily create obstacles in our path and then enjoy overcoming them* [emphasis mine]. In the higher animals and in humans, it is of supreme evolutionary value." After all, think of any sport or any game, and you'll discover an obstacle in the form of a rule (you have to touch all the bases to get home in baseball) or physical challenge (the basket being so many feet high in basketball, or the hockey goal being just so many feet wide) without which there would be no challenge, hence no game, no sport, no fun.

Play, then, is not just going from point A to point B, or getting goal C, but the way in which we do these things. Play is therefore not what we do, but *how we do it.* In play we seek to create new ways of relating with people, words, actions, ideas, images, things, and ourselves. And we do it by creating obstacles or challenges to overcome, by freeing ourselves from arbitrary rules, and creating new ones in order to expand our range of possible actions. And by adding a new object or new rule, we've created a whole new challenge and experience.

In a very real sense, then, all of the activities in this book are ways to galumph through the everyday situations of life, to enjoy the doing of the very ordinary stuff of life by making games out of it—by adding, ironically, yet another obstacle to our path.

> Play is the fount of creativity.
>
> —Stephen Nachmanovitch
>
> • • • •
>
> Genius is childhood recaptured.
>
> —Baudelaire

Play and Creativity

Play, when it's really play, and not performing a game in a mean-spirited way, not only makes us happier, but it also releases our creative juices. Indeed, play is the fount of creativity. After all, creativity is all about the use of imagination. But what is imagination other than *playing with ideas for its own sake, for the joy of it, for the opportunity to challenge one's mental abilities?* Play, therefore, is at the source of what leads to new discoveries. No wonder Einstein said, *"Imagination is more important than knowledge."*

> Play is the wind of creation blowing through your heart.
>
> —Wavy Gravy

The more you discover about play, the more you realize that play is perhaps the most important thing there is. *Playfulness is the pool out of which all creativity emerges.* Creative work is play. The playful attitude is the root from which original art and science springs. It is the raw stuff that the artist and the scientist channel and organize with all their learning and technique. It's free speculation, using the materials of one's chosen form. The creative mind plays with the tools or instruments it loves. Scientific research is really play with whatever variables in the universe the scientist chooses. Technique itself develops from play, from trying out something new, and persistently experimenting and playing with our tools. Artists play with color, line and space. Musicians play with sound, rhythms and silence. Children, of course, play with everything they can get their hands on. And through this book, you get to play with any of the objects, sounds,

> God is the poetic genius in each of us.
>
> —William Blake

18

people, and actions that make up your own life. *You get to be an artist with your own life.*

Many go even farther and say that play is one of the highest spiritual forms of being, or even divine energy itself. After all, as John Bradshaw points out in the foreword, children are close to the divine, that's why we say they are *"spirited."* When we are in the state of play, we lose ourselves or our self-consciousness, leading to such a deep sense of aliveness that it can be a deeply spiritual experience. This close relation of play or childlikeness to divinity is seen in a wide variety of religious teachings, from those of Jesus ("ye shall be like children") to the Hindu religion, which sees the universe as the playfulness of God himself.

In spite of how absolutely necessary play is to creativity, to acquiring new knowledge, and to spirituality itself, we adults often think of play as frivolous, unproductive activity, "just for kids," or at best, something we can allow ourselves to do three or four times a month. That attitude, I believe, starves our souls to death long before we physically die. Sadly, the majority of Americans wait until they are in their fifties or even sixties to give themselves permission to play and express their buried longing for creative expression.

In my playshops, I often ask participants to think of just one of the most outrageous things they have done in the past five years, and then the past ten years, twenty years, all the way back to their teens. By "outrageous," I mean a time of intense playfulness, involving either some risk of embarrassment or even some physical risk, when you felt incredibly alive, like riding nude on a horse on the beach at night. Or like Maude in the wonderful movie *Harold and Maude,* who goes to funerals of people she doesn't even know just to feel how lucky she is to just be alive. Or getting into an empty elevator with your partner or child, hitting the button for every floor, and then start singing a happy song together and see if you can do it without stopping, or as a bet to see who chickens out first when the doors open. It always amazes me to hear that the vast majority of people haven't done anything outrageous since they were in their teens or twenties. And most of the participants are in their forties or older. If we asked the question, "Are we having fun yet?" most people, if they were honest, would have to answer, "rarely."

Myths about Playfulness

A big part of our problem with play is that we hold certain ideas about it which are myths. The following are those that I feel are most destructive to playfulness and which will keep getting in your way until you can see through them:

Myth I: Play is doing a game; games are always play.

Myth II: Play should take little effort.

Myth III: Play can only happen in certain situations.

Myth IV: Play is primarily for children, not grown-ups.

Myth V: Playfulness can't be learned or developed.

Myth VI: Play is only fun if it's spontaneous.

Myth VII: The more money you haver, the more fun you'll have.

Myth VIII: Play takes extra time.

> Games and other forms of play are only the packages for providing the experience of playfulness.
>
> —*Mihaly Csikszentmihalyi*

Myth I: Play is doing a game; games are always play.

"Play" is not the same as "game." As I mentioned above, play is the free spirit of exploration, doing and being for its own pure joy. Play, or to be more exact, "playfulness," is really an attitude, a way of doing anything. A game, on the other hand, is a specific activity defined by a set of rules, like baseball, writing rhyming couplets, or any of the games in this book. As Dr. Csikszentmihalyi states, "Games and other forms of play are only the packages for providing the experience of playfulness."

If you are going to engage in a game, you should do so in a playful way. But

unfortunately, all too many kids and adults engage in them merely as exercise, drudgery, bids for social prestige, methods of domination etc.

In *Simple Fun for Busy People,* I am encouraging you to engage in the spirit of lighthearted playfulness when you do the games, or you will miss the whole point. Just be intrigued with the "what-happens-ifness" of the new challenges or obstacles you're given by the games in this book.

For example, *what happens* if the next time you eat dinner together, you first write your names on slips of paper, mix them up in a cup, and then act like whomever you draw? What happens if the next time you go to bed with your partner or put your kid to bed, you see who can get each other's socks off first? If these games become only a competition or just another thing you have to cross off your to-do list, this book will just become another job, and you will defeat the whole purpose.

Myth II: Play can involve little effort.

This is an insidious notion, because it permits the drug of television and other passive forms of leisure to be considered play. When you watch a child play, he's constantly dealing with challenges. He just happens to be loving it. Why? Because he's in a state of "flow." But what is flow?

Play as Flow

For more than twenty-five years Mihaly Csikszentmihalyi, a professor of psychology at the University of Chicago, has been engaged in an epic study of happiness and the characteristics of states of happiness, particularly in people who have achieved great accomplishments in a wide variety of human endeavors. In his book *Flow: The Psychology of Optimal Experience* and his recent book *Finding Flow,* he offers the fruits of this research. His basic explanation of fun and happiness is as follows: in any situation a person must pit his/her personal ability against a degree of challenge. Ability and degree of challenge rarely coincide. When challenge is way below ability, when it's "too easy," we get boredom. When challenge exceeds ability too much, we get anxiety.

But when challenge and ability are in close balance, as in the figure below, a person's feelings go somewhere else—and they are experiencing what Csikszentmihalyi calls the state of flow: "a state that is quintessentially in the moment, full of joy, satisfaction, affection, freedom, the feeling of being truly alive."

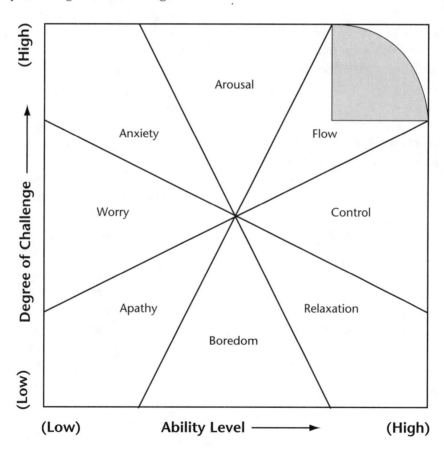

(Courtesy of Csikszentmilhalyi, M., Carli, M., and Massimini, F.)

21

So, to ensure your play time is fun, that you are in the flow, so to speak, be sure to do your best to match each person's ability to the challenge in the game or activity. I do my best to suggest some ways you can do that when you have younger children in your family.

Take an obvious example: We have a dishwashing game in Chapter 15. A child who is too short to reach the sink, or not coordinated enough to do a good job, would not experience "flow" if he or she were washing dishes. He'd experience anxiety. Conversely, an older child or adult who has had plenty of experience washing dishes would most likely experience boredom. For the adult to experience "flow" as a dishwasher, you'd have to add some extra challenge.

The Most Important Rule of Play

The most important *"Rule of Rules,"* then, *for all games to be playful is to be sure to matchd game's level of challenge to the ability person's level for minimum boredom, minimum anxiety, and maximum fun.* This is necessary both in relationship to the game itself, and perhaps even more importantly, with respect to differences in ability levels between the players. We'll talk more about this critical rule in Chapter 5 when we discuss the most common barriers to play. *Just remember that play will never occur if there is too big a gap between ability and challenge.*

Myth III: Play can only happen in certain situations.

Since we learned that playfulness is really an attitude, and since an attitude can apply to almost any situation, it should be obvious that playfulness can occur virtually anywhere. All you have to do is watch a three year old in virtually any situation to see that play can happen anywhere, anytime. You can also dispel your doubts by looking at this book's table of contents and then turning to whatever chapter most intrigues you: "Waking Up in the Morning", "Riding in the Car", "Eating Dinner", "Doing Chores", "At the Office." It should quickly become obvious that playfulness can occur almost anywhere. I've even heard of people on their deathbed who made their last words a joke that left everyone laughing. After writing this book, I better do that too.

Myth IV: Play is primarily for children, not for grownups.

A corollary myth to the above is that play is only for certain times of our lives, specifically our childhood or occasionally vacations or weekends. Though the primary characteristics of play which we mentioned earlier are those positive characteristics we associate with children, they are characteristics we can retain and develop throughout our life. The famous anthropologist Ashley Montague, author of *Growing Young,* puts it eloquently this way: "The truth about the human species is that we are intended to remain in many ways childlike: we were never intended to grow 'up' into the kind of adults most of us have become. We're designed—in body, spirit, feeling, and conduct—to grow and develop in ways that emphasize rather than minimize childlike traits. By learning to act more like a child, human beings can revolutionize their lives and become for the first time, perhaps, the kinds of creatures their heritage has prepared them to be—youthful all the days of their lives."

So the next time some uptight person, adult or child who "grew up," accuses you of being "childish" when you're simply playing, be sure to say, "No, I'm being *childlike*," and that you've simply decided to live your life before it's too late.

A corollary to Myth IV is that *"play and work don't mix."* Just as I pointed out earlier that work is in fact necessary to play, play, if not necessary, can certainly benefit work. I give many examples from corporate life to prove this in Chapter 12 ("At the Office"). But let me just say two things here: First, as adults, most of us have to somehow relearn or recapture the playful spirit that originally existed in us as children, but somehow got deactivated. When we unlock that spirit within us, we can be playful, no matter what activity we're engaged in. Even the most challenging work can be approached with a playful spirit and, therefore, become play.

Second, in the past ten years, teams have become the dominant vehicle in reengineering the workplace. Through teams, companies are able to find the most creative ways to produce more and better

goods or services at less cost with fewer people—usually fewer managers. With work teams, cooperation is the key to success. How does a company whose executives and other workers have spent their lives competing with each other suddenly get them to cooperate? The answer has usually been through team building games that are fun to play, and require cooperation for success, and conversely lead to failure if team members act on their own.

According to Ken Hill, professor of management at University of California School of Business Administration: "By making the learning environment fun as well as educational, people feel less fear of failure, are more willing to be creative and innovative, and come away from the experience with enthusiasm to try what they have learned back in the workplace. When people laugh at themselves, and have fun along with others in the training experience, their learning is enhanced and teamwork is encouraged."

Myth V: Playfulness can't be learned or developed.

Hogwash. Human beings are learning machines. If Psychology 101 teaches anything, it teaches that almost anything can be taught, given sufficient reinforcement contingencies. What we also know from Psych 101 is that you can't learn to be playful using force or punishment. Using punishment only teaches fear and creates undue anxieties and inhibited adults, just the opposite of playfulness. So it is extremely important to avoid creating conditions that lead to hurt feelings or continual loss (unless of course *everyone* is continually losing, and even this is not good for too long).

If you or your spouse might already be somewhat inhibited from early unpleasant or anxiety provoking play experiences, I suggest using the noncompetitive games in this book first, and then gradually working in competitive games under carefully controlled conditions that ensure plenty of winning. Chances are that those early traumas were with highly competitive people playing competitive games. More on this in Chapter 5.

Myth VI: Play is only fun if it is spontaneous.

If that were true, dances, dates, and major league sports events would disappear. Wednesday night poker clubs, bridge clubs, Friday night out, and bowling leagues would never be seen. The list is endless. Much of the fun people have is planned and in fact are weekly rituals. This myth probably arose from the fact that some of the best fun occurs without being planned, or as an unexpected event within the planned fun activity.

But the key condition for fun to occur, as I explained above in my explanation of "flow," is not spontaneity, but rather balance: balancing people's abilities with the challenge. Planning can only help promote balance.

There is much to be said, however, for spontaneity, and unfortunately most of us have lost it. But this trait, like any other, can also be developed. In the beginning, as with any newly acquired skill or newly developing muscle, playing these games may feel forced, unnatural. But that's okay. In the beginning, you have to plan the conditions where spontaneity can later occur on its own.

In music and theater we call spontaneity "improvisation." But as any good improvisational musician or actor will tell you, you can only "improvise" if you know your craft, if you have the basic skills down. I think spontaneity in life, or "playfulness," is very similar. A small child naturally seems to have this gift without any practice. But for older kids and for us adults, the more practice you have at play, the more natural you can again become. In other words, I think playfulness is much like a muscle: the more you use it, the stronger it becomes.

Being able to be spontaneous in life also means being able to have fun almost any time and any place: in other words, in almost any situation. And that is exactly what this book offers—countless ways to have fun in almost any situation, whether it be waking up, answering the phone, settling an argument, or even watching TV.

Think of the games in the book, then, as exercises to condition your new "play or creativity muscles." Sooner or later, your muscles will be in top form and you won't have to use the same exercises any longer unless you want to. And with these new developed "muscles of play," you will be able to create different, unique games of your own. As the doctor of my 90-year-old mother often says, "You're never too old to strengthen a muscle."

Flexibility and the Willingness to Explore

Perhaps the most important conditions for spontaneity are flexibility and the willingness to explore. It's next to impossible to have playfulness, and certainly spontaneous play, without flexibility and the willingness to explore or "try out" stuff.

Being flexible and exploratory means, among other things, that we are willing to let go of (at least temporarily) our view of how things ought to look, ought to proceed, or ought to turn out. It means being willing to give up what you think ought to happen first (even if you're sure you're right).

Flexibility also means, among other things, not getting too attached to the rules of any particular game. The point is to create a stronger connection to those you love. If your son begins one way and then goes off in a different direction, try following his lead rather than insisting that he get back to the "real" game. His game could be more fun! I'm not saying you don't need rules; on the contrary, there is usually more freedom within structure than without. I'm only saying that one must be flexible in changing the structure.

> The best things in life aren't things.
>
> —*Anonymous*

Myth VII: The more money you have, the more fun you have.

First the research. I wouldn't want you to just take my word for it. By now one or two of you might be thinking I'm a silly fool. Without going into all the studies on happiness over the last few decades, some of which I refer to in our resource guide, let me again just mention two of Dr. Csikszentmihalyi's findings. First, it's true, as you'd expect, that people who live in nations that are materially better off and more stable rate themselves as happier, i.e. Norwegians are happier in general than Greeks or Portuguese. But this is not always the case. For example, the much poorer Irish seem to be happier than the Japanese. And within the same society, there's only a very weak correlation between finances and satisfaction with life. Billionaires in the United States are only infinitesimally happier than those with average incomes. In fact, while personal incomes doubled from the late '50s to the '70s, the proportion of people saying they are very happy has remained a steady 30 percent.

As for myself, I believe so fervently that "the best things in life aren't things," that it's my company's other motto. The great thing about playfulness is that it takes no money and no special equipment. All it really requires is a reconnection to your true self, to the child within you. That's all. And that's a lot, considering all the years that child within has been suppressed for so many of us. It reminds me of the attorney I once met to whom I showed a video of families and some celebrities playing some of the new game ideas in this book. He said he loved it, not just because of the ideas, but more importantly, because he felt it gave him "permission" now to suggest his own "wacky ideas" to his wife and kids without them thinking he was too silly or nuts.

Putting it another way, the most powerful muse or inspiration of all is your own inner child. And more often than not, all that is needed is permission, permission that you can trust, for that child to come out. The talented writer, artist, or otherwise highly playful adult is simply someone who continues throughout life to contact this child, the self who still knows how to play.

Myth VII: Play takes extra time.

Since playfulness is an attitude or perhaps even the "possession of the spirit of the divine," rather than any particular activi-

> Some parents think that the more elaborate, the more expensive the plaything, the more fascinating it will be to children. That is simply not true. What children love most of all, and what will keep them busy longest is an opportunity to be creative, and this is why a box of crayons, a wad of paper, and a box of good blocks will keep children imagining and building week after week, month after month.
>
> —Dr. Benjamin Spock

ties or games themselves, it's the expression of how any activity or game is done. So play and playfulness don't really require extra time to fit into your schedule—they're part of all of your activities. And that's the point of this book—to give you more than three hundred examples of how to express that playful attitude in almost all the ordinary situations of everyday life. *So it is not just doing these games that will make you playful, but doing them in a playful way.*

The most important thing to remember in all of this is to get into the attitude of playfulness. Your true nature is playful, creative energy. You came in with it, but may have lost it somewhere along the way. Or more accurately, we all lose it and find it again and then lose it. But it is your birthright, and you can reclaim it. Life, this ongoing panoply of thousands of miracles constantly occurring inside and around us, is not to be lived in boredom or in quiet desperation, but full-out, alive, filled with awe and wonder. I started this book with a statement from Helen Keller because I think she said it best: "Life is a daring adventure, or it's nothing at all!" So, let's adventure, let's play!

Please note: I have also suggested several books in the Resource Guide (Appendix D), that can provide much more help than this chapter in overcoming one's blocks to playfulness and creativity.

CHAPTER 4

If You Play with Me, I'll Be Your Friend:
Why Play Is So Important & How It
Strengthens Relationships

You can learn more about a person in an hour of play
than in a lifetime of conversation.

—Plato

You'd think that since play is fun, I wouldn't have to tell you all the other reasons why it's good for you. But so many of us adults are so darn reluctant to play, that I figure I better lay out my top twelve reasons, just in case you need to justify yourself to your older kids or spouse who think you're being too silly.

First the research: Considering how fundamental fun and play is to happiness, you'd think all these psychologists would have done loads of research, especially when you consider how fun it would have been to do the experiments. Alas, little research has actually been done on play in the halls of academic psychology. One of the few social scientists who has done significant work in examining the role of play in marital and family well-being is Dr. Dianne Smith of Brigham Young University, and one fact she recently uncovered in her research shows how dismal the situation is: in seven of the leading college texts on family psychology, there are only twelve pages on the importance of play.

On that cheery note, I shall do whatever I can in this chapter to begin to fill the void. I think this chapter alone will equal or surpass everything those psychologists have done all these years. Here then is a quick list of some of the major values of play, which I believe easily translate to a strengthening of couple and family happiness and closeness. And if you check out my bibliography on play in the back (Appendix D), you'll find the proof of what I say.

> That it will never come again is what makes life so sweet.
>
> —*Emily Dickinson*

1. Play makes us happy.

Though you'd think every man, woman, and child would know this, people seem to have forgotten. Instead we're rapidly replacing play with passive spectator forms of "leisure." It's no secret that most adults and much of our youth today have simply forgotten how to play, and accept sitting in front of a screen watching others joke and play and be challenged, as "play." This is distraction, not play. And we are living in the "over-distracted society," numbed by the TV drug. Our society has elevated distraction to an art form. In fact, America today might be more aptly called an "entertainment state" rather than a democracy.

As I mentioned in the previous chapter, the scientist who has studied happiness and play more than anyone else in America is Mihalyi Csikszentmihalyi. He, along with virtually all other scientific researchers for the past thirty years on this subject, clearly demonstrate that the people who are happiest are not those who engage in passive non-challenging forms of "entertainment" (TV and movies), but those involved in pursuits which challenge us, while maintaining a balance between our abilities and that challenge.

Joel Hektner, an associate of Csikszentmihalyi, in a two-year longitudinal study of teenagers, found that those teens whose experiences of flow (high skill, high challenge experiences) increased, reported significantly higher levels of concentration, self esteem, and enjoyment. In another and more recent study of more than two thousand teens, the teens reported that almost half the time they were involved in *games* or *sports*—in other words, where their skills were *challenged*—they experienced flow. Whereas they experienced flow only about 13 percent of the time when they watched TV. Considering the total lack of challenge in watching TV, and the virtual absence of any significant brain activity during TV watching (see number 10 below), I am surprised the teens reported *any* flow experiences while watching TV. I think they just didn't want to admit what a huge waste of time it was.

2. Play enhances flexibility and the ability to deal with crisis.

A playful person, as opposed to a rigid one, is far better equipped to roll with life's inevitable punches. The only thing certain in life is change, and if we are stuck in a rigid view of ourselves and life, we are bound to be disappointed. Often the best solutions come from a "wacky" perspective, by getting as silly as possible.

Though there is not a lot of experimental research on play's relationship to family and marriage, there is plenty on its value to problem solving, flexibility, and ability

to deal with crisis. Play keeps you on your toes, which is why at IBM and in so many other Fortune 500 companies, executives have all kinds of toys by their computers, in the executive meeting rooms, and basketball hoops and foam basket balls close to their desks.

Play, which includes humor (since humor is just playing around with words) helps individuals through crisis and change. Because it facilitates the release of tension, fun and humor increase employees' ability to cope with stress on the job and to remain flexible, creative, and innovative under pressure—central features of a strong, resilient corporate culture. Organizations that integrate fun into work have lower levels of absenteeism, greater job satisfaction, increased productivity, and less downtime.

> Romantic love is one of the most powerful needs for pulling us out of literal life and into play.... To be in love is to be in play.
>
> —*Thomas Moore*

3. Play keeps couples together.

In the early '80s, Drs. Howard Markman and Andrea Van Steenhouse from the University of Denver studied over two thousand "happy" couples through a survey conducted by one of Colorado's two major dailies, the *Rocky Mountain News,* to determine the secrets of their happy marriages. According to Markman, "Among all the variables, the amount of *fun* these partners had together emerged as the strongest factor in determining their overall marital happiness." This also seemed to be the primary variable distinguishing "super marriages" from just good ones; good marriages became great marriages when they were able to preserve both the quantity and the quality of the fun they had when they started.

Most couples start out having plenty of fun during courtship, because fun provides the intimacy and strengthens the bonds as nothing else does. When my wife and I got married, one thing we said in our vows was this:

Karen: "It is that little boy in you who makes the little girl in me feel safe enough to come out and play."

Gary: "...and it is the little girl in you who inspires the little boy in me to want to play and to show you each new and endless wonder my eyes, ears, heart, and mind discovers, or which my being loves to create."

It is perhaps the greatest tragedy of most marriages that something that was so pleasurable and so important in developing the relationship in the first place, seems to become so much less prevalent within a few years. Why does this happen? What are those barriers to fun later in marriage? Most will say the biggest one is time. And

that's why you very wisely bought this book.

When couples first fall in love, and say they "click" with each other, they are describing their being in flow together. One of the biggest tragedies in life is this loss of flow from the marriage partnership. As we learned in Chapter 3, this is due either to too much stress and anxiety, because the challenges become too great, or to too much boredom, because the challenges are not enough. The breakthrough in this book, then, is to realize that if we simply add a little challenge to the otherwise mindless routine rituals of everyday life, we could put people back in the flow. In other words, we can make the activity fun, without needing more time.

More evidence for the importance of play to marriage longevity: Mormons have one of the lowest divorce rates of any religious group in our country. One of the reasons for this, they believe, is that it is a religious duty for families to spend time together at least one evening per week— "Family Home Evening." A good chunk of this evening is usually spent in play.

Virtually all of the social scientific literature on the effect of couple play on marital happiness and longevity since the early '80s shows that husbands and wives who share leisure time in joint activities tend to be more satisfied with their marriages. One interesting study by Charlotte Reissman made a distinction between pleasant activity, such as TV watching, and exciting, flow-type activity in a study of fifty couples over ten weeks. Marital satisfaction was not significantly higher for the "pleasant activity" group compared to those couples who spent no leisure time together at all, but was significantly higher for the "exciting activity" group.

According to Dr. Richard Simon, editor and founder of *Family Network*, one of the country's leading journals of couple and family counseling, "As our society seems to be getting more and more stressed out, marriage and family therapists are increasingly using methods of intervention that help couples learn how to play more and play better together." Reestablishing couple playfulness is also a primary goal of sex therapy. I'd say that's another pretty good reason to play.

> Why should we use our creative power?. . . Because there is nothing that makes people so generous, joyful, lively, bold, compassionate, and so indifferent to fighting and the accumulation of objects and money.
>
> —*Brenda Ueland*

4. Play teaches basic morality.

The principles for successful play are the same as for a moral life. Here are just a few:

1) Take turns. Almost all games require one to take turns if play is to be fun for everyone. This is such a deceptively simple rule, but so often forgotten, as much by adults (who, for example, tend to monopolize conversations) as by young children.

2) Consider the other person's feelings. You can't become a good player without knowing when challenge is out of balance with ability. Role playing, for example, is a powerful training ground for developing empathy and the humility to see ourselves as others see us, another ability or sensitivity that must be cultivated to create a considerate human being. The "Be Each Other Game," in Chapter 9 is a good demonstration of this.

3) Be a good sport about losing. In games, as in life, you win some and you lose some. You try your best to learn from your mistakes. But if you discover the game is rigged, that it is unfair, you stand up to stop the injustice, which brings us to our last, but certainly not least important, rule. . . .

4) Don't unduly take advantage of, or exploit, another person (or class of people) for your own advantage. In fact, help the underdog. If it's no contest, it's not fun, it's sadism. Games are meant to be played playfully, not with an exploitative or "win-at-any-costs" attitude. This is

really a corollary of the rule about "flow," the Rule of Rules: Always keep a balance between abilities and challenges. If one player has little or no chance of winning, if there's not an even playing field, there's injustice in the game, and the fun disappears. We can imagine how this rule applies to life, too, for the majority of working class people and the increasingly growing population of those in poverty. (As of 1997, 26 percent of America's children now live in poverty.)

Concerning teaching moral behavior and play, it's worth at least mentioning that much of the effort parents put in to teach kids how to play often does the opposite of the above, through overly competitive sports run by adults who put winning before fun. Involving kids in these games teaches them to exploit and to feel fine about others always losing.

For a scientific grounding for the relation of play to moral development, I suggest Piaget's classic *Moral Development of the Child*, where Piaget demonstrates how learning the rules of playing games enables the child to internalize moral commitments.

5. Play increases creativity, productivity, and creative problem solving.

With all of today's time and money pressures, families can use all the help they can

According to Dr. William Fry of the Stanford University Medical School, laughter can boost cardiovascular fitness by lowering blood pressure and heart rate. It also reduces pain perception, stimulates blood flow, strengthens the immune system, and reduces levels of hormones that create stress, all of which could have positive effects on a person's creativity and productivity.

—*Bradford Swift*

get in creative problem solving and in becoming more creative in general. Adding play will definitely help. There is abundant research showing that creativity in problem solving is directly correlated to play and playfulness, and more importantly, that whatever promotes playfulness also seems to promote creativity in general and problem solving ability in particular.

This should also be no surprise, considering that the major traits associated with creative people are those we also normally associate with highly playful kids and adults: curiosity, preference for challenge and risk taking, high tolerance for ambiguity, openness to experience, possession of unconventional values, tendency toward divergent thinking, tendency to practice with alternative solutions, independence of judgment, and self-confidence. Being disordered (messy) is also typical of highly creative people.

For example: A study several years ago examined how young children learned to problem solve with a set of construction sticks in order to reach an object. Toddlers allowed to play around freely with the sticks were much faster in learning to reach the object than toddlers in control groups who were given other kinds of help, including one group that actually got to watch a man modeling the correct problem-solving behavior.

Productivity is often king for adults, so the following study should be of interest: In the nine months that followed a "playshop" conducted by M. C. Metcalf at Digital Equipment Corporation in Colorado Springs, twenty middle managers increased their productivity by 15 percent and reduced their sick days by half. Employees from the Colorado Health Sciences Center in Denver who viewed humorous training films and attended fun workshops showed a 25-percent decrease in downtime and a 60-percent increase in job satisfaction. Dozens of additional examples from the corporate world can be found in Hemsath's *301 Ways to Have Fun at Work.*

6. Play enhances family cohesion.

Why is it that people's fondest memories of family life are invariably moments involving play? That's because these activities create bonds and encourage the honest

> The family that plays together, stays together.
> —*Anonymous*

expression of feelings, including the constructive expression of anger. With an ever-shrinking amount of time, money, and energy, parents and children desperately need to reconnect in ways that are meaningful and that don't cost a fortune or require additional scheduling in an already overloaded calendar. Simple activities done in the course of an average day can go a long way toward creating a family that wants to be together. I firmly believe that the couple or family that plays together is probably the most likely to stay together.

7. Play reduces sibling rivalry and other family conflict.

A great way to reduce sibling rivalry and to modify any person's behavior is to "catch the person doing good." In other words, praise them for being good, rather than complain or punish when they make a mistake. And a great way to do this is to involve the siblings in cooperative games, that are noncompetitive, and then reward or positively recognize them during their cooperative behavior. The majority of the games and activities in this book are noncompetitive. Just inviting the siblings to play these sorts of games together will reduce sibling rivalry and create more bonds.

You need only look at Chapter 18 to see several examples of specific games that can be extremely valuable methods of conflict resolution, whether between kids or adults. The resource guide in the back of the book has additional valuable sources.

> I tried to teach my child with books. He gave me only puzzled looks. I tried to teach my child with words. They passed him by often unheard. Despairingly, I turned aside. "How shall I teach this child," I cried. Into my hand he put the key. "Come," he said, "play with me."
>
> —*Anonymous*
> *(courtesy of Louisiana*
> *Children's Museum)*

8. Play helps develop communication skills.

Many verbal games in this book, particularly the role-playing ones, can powerfully increase language skills, which will lead to later success in reading and writing. That's because there is abundant research showing that, in addition to drawing and painting, the activity that best predicts later writing and reading success is dramatic play. The theory behind this is that the first time children begin to get practice holding symbols in their mind is when they are pretending they are somebody else.

Though there has yet to emerge sufficient research, it is only common sense that those forms of play that enhance the child's self-esteem will also improve the child's performance in school, since research shows that increased self-esteem leads to improved school performance.

9. Play reduces TV addiction.

I am quite confident that ten to fifteen years from now, and I hope much sooner, we'll be talking about TV addiction the same way we're talking about cigarette smoking today. One of the major causes of the loss of family cohesion is television. If you don't recall what happened when a TV set was first introduced into your home, see the scene in the movie *Avalon* where the camera pans from the dining room table (which each evening had been the center of warmth, excited conversation, family interaction, and creativity) to the den, where we see the family now mesmerized into passivity and silence in front of the TV. One of the good things about the days of yesteryear is that without television, parents and children interacted a lot more. In the resource guide (Appendix D) at the back of the book, I suggest several excellent books to help you further in eliminating addiction to this drug.

When you are joyful, your body chemistry is different, and it helps your body. Your body literally knows when you're happy; it's not just in your mind.

—*Bernie Siegel, M.D.*

10. Play helps prevent and heal disease.

I doubt it's a coincidence that America leads the world in both heart disease and workaholism. From Norman Cousin's breakthrough work *Anatomy of an Illness* to Dr. Bernie Siegel's *Love, Medicine, and Miracles* to more recent reviews and experiments, there is abundant research to show that retaining our youthfulness of spirit positively affects our physical development, rate of aging, susceptibility to disease, and ability to overcome everything from heart disease to cancer in dramatic ways.

There is even more research demonstrating the influence of mind and feelings in general (for example, relaxation techniques and autohypnotic suggestion) upon prevention, remission, and complete recovery from major disease, particularly cancer. To name one of dozens of excellent studies, Dr. David Spiegel at the Stanford Medical School showed a twofold increase in survival time in women with advanced breast cancer who had received group therapy and autohypnotic techniques, compared to a control group who had received standard medical therapy alone. Social activity has been shown to reduce incidence of colds and disease in general, above and beyond what has always been known about the healthful effects of regular exercise. And play, of course, often involves physical exercise.

11. Play promotes mental health and psychological healing.

Can you think of anyone you'd consider happy—in great psychological health—who didn't have a great sense of humor or a playfulness about them? As one would expect, playfulness becomes especially important in making friends, staying in touch with feelings, and in dating during adolescence.

The psychiatrist Donald Winnicott thought that the whole goal of psychological healing was to bring the patient out of an inability to play, into an ability to play. He said that only in playing can a child or adult be creative. And that only through creativity can one discover and use the whole self.

Unless we understand this importance of play, there won't be the motivation for relearning this lost art we once all had as children. Until we reconnect with the fundamental importance of play, we cannot foster it in our children. And unless it is cultivated, encouraged, and rewarded (instead of squelched) in our children, we will continue to create people who are cut off from their wholeness.

12. Play helps our entire society evolve and productively respond to changing conditions.

As we saw in the previous chapter, playfulness is the fount of all creativity in the arts and sciences. It is what fosters our species' ability to respond in endless ways to constantly new experience. This is the evolutionary value of play: it makes us flexible. By reacting to reality in ever-new ways we keep ourselves from becoming rigid, which is important, for when a species becomes rigid in response to changing conditions, it dies out.

Through the social invention called "democracy," individuals and whole societies get to experiment with all sorts of combinations and permutations of rules, rights, privileges, technology, thought forms, and images. This would not be possible in a world that functions only in terms of immediate survival, or what seems to be most efficient at the time to any one person. A creature that plays is more readily adaptable to changing contexts and conditions. A civilization that plays is likewise more adaptable to changing conditions. And the greatest social invention to allow for that play, for that continual experimentation to occur, is democracy.

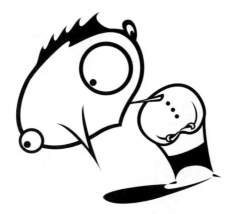

CHAPTER 5

For Better or For Worse but Can't We Have Some Fun?
Barriers to Couple and Family Fun

To laugh is to risk appearing the fool.
To weep is to risk appearing sentimental.
To reach out to another is to risk involvement.
To express feelings is to risk exposing your true self.
To place ideas and dreams before a crowd is to risk their loss.
To love is to risk being loved in return.
To live is to risk dying.
To hope is to risk despair.
To try is to risk failure.
But risks must be taken, because the greatest hazard in life
is to risk nothing.
The person who asks nothing, does nothing, has nothing, and is nothing.
They may avoid suffering and sorrow,
but they cannot learn, feel, change, grow, love, live.
Chained by their attitude, they are a slave.
They have forfeited their freedom.
Only a person who risks is free.

—Anonymous

I t's great to know that play is so valuable for us. It's like in the sci-fi satire movie *Sleeper,* where in the future they discover chocolate and ice cream are actually good for your health. But knowing why play is so vital isn't necessarily going to make us more playful. All the insight in the world, unfortunately, can rarely change a habit. If you're any older than five or six, you've probably already developed various patterns of resistance to play, resistances that need to be unlearned and replaced with "playful" behaviors.

And because it is so often that opposites attract, it is probably the case that one spouse is less playful than the other. This dilemma was both humorously and tragically portrayed in Robin Williams' movie *Mrs. Doubtfire.* Whether or not one of you is more playful than the other, or the two of you both find it difficult to get out of your "serious adult attire" and put on your "child's garb," you can benefit from the following tips. Whatever you do, don't start arguing about who is more playful. I'm sure in some situations and on some days either of you can be the most playful. It just almost always depends on the situation.

But before getting to some practical techniques that can bring both of you into a playful mood, and help overcome various barriers to play, let's first look at some basic understandings, especially about male/female differences when it comes to play.

> In our play we reveal what kind of people we are.
>
> —*Ovid*

People Are Different

Just as we are different in our communication styles, food preferences, and TV show preferences, we're also different when it comes to play. Yes, it's true. For example, many people prefer more structureless or more process-oriented activities, without specific goals and clear rules, like talking, hiking, camping, acting, meeting new people, free style dancing, shopping, or massage. Others prefer their play or fun to be very structured with specific rules and goals, like tennis, crossword puzzles, chess, ballroom dance, or basketball.

We see those differences early in childhood between different children. Some will very much gravitate to construction type activities, whereas others prefer pretend or dramatic play activities. Some, of course, might like both equally. Similarly, when it comes to competition. Some kids love competition, and others detest it. Another influence might be culture. For example, if your marriage is intercultural with someone from a cooperative-type culture, they might not be as comfortable with competition as most Americans are, and this might create some big differences.

In any case, we should be careful to not simply discuss these differences as a matter of gender, since that would deny the much greater variation that occurs from individual to individual. And those are the differences you as a husband or wife, son or daughter, must discover. My wife, Karen, for example, is much more competitive than I am. So whenever I want to get her more excited about playing with me, all I have to do is put a competitive spin along with some kind of bet (reward for the winner or chore for the loser) on it and she's almost always game. The point is that your mate might have some very different play preferences than you, that have nothing to do with gender.

Whatever the individual differences, all humans seem to seek the "flow" experience, but seek it out through different types of fun. The trick, then, is to take the differences into account when you create the rules of the game, and to balance abilities and challenge levels.

Your mate might also have very different play preferences, because of early childhood experiences with siblings or other kids. For example, she might vastly prefer mental games to physical ones because of being shamed by the neighborhood kids over her softball throwing, or prefer artistic to dramatic play because of being laughed at on stage. There are always very good reasons for people being the way they are.

So the point here is that it is important to discover the peculiar preferences your spouse or partner has for play, perhaps in part because of his gender, but more likely because of his unique childhood experience and his genes. And to find out just what those preferences are, you need to do a Play Inventory.

> It is a paradox of creativity that we must get serious about taking ourselves lightly. We must work at learning to play.
>
> —*Julia Cameron*
> *from* The Artist's Way

Take a Play Inventory

This is probably the best first step to take if you want to learn how to maximize the playfulness of your mate with you. Taking a Play Inventory involves making a list of all the things that the two of you like to do to have fun both together and also separately. Then list what you enjoy about the activities you chose. Is it because they are mentally or physically challenging? Laughter-creating? Do they have a lot of structure or a little? Do they involve words, or making things with materials?

Based on what the lists reveal about each of you, now you have a better idea of the types of things you each find fun to do. In coaxing a reluctant partner, it's much better to tempt them with a type of game they might enjoy. Once you know what those preferred forms of play are, you can begin to play. That now brings us to the quality of the invitation.

The Quality of the Invitation

The invitation is critical. If you meet your partner at the door after a day of intense mental activity and blurt out, "Hi, honey, wanna play chess?" the response will probably be, not only no, but "hell no!" No, that isn't the way to do it. A safer and more promising approach would be to first wait till dinner, and see if they'd like to try one of the more feel-good dinner games like "Family" or "Couple Treasure Chest" in Chapter 9 ("Mealtimes"), where you could just hear and express some good feelings without having to do anything mental. Alternatively, if you didn't want to wait until dinner, your partner might really be in the mood right now for a light physical game, like some of those in Chapter 13 ("Waiting Around") or "Paperball Basketball" in Chapter 14 ("Popular Sports"). Or maybe, you just need to have patience and wait. Maybe you both have been around people so much for the past ten hours, you just need a half hour of alone time and then you'll be ready for a rousing round of "Knock Your Socks Off" before going to bed.

So, be flexible. Both of you need to be flexible. First, be sure you have read the previous chapter and agree that play is vital to your health and well-being. And remember the invitation to play needs to honor each person's "freedom of choice." Play and force never go together. Sometimes we're in the mood to play and sometimes we're not.

When it is your idea to play something, offer the invitation like this: "Honey, would you be willing to try something fun with me for just five minutes?" Touching and eye contact are good ways to establish a viable connection. Be sincere and incorporate humor, not somberness, making sure they know that you are taking their feelings and state of mind into consideration. If the answer is no, or "not right now," be okay with that. But chances are, once you back off, a few minutes later your partner will probably ask you what it is, right? (Doesn't this start to remind you of your dating years?) Then you can say it's just a little activity you got from the *Simple Fun for Busy People* book, and you wanted to try it out before you included the kids, or that you thought it sounded more fun for a couple, and just wanted to try it. From here, they'll probably ask you what the activity is. You tell them, and then they will say yes or no.

Remember, if your mate is still not in the mood to play, odds are you'll do more harm than good trying to push your agenda. At the moment, the challenge is too beyond their ability. So by definition, there's no way that they can get into a flow experience right now. And no flow, no fun. You'll most likely need to figure out what's under the resistance and try to talk about it, when and if they're ready. (See "Isolate the Resistance" below). If your resistant partner is a woman, it's even more likely that she needs you to just listen to her for a while, and hear whatever frustrations or joys she needs to share.

42

But by all means, to the extent you can, ask spontaneously and with enthusiasm. I'm sure you can think of many times you had to be nudged a little to do something, and you were soon happy for it.

And if you have confidence and get in touch with your own excitement you felt when you first read about or actually played the game, it can often be contagious, especially if you're only asking for a five-minute time commitment. Pique their interest by giving them just a taste of the tantalizing whole, so that they will be seduced into jumping in with you because you've gotten them so curious. For example, if you want to try the decision-making game "Thumb-Hat Wrestling" (Chapter 17), you might first ask your mate if they have any decisions they'd like to make right now about anything. If the answer is yes, you might then say, "Well what if I show you in one minute a real fun way I could help you with that by using our thumbs? Your thumb and my thumb (as you grasp hands getting into the "thumb-wrestling position.")

Here's another example and another important rule regarding the art of the invitation to play. When it is your idea to play, you should take on the major responsibility of providing most of the elements necessary for the game, particularly if your partner might still be stressed out from the work environment they were just in. For example, take the "Combo Song" walking or riding game (Chapter 7). If you want to play this in the car after having picking up your mate from work, you're the one who should do the lion's share of work. First, you want to give them a chance just to talk about the day, and for you to just listen. When they're done talking, your invitation might go something like this: "Honey, I've got a new game that just might make you feel better. All you have to do is give me a very morose topic, like 'the car sounds like it might need a major engine job soon,' and I'll sing it to a tune like 'Jingle Bells.' Okay? Any depressing topic you want."

> By holding lightly to an attitude of gentle exploration, we can begin to lean into creative expansion. By replacing "no way!" with "maybe," we open the door to mystery and to magic.
>
> —*Julia Cameron*

Isolate the Resistance

What if the other person is still resistant much of the time? In that case, it's good to isolate the reason for the resistance, the particular barrier or "block" that is operating here, and as soon as you can. Is it a control issue? Are they deeply attached to winning? Are they afraid of losing? Are they annoyed because it was not their idea? Do games call up something from their past? Maybe, because they lost track of the time or lost some valuable object while playing as a child, they were beaten by a parent, or emotionally abused and humiliated. Talking and careful listening will hopefully uncover the source of the resistance.

If, for example, you discover she had some awful experience with competitive games or with word games as a child, you now know that you need to stay away from this sort of game for a while, and play noncompetitive win-win games (see below) until you can gradually desensitize her from this fear.

Following is a list of many of the primary barriers or blocks to play (and creativity). Hopefully you can agree on one or two of these that pertain to your situation, and start dealing with the problem by talking about it, in a nonjudgmental way:

Blocks to Play and Creativity

Self-imposed or Development-based Emotional Blocks

Workaholism (probably the number-one barrier, and an even more rampant disease than alcoholism)

Self-censorship (being too judgmental of oneself)

Alcohol and other drug addictions

TV addiction

Overcompetitiveness (needing to compare oneself to others)

Fear of failure

Wrong livelihood

Information addiction/infoglut (Internet junkie)

Addiction to consumerism

Couple-Dynamics Blocks

Poor play technique (not keeping the players well-matched)

Unresolved major conflict(s)

Lack of agreed-upon conflict resolution method(s)

Judgmentalism (your partner is too judgmental)

Control issues (your partner is too controlling)

Intellectual Blocks

Ignorance of each other's play preferences

Lack of intellectual challenge

Self-defeating Belief Systems Blocks

"Playing is for children."

"I am not creative."

"I can only be creative in one or two areas."

"My creations or play has to be perfect or at least first rate."

"I can't look foolish."

"I have to first get good at it before trying it."

"It's not good to make mistakes."

Economic System-Based Blocks

Top-down demand for long work weeks

Lack of job security (merger mania, corporate greed)

Absence of guaranteed health care (unlike in other Western democracies)

Stressful job situation

Acceleration of pace of life by those "in control"

Since this book is really a book of games and not a therapy book, per se, the best I can do here is simply bring up these demons to point you in the right direction. There are, for example, several books (*The Artist's Way* in particular), that are very helpful in overcoming some of these blocks. And of course, if you look, there are excellent teachers in adult education and university extension, as well as private classes that can be very inspiring to help you overcome many of the above personal belief blocks. But an understanding and supportive partner who can listen well and knows some of the techniques I describe below, and most importantly knows how to really listen, can be one of the most important keys to helping you overcome your blocks. For now, I'll just leave it to you to discuss them with each other, right now if you're comfortable, or soon. A good time, of course, would be the next time they surface. And you might want to agree now to have the discussion then.

One Short Note on Alcoholism, Workaholism, and TV Addiction

The first two diseases are two of the most intransigent, and will probably require group self-help programs such as Alcoholics Anonymous. The other block may or may not require professional intervention. TV addiction, in my opinion, is the most destructive force to couple and family play and creativity. Fortunately, you can cure yourself and your family without outside intervention or help. Since there already are some excellent books out to help you kick your or your child's or spouse's TV addiction, I strongly suggest getting one at your earliest opportunity. In fact, the use of one of these books in combination with this one would be the most powerful combination.

The most important rule when playing: KEEP IT WELL-MATCHED

This is the simplest, but probably most important single thing you need to remember when playing the games in this book, to ensure that it will be a fun experience for everyone. Conversely, if you have someone who has to struggle much harder than the rest, it will be a very unpleasant experience for that person and could kill the game for everyone else. So I cannot stress the importance of this "Rule of Rules."

Take Small Steps and Work Together on It as a Family

As for the rest of the above-mentioned blocks, try first using small steps, as with any phobias or habits, and give lots of praise for any movement in the right direction. These blocks, along with TV addiction, also respond best to a whole-family approach. The whole family should be involved in the process. For example, if your spouse's major fear is fear of failure, it's important that everyone in the family realize the importance of playing noncompetitive games for a while until your spouse can, in small steps, with lots of support, be desensitized to competitive games. Here are some other helpful techniques:

Help Them Get in the Mood

Besides discovering the barriers, and working around them, or helping your partner to overcome these barriers, and besides the quality of the invitation itself, there are a number of other things you can do to get them into the mood. Again, keep in mind that there will be individual and perhaps gender differences here. But in most cases, good warm-up activities include offering a shoulder massage, telling a joke, just going for a short stroll, or giving the reluctant partner a surprise gift of flowers or chocolate, are all usually helpful ways to get them into a more relaxed and open mood. If you're dealing with another adult, getting someone into play is a process perhaps no different than getting them into romance. (In fact, it's so similar, you might often never get to the games in my book!)

If They Aren't in the Mood to Play, Find Out What Mood They're In

Now the above warm-up activities will certainly do a lot to change another person's mood if they are sad or mad. But obviously if someone if feeling sad or mad, they are not very likely going to want to play much, if at all. So simply out of caring, sensing their hurt or anger, and out of respect, I hope you will first try your best to listen to what they say is saddening or hurting or frightening them. (Yelling "Snap out of it!" works well in the movies, but rarely in real life.) Once they are heard, and perhaps given a little more time to process, they may still not want to play. But the odds will be much more in your favor.

Keep It Simple

If you are successful and your partner is now willing to hear your game idea, be sure your first idea for a game is a simple one, involving just one or two rules. And then be confident about giving those rules. Remember, trying to play without rules only generates stress and confusion. Playing a game with a few simple rules usually reduces anxiety. One of the reasons the activities in this book work so well with adults is that they create what I call "structured spontaneity." I give a few rules or boundaries within which you can be as free, spontaneous and creative as you choose. Generally people of all ages feel more comfortable within a structure, even a loose one, than without any at all. But if we give a structure, we should always be flexible about changing it, so that our fellow player(s) can feel it's their structure, too.

Choose Win/Win (Noncompetitive) Games or Keep the Players Well-Matched

I'm not one who thinks competition is bad. It's the obsession with winning that can be. The vitally important thing is to make sure the game is well-matched. A well-matched game can really make a game take off; it makes all the difference between a game that's fun and one that's not.

On the other hand, if you're playing with someone (most likely your partner) who has had some terrible childhood experiences with competitive games, it's probably safest to start with noncompetitive games. And most of the games in this book are in fact noncompetitive (though we often explain how to make them competitive).

In helping someone like this to be more playful, do your best to create the kind of fun that brings you closer, instead of dividing you into winners and losers. Choose noncompetitive games, at least to start.

It's the kind of fun that is healing for people. The win/lose mentality is part of the problem. Win/win is what is needed in play and in all our human interactions. Everyone is special and unique and contributes in their own way. Make sure you allow room for that.

Fake It Until You Make It

In trying any of these techniques, I suggest for best results you playfully adopt the "fake it till you make it" attitude. Any habit, good or bad, had to be learned. And you learned it by practice, practice, practice. If that prospect is too scary for you, consider the scarier prospect: continuing to fossilize your heart and body and mind, with an ever-shrinking compass of available variety, till you die.

You might say, "But isn't playfulness supposed to be more natural?" Not when you've unlearned most of it through family and school pressures. But everything we now do that feels natural once felt unnatural and took practice to learn. So, if you just fake it till you make it, pretty soon it will feel more and more natural and before long, you will have incorporated a much more playful spirit into your life. And as you become more and more playful, your creativity will blossom and you will feel more and more alive. You will have returned to your birthright—your true nature.

Remember, everyone's different, so don't be afraid to discover your rhythm of play. If you aren't a morning person, play at night or after you've had your coffee. This is about giving ourselves and those we live with permission to connect in a more joyful way, not about rules as to when, where, and how.

Become More Playful Yourself

Another way you may be successful in becoming more playful yourself and/or helping your partner be more playful is to learn a new activity together, maybe something that is outside your comfort zone just a little bit. Learn to ride a unicycle, juggle, skate, play volleyball, or whatever. If it's something that your mate might be a little better at than you, all the better. She or he will feel more relaxed and therefore more able to be playful.

The main goal is to do it for yourself. They may join you, or—more importantly—they may discover something else totally different that they'd like to do. And that's great.

Start Playing with Another Family Member

A good way to seduce a reluctant partner is to let them see you playing something with the children. If you think your child's invitation might be more effective than your own, invite (whisper) your child to invite your mate to play.

An almost surefire game at dinner is "Be Each Other," which I describe in Chapter 9. Each member of the family pretends to be someone else in the family. At dinner one night, just suggest it off the cuff (you may arrange it before with your kids if you like). So, all during dinner, you would be each other. Chances are, the reluctant partner (or child) would see all the fun you're having and join in without even being asked.

> If you ask me what I have come to do in this world, I who am an artist, I will reply, I am here to live my life out loud.
>
> —*Emil Zola*

Dare to Grow Young

We need to realize that our culture is in effect engaged in a conspiracy against being human; it puts down all those wonderful promising traits, those capacities for development that children are born with and which they ache, literally, to turn into abilities. We kill these capacities by the way in which we teach children at home and in school. It is a conspiracy against learning not only how to grow up, but how to grow young!

Today we know more. Today it is time to reconnect with our own uniqueness and childlike qualities—to tap into our creative spirit, and to help our children do the same. We can, as parents, encourage our children to explore imagination and creativity and express their unique, God-given talents in their own way. Encouraging our children, we can encourage ourselves.

Inside each of us is our own genius, just waiting to be accessed. It takes the willingness to live life improvisationally—in the moment, not every moment, but certainly far more than most of do today. We can break out of the small, rigid mold that we have been poured into and dare to live our lives playfully. It requires listening to our inner voice, the one that knows. It is the life force speaking to us. Can you hear it? If you're not sure, the games in the chapters that follow are vehicles that can take you to where you can.

CHAPTER 6

Waking Up in the Morning & Going to Bed at Night

Alas, Alas for those who never sing but die with all their music in them.
—*Oliver Wendell Holmes*

Knock Your Socks Off

The Undercover Penny

Wake Up Singing
(a.k.a. Shower Song)

Three Shots (or The Gun Game)

Make Up A Story

Surprise Wake-up Call

Surprise Gift

General Benefits

Besides transforming the ordinary situations of waking up or going to bed into extraordinary experiences for a couple or a family, all of these activities, used as wake-up games, are great ways to get you and your mate's brains going in the morning, and both of you out of bed in a good mood to start your day. Used as going-to-bed games, these also serve a great incentives to get your significant others to bed on time.

Knock Your Socks Off

Thank You:

The "Guru of Play" Bernie De Koven of Palo Alto, California, a husband and father of two children, who has invented as many games as anyone I know, and was once my mentor.

Benefits:

Because kids love this game so much, it's a great incentive to them to both take a shower and be in bed on time. And let's face it, anything that gets them to take a shower or go to bed on time is a very good thing.

Many parents, however will prefer version #1 (under "More Fun Ideas", below), using the game as a "Wake Up Game," because it's so energizing. (I've heard of some people playing it so hard when they awoke, they had to take a nap!) Feel free to try it either way, whichever best suits your needs.

For many of us guys, and perhaps many women too, our most wonderful childhood memories with our fathers were when we roughhoused with them. This game creates those kind of strong bonding experiences. And I suspect the research will someday show such play is just as powerful in bonding moms and kids. It can't be an accident that roughhousing is the most common form of play between parents and offspring in the animal kingdom.

This game is a great way for couples to get re-energized before going to bed, if you know what I mean.

Equipment Needed:

Just socks, clean socks (and a clean body, hint, hint)

How to Play:

First, parent and child (or both partners) face each other on all fours atop a large bed or blanket on the ground. (You can make up whatever starting position you want.) Next, see who can pull the other's socks off first.

You must stay on the mattress or blanket, or else. Or else . . . what? Well, you could get one free tug on the rulebreaker's sock. (Or a tickle or . . .)

The winner is whoever wins two out of three matches, or three out of five, or really anyone who enjoys themselves.

Warnings:

There are of course risks of injury in any physical game. So it is always important to use common sense when playing any of these games. Be sure not to have any furniture, sharp or hard objects, or fragile items with you or near the bed that you could possibly hit with your head or foot, or any other part of your body.

Keep your head far enough away from the other person's knees and feet. (Or to be 99 percent safe, wear a helmet with a face guard.)

When playing with kids older than age ten, you might find it prudent to pair off by gender.

Be sure you don't have a bad back or any other serious bone, muscle or internal problem. Use common sense.

Helpful Hints:

Don't forget the Rule of Rules: Be sure all those playing are well-matched. If not, handicap the advantaged.

The bigger the bed the better.

Handicap Ideas:

If someone is a lot better, you could handicap that person by having them use only one hand; or using their nondominant hand; or putting socks on their hands; or taking off one of their socks to begin with; having them wear shorter socks; pulling both off partially. You get the idea.

More Fun Ideas

1) Use this as a wake-up game by playing it in reverse (especially if you're both ticklish). The object is to get both socks on the other person's feet first.

2) For adults, needless to say, socks need only be the beginning.

The Undercover Penny

Thank you:
   Lisa Kirnin of San Francisco, California.

Benefits

Same as Knock Your Socks Off, except that you can actually make money on this one.

Equipment Needed:

a bed and a penny

How to Play:

Two people play this game. One person throws a penny under the covers. Both scramble to find the penny, hopefully without bumping heads.

The one who finds the penny and picks it up wins! So, what will the prize be? That depends who's playing. Best two out of three or three out of five wins whatever you decide.

Warnings:

Be sure not to have any furniture, sharp or hard objects, or fragile items near the bed that you could possibly hit with your head or foot. Be sure to keep your head far enough away from the other person's knees and feet. Or to be 99 percent safe, wear a helmet with a face guard.

When playing with kids older than age ten, you might find it prudent to pair off by gender.

Be sure you don't have a bad back or

any other serious bone, muscular, or internal problem.

Also, I've had reports that sometimes this game doesn't get beyond the first penny under the covers with some couples. So, use your own best judgment here.

Helpful Hints:

Shower beforehand. Have enough light on so you can see. And be sure you don't already have change in your clothes that might fall out and confuse matters.

More Fun Ideas

Try tossing two or three coins at once, and see who can find the most.

Wake Up Singing (a.k.a. Shower Song)

Thank You:

David and Joanne Kleijunas of Oakland, California, who actually have kept a diary of their song combinations since they started doing this. Just as many couples agree never to go to bed mad at each other,

David and Joanne used their imagination to come up with a way to (almost) always wake up feeling happy!

Benefits

1) A great way to start your day off with a smile or a laugh. It's also a wonderful way to expand and refresh your song repertoire.

2) For adults, a good way to begin to re-experience the joy you once had in singing.

3) For adults and kids, if you learn the start of a song that's a hit with the other generation, you'll get a huge number of brownie points.

How to Play:

As soon as you wake up, each of you think of a song that you know the melody of and at least the first few words.

When you've got one, ask your partner if they're ready, meaning "Are you now ready to start singing your song?" (Remember, you do not need to know the entire song by heart, only the beginning.)

Don't tell each other what your song is.

Then, one of you says, "On your mark, get set, go!" (You can alternate this role from day to day.) On "Go!," you both proceed to sing out your respective songs simultaneously to each other, as

54

authentically and in character with the original singer's performance as you can. The more you ham it up, the better! You'll laugh your way into the day.

Helpful Hints:

For adults, be sure to reassure your play partner that they don't have to be able to sing or know any more than the first few words. They can hum the rest. If you're desperate, and your partner seems to not have a clue, you can start teaching them song beginnings. (That could actually be more fun than this game!) Just be sure it's a song they like a lot.

If you know a radio station that plays music your partner likes, put it on, and record a few that they like. Or maybe you already have a cassette or CD of songs they like. Once your non-singing partner manages to learn one song, or even the beginning of one, the rest gets much easier.

Handicaps:

None here. We think being half asleep is enough.

More Fun Ideas

1) Agree the night before on a song and do that song simultaneously.

2) Try learning an additional word or line each morning till you can both sing a song together in its entirety.

3) If you like your partner or child's choice, you can just join in and sing their song together.

4) Adults, you can play this when you first meet in the shower together. Hence the name "shower song." Or skip the shower and just do it when you first meet in the bathroom.

5) Parents and kids: Do it when you first meet at breakfast, or in the car while driving.

6) See who can name the other person's song first.

7) Do this when you call your partner or child on the phone. Make it the first thing you do after you say, "HI!" In other words, you say, "Hi, Are you ready?" And when they are, you do the "on your mark, get set, go" routine.

Three Shots (or The Gun Game)

Thank you:
Wavy Gravy, Founder of Camp Winnarainbow, poet, clown-activist, and great humanitarian of Berkeley, California. Thanks also to the Committee, the precursor to Chicago's Second City.

Benefits
1) Good way to get your kids to bed.

2) Good way to add humor to getting your spouse going in he morning.

How to Play:

This game can be played any time of the day. You could even use it as an office game. And it certainly works as a "leaving or coming home" game, because the whole idea is to surprise the people you shoot. They should never know when to expect it.

Everyone has an invisible gun, and everybody has three shots a day. You sneak up on people and pretend to shoot them, and then they have to die the most dramatic death that they can imagine at that time, coughing, groaning, flailing arms, falling to the ground and gasping—the whole enchilada.

Warning:

You can't shoot if they're carrying anything hot, or breakable like a camera, or if they're doing an important job.

More Fun Ideas

If you use this upon waking up, just announce that you wounded the victim and tell them where you hit them, so they can still get out of bed and get dressed, albeit in pain and hobbling. Ironically, by handicapping someone in this way, but making them laugh, they'll probably get dressed and ready faster than without any encumbrances.

Make Up A Story

Benefits

1) Encourages imagination and spontaneity.

2) Develops verbal fluency and love of language.

3) If we ever run out of paper and trees to make it out of, a good storyteller will be very much in demand.

How to Play:

Just decide who starts, and start telling a story one sentence (or one word) at a time. Each person says his or her sentence, and then the other person picks up the story, connecting as much as possible with the thought and character(s) of the previous sentence.

Helpful Hints:

Don't try too hard or think ahead. Just listen well and let whatever comes up come out. Pick some parameters in advance, like the topic, or the two or three main characters, and perhaps two or three objects that the story will have to involve. You'll quickly find that everyone will have more freedom to create with these limitations than if there were no limits at all.

If you're doing the one-word version and one of you accidentally says two words, just use the first one.

If you're playing with a young child or anyone having a hard time, tell them that they can always try the word "and," if they get stumped. It's good to give a three-second time limit to keep the story moving, with perhaps more time for young children.

Warnings:

Don't be judgmental: it's is the worst enemy of creativity. Adults playing this game with children should be prepared for kids to come up with lots of stuff that is normally censored (for example, references to various body excretions). Those have to come out, pardon the pun, if the creativity is going to come out.

More Fun Ideas

1) Let each person do three words only.

2) Once you're both warmed up and into the swing of it, and doing one sentence at a time, try taking on different accents (Italian, French, German) or dialects (Brooklynese, Southern). This will add a lot of humor to the proceeding and might also make it easier to get into the swing of things.

Surprise Wake-up Call

Thank You:

Carolyn Permentier from Arlington, Virginia. I don't remember who invented this first, but we sure had a lot of fun testing it out.

Benefits

1) Gets you up quickly and with a laugh. When you laugh, the muscles in your face bring more blood into your head!

2) Develops your repertoire of "voices" or characters, which can come in very handy in many other areas of life, especially if you want to provide interesting alternatives to watching television, like making up a story, skit, or talk show with various characters.

3) If you let whoever tends to sleep too long be the caller, it might be enough of an incentive to getting them up on time, or even earlier than usual.

How to Play:

Arrange with another family with whom you're close to take turns giving each other wake-up calls.

For example: wives call Mondays and Wednesdays; husbands call Tuesdays and Thursdays, responsible kids call Fridays (this can be a reward for the kids).

The idea is for the "waker" to pretend he or she is someone else like the president of the United States; Fidel Castro (if you can speak Spanish); Inspector Clouseau (if you can do a French accent); a very sexy admirer from the company the "wakee" works at (be careful with this one); the guy who's trying to give you a free newspaper subscription (you of course make it the National Enquirer to add some pizzazz); a market researcher doing a survey on whatever sensational topic you can imagine; that Publishers Clearinghouse Sweepstakes guy offering you a million bucks.

Warning:

Double-check that you are calling at the precise time when the wakee wants, and not sooner or later. Slipups could be detrimental to neighborly relations.

This is probably not a game for weekends, when most people prefer waking up naturally!

Helpful Hints:

If you feel awkward or shy, try role-playing with a friend.

More Fun Ideas

Pretend you're one of the most famous people alive (or secretary thereof) within the occupation of the person you're calling. For example, if you're waking up someone who is an stockbroker, you could say you're the assistant to the president of Merrill Lynch, who's heard about how well they've been performing and wants to offer them a position in New York. Or if you're waking up an attorney, you could say you're Alan Dershowitz or his assistant. You got the idea.

Surprise Gift

Thank you Karen Ehrlich for this one.

Benefits

1) We can all do with more pleasant surprises in our lives.

2) This is a fun way to reinforce a desired habit, (e.g., getting to bed on time.)

3) It's also a wonderful way for couples to show their gratitude for each other and to nourish their love.

How To Play:

For couples: Sometime in the evening, slip a love note or other surprise under your mate's pillow. When you go to bed, just tell them that there's a surprise under their pillow.

For kids: Let them know that sometimes, but not always, as long as they get to bed on time, there will be a surprise for them under the pillow when they wake up the next morning. Then after they've fallen asleep, slip the surprise under their pillow for them to discover the next morning. The surprise could be a new book, a little toy, or a coupon good for their favorite breakfast item or whatever, depending on their age.

We'd love to hear your own inventions of new and free ways to have fun waking up or going to bed. You'll be delighted and so will perhaps millions of others. Please see the end of Chapter 20 for details on how to send in your ideas and how we'll reward your effort and ingenuity.

CHAPTER 7

Riding in the Car, Walking, or Biking

Play is often talked about as if it were a relief
from serious learning. But for children play is serious learning.
Play is really the work of childhood.

—*Fred Rogers*

The Alphabet Game

Three Best Things

Last Letter-First Letter

Hinky Pinky

Slow Bike Race

Read My Mind

The Special Combo Song

Three Word Song Make-Up

Alphabetical Song Game

Stop Light Jokes

Zen Seeing

Alliteration Road Game

Verb Travel Game

Colors

Help Me Rhonda

Interview the Experts

Color Car Windows

Wheel of Fortune

Make Up a Story

Character in the Car

Word Pairs

General Benefits

All of these games can remove whatever boredom that may arise riding in the car, or even during a routine walk or bike ride. Many of the Mealtime games in Chapter 9 work just as well here, and most of the games here can also turn other common situations like eating dinner or waiting around into fun opportunities.

Finally, aside from Zen Seeing, Slow Bike Race, and Wheel of Fortune, all of these activities are valuable for language and knowledge development, and in some cases, dramatic skill development.

The Alphabet Game

Thank you:
Bob Cambanes of Brooklyn Park, Minnesota.

Benefits

1) Helps the time pass much more interestingly in the car or on a walk.

2) Develops verbal fluency, vocabulary, and strengthens love for language.

3) Provides extra conversational structure for family members who might otherwise be a little shy, or, on the other hand, who might want to bite your head off. (I recommend it more for the shy situation, however, than the angry one.)

How to Play:

Pick a topic and choose someone to start the conversation. Whoever starts talking has to start their sentence with the letter A. The next person has to start their sentence with the letter B, the next with C, and so on.

It's best to determine the order ahead of time, say clockwise or counter clockwise, so everyone gets a turn.

You also should announce in advance that the X and Z are excluded, and for the first two or three times, maybe those stumpers Q and J as well.

Decide if you want to make it competitive by giving points (see below).

Helpful Hints:

1) If you have a much younger child for whom this is too difficult, or a shy grandmother or grandfather, have them be the "scorekeeper"— announcing in advance which letter of the alphabet is next, and whose turn is next.

2) The trick to keeping the game from getting bogged down is to tell people ahead of time to *anticipate* their letter—to start thinking of how they will start ahead of time.

3) Another very helpful tip to make this game go smoothly and quickly, and to keep the conversation on the same topic, is to come up with word phrases that are reacting to the person who spoke before you. Here's an example: Although I agree with you ... But you forgot ... Could you elaborate on that point about ... Don't you think that ... Even if you did ... For whatever it's worth. ... and so on and so forth.

4) Younger or less fluent players could be allowed to use a dictionary.

If you have a teenager who refuses to keep to the rules of this simple little game, or has not yet mastered the alphabet, just pull over to the side of the road immediately, let the teenager out, and speed away very quickly. (If your kids are reading this with you, tell them the author's just kidding. Really. I am.)

More Fun Ideas

1) Give extra points if anyone (a) compliments the driver in their sentence; or (b) uses a real word that no other children her age or older can define.

2) Require that the each person start their sentence with the last letter of the last word of the person who spoke before them.

3) See how fast you can get through the alphabet, and then try to beat your record, offering a special reward if you do.

4) For more advanced players, pick an object like water, sun, flowers, dogs, etc. and whatever you say, you must make some reference to that object. So if you were about to say "After school let out, I met Sally," and the object for the game was "sun," you might now say, "After school let out, I met Sally, who has hair as bright and golden as the sun!" The person responsible for the letter B might respond: "But when I started to talk to her, the sun was in my eyes." And person C might respond, "Carefully, I

bet, you maneuvered yourself into another position that got the sun out of your eyes?"

> Get everybody on the bus to sing with you. I know one bus driver when he saw a conflict between two men sang, "You Are My Sunshine". So imagine getting the whole bus in the morning singing "You Are My Sunshine". I had a whole airplane sing "Happy Birthday" to me because I said, "It's my birthday, I'm in the air, I want to celebrate". Everybody in the plane was changed by that experience. Often my wife next to me says, "You going to do it?" I say, "Well, I'm not sure." She says, "Do it!"
>
> —*Bernie Siegel, M.D.*

Three Best Things

Thank you:
Michelle Ballew, Tacoma, Washington

Benefits

1) Makes you feel gratitude for your daily blessings, and see how the "little things" can be as significant as

what you always thought were the "big" things.

2) Makes walking more fun, so you end up exercising more.

3) Makes you appreciate those other people, more than you might have otherwise, who've been the source of your "best things" during the week.

4) Can enlighten you about what you are failing to appreciate.

How to Play:

Very simple: While in the car or taking a walk, just share, taking turns, the three best things that happened to you during your day.

I do this with my wife, Karen, almost every day during our walk before dinner (which also keeps us from gaining weight). If we miss our walk, we do Three Best Things during the dinner.

More Fun Ideas

1) I tend to ask too many questions all the time, and she tends not to ask enough. So lately we've added this variation by adding this rule: I can only ask two questions about each of her best things, and she must ask at least two questions about my three best things.

2) Every so often, Karen will get especially playful and surprise me by announcing the game as "Eight Best Things!" And then we both have to

find that many things. This variation is especially powerful in forcing you to really start seeing and appreciating the small things that happen every day.

Last Letter-First Letter

Benefits

Expands one's vocabulary and knowledge of animals, historical figures, etc.

How to Play:

Decide who starts and your order (clockwise or counterclockwise).

Then whoever starts says the name of an historical figure (or animal, flower, food, etc.), and the next person must say the name of another historical figure (or animal, etc.) that starts with the last letter of the previous person's word. For example, if the first person says "Martin Luther King," the next person could say "Ghandi." If the first person said "tiger," the next person could say "raccoon."

More Fun Ideas

Make it competitive by giving points, and give an extra point whenever the person giving the historical figure's name, can also describe the figure's historical significance.

One thing you can do when you're traveling and the parent has a very good idea of what they want to see in a certain museum, but knows that the children will get restless, is for the parent to buy a stack of postcards of the pictures in the museum's store, and then give one stack to each child, and see how fast, or how well each child can find the original picture on the wall they've now had a postcard view of. This can keep them busy for a very long time.

—*Dr. Benjamin Spock*

Hinky Pinky

Thank You:

Bernie De Koven, "the Guru of Play," again gets my thanks. Bernie can be found, by the way, at his Web site. Just go to any search engine and search on the phrase, "Dr. Fun."

Benefits

Offers the same verbal benefits as the Alphabet Game, and also develops the ability to rhyme. And you just never know when you might have to think up a poem or make up a song.

How to Play:

This game uses charming rhyming word pairs you've only dreamed of creating. Okay, this can be a very cute game. So please pardon a digression into momentary partial cuteness: Sly guys and gal pals! Let's play a fun one! It's not a tame game. Here's the hot plot! Spot sees the hot plot! See the hot plot of Spot! See Spot go splot!

No, seriously. This game can be quite mentally challenging. Here's how it works.

A Hinky Pinky is a noun-adjective pair that rhymes. A pair with one syllable is called a "Hink Pink" (nice mice, hot pot, fat cat); with two syllables, it's a Hinky Pinky (funny bunny, pretty kitty); with three syllables, it becomes a Hinkety Pinkety (merrier terrier). Hinkety Pinketies are, of course, the most challenging.

Whoever is "It" thinks of a pair of rhyming words and describes the pair in a sentence or two. The other players try to guess what the pair is. First to guess will be "It" next. Being "It" is significant. Being "It" is life-impacting. Being "It" means you'll be referred to for several minutes as a pronoun for inanimate, sexless objects. Here's an example:

Mom is "It." She thinks long and hard for several minutes. "OK, here's a Hinky Pinky," she tells the kids. "A very relaxed low calorie dessert." "A flustered custard?" Susie guesses.

"Nope! but you're getting close."
"A half-dead shortbread?" tries Junior.
"Wrong! but that's very clever."
"Give up?" Mom is resonating with

pride and joyous emotions.

"Mellow jello!" Susie exclaims.

"Yes!" Mom says. "Congrats. You're It."

Warn everyone that some people find it easier to guess the answer while others find it easier to think up the challenge.

Helpful Hints:

If you have two or more children and one is much younger, give the younger his or her own Hink Pink to solve, without help from the older; otherwise you'll be creating a frustrating situation. Or to make it even easier, just ask the younger to think of words that rhyme with whatever word you want to throw his way. Once he comes up with one that makes a good Hink Pink, write it down, and later on, after every- one's talked about a zillion other rhyming pairs, pass him the one he thought of and ask him to be It.

> **Don't forget the Rule of Rules:**
>
> Be sure all those playing are well- matchhed. If not, handicap the advantaged. Remember: Be imaginative in your rewards. See Appendix A.

Slow Bike Race

Thank You:

Christine Lavin, one of our country's most insightful and humorous singers, of New York City.

Benefits

1) You mean outside of the fact that it's very funny? Well . . .

It gives you some perspective on what I mean when we talk about winning. If Vince Lombardi had known about slow bike racing, he probably wouldn't have been so cranky all the time. All that yelling couldn't have been good for him.

2) It also shines a little light on our relationship with that old nemesis, time. I mean, who's really chasing who here? Is time catching up with you, or is it just trying to keep up with you?

3) Helps people learn to literally bal- ance discipline with spontaneity.

4) It is much safer than speed bicycle racing.

5) Develops balance and makes a great metaphor for emotional balance, as participants must learn to match discipline with spontaneity.

6) Why else play this game? Obviously, because sometimes you just need to slow down. Way down. This will do it.

Equipment Needed:

Everyone in the race should have a bicycle. That way it's fair. If you don't want to be fair, that's all right too. But the game's name does carry a general implication of bicycle availability.

How to Play:

Everybody's done this game in some form, but probably not on a bicycle. You did it when you were a kid, remember? The object is to race, not as fast as you can, but as slow as you can. Whoever gets there last wins. I don't recommend having more than one of these a day, however. Trust me.

Pick out a goal, or finish line marker, about 100 feet away from your starting line. Anything will do: a tree, parking meter, wall, or even a very lazy person who you're sure won't move. (Do not tell them why you chose them. Show tact and commend them for their patience.)

Give the signal: on your mark, get set, SLOW!

Each racer begins pedaling his or her bicycle toward the finish marker as slowly as possible without feet touching ground or falling over (or perhaps for beginners, without feet touching ground or falling over more than two times). If those feet hit the ground, that's a stop, and the stopper must immediately pedal one bike length forward (or you might try making it two bike lengths, or most simply, must bike one bike length in front of the most forward person). The last person to the finish marker wins.

Just as in life, it will be considered unfair if you should lengthen your path by going astray. However, just as in life, it could also be more fun to go astray, depending on where you stray to and who you stray with. I leave this rule in your hands, since who is actually astray is a nasty tactical question at best.

Warnings:

Don't play on the street or on heavily traveled sidewalks, and be sure to wear knee and elbow guards if you're prone to falling. Pushing or pulling your competition is not allowed. And don't play if you have knee or muscular problems, or any skeletal problems, since falling off of a nearly stationary bicycle can still cause problems.

Helpful Hints:

Warn beginners to be sure to move a little or else they'll fall over. Kids too young (or adults too fragile) to be able to do this can be given the referee role, in charge of yelling on your mark, get set, go!, citing players for penalties, and announcing the winner. They can also be given the "tick-ler" role to handicap the better player(s).

More Fun Ideas

1) The slow pogo stick race, and for the truly gifted, the slow unicycle race.

2) Try experimenting with the following handicaps, especially if very young children with less developed balance ability are playing. Handicaps can be include slight pushes or tickles by family or friends who are watching, or by mechanical means. Other possibilities include having to hold balloons under your armpits, having to play a kazoo while racing, or even having to hold a hard-boiled egg between your teeth without biting it in two.

Research Note

So far, not a single slow bike race run in this country has ever not ended. But that does give you something to shoot for.

Read My Mind

Thank you:
Fred Schildmeyer, wherever you are! (I wish I knew)

Benefits

1) Improves visual imagination and memory.

2) Replaces kids complaining, arguing, fighting, begging for money, etc.

How to Play:

A person thinks of a mental picture and then everyone else asks the person questions till the picture can be guessed. The first person to guess the other's picture wins whatever you all decide on.

Example: Sally pictures in her mind the cover of her "Lion King" book. Everyone else has to guess what she is seeing in her mind, by asking questions such as:

Dad: "Is it outdoors or inside?"
Sally says, "Outdoors."
Mom: " Is it city, wilderness, or rural?"

Sally says, "Wilderness."

Dad: "Does it have a human, an animal, or only plants in it?"

Helpful Hints:

Don't be extremely detailed. If someone guesses the basic situation, that's enough. Don't expect people to guess colors or jewelry, for example.

If there is a big age spread, you might want to whisper to the youngest a hint or two (e.g. a growl sound for the above picture), and then ask him/her to wait till everyone has had at least a couple of questions before they start asking questions.

If those guessing are simply having a difficult time, give more clues (see #2 under "More Fun Ideas" below).

You'll just have to experiment a bit to see how low in age you can work with, when you have older kids involved.

More Fun Ideas

1) Everyone thinks of a picture simultaneously, and everyone tries to guess everyone else's picture. Of course you'll need pen and paper to keep track of the clues. And whoever guesses a correct picture first gets the Big Reward.

2) Give your hints in creative ways, for example, by whistling a tune that provides a hint. For example, if my picture is of myself singing in the rain, or just being in the bathroom shower, I could whistle "Raindrops Keep Falling on My Head," or if I get desperate, "Singing in the Rain."

3) If you have four or more players (an even number is best), cut out various pictures from magazines and/or newspapers, fold them and put them in a cup to be drawn later, or just put them face down. Get into pairs like in the game Pictionary and then, on the count of three, have one person from each pair simultaneously look at one picture (one of those drawn from those cut out of the paper), and then go back to their partner and proceed to see which couple team can get the picture guessed first. Think of this as a "verbal Pictionary!"

4) Limit the field of choices to a picture (other than of a person) in the newspaper or a section thereof. This will help get the right answer much more quickly and make the game move much faster.

The Special Combo Song

Thank You:

Again, Carolyn Permentier, Arlington, Virginia.

Benefits

1) Develops love of language and, we should hope, song.

2) Develops mental and verbal dexterity and spontaneity.

3) Is almost always much funnier than anything you'd hear on the car radio.

4) Could reveal things deep inside your mate or child you never knew were there! (Don't forget, "The truth shall set you free.")

5) Could lead to a whole new career as a humorous song writer or singer.

How to Play:

This unlikely match is likely to be for the more courageous, for it not only involves song, but also mental dexterity. But remember, as Anaïs Nin once said, "Life shrinks or expands in proportion to one's courage."

One person gives the other a particular issue or topic, and the name of a familiar song for which those playing would know the melody. For example, "Mary Had a Little Lamb" is the melody and "homework" is the topic. Using the melody of the song, the other person must make up lyrics for the topic and sing it. Here's what my wife came up with when I gave her this combination:

Mary had to do her homework,
do her homework, do her homework.
Mary had to do her homework, which
made her very smart.

Every day she finished her work
finished her work, finished her work.
Every day she finished her work, so she
could go and play.

Here are some more examples of topic tune combos:

The tune is "She'll Be Coming Around the Mountain" and the topic is "family or couple arguments."

The tune is "White Christmas," and the topic is the war on drugs, or welfare cuts.

Helpful Hints:

You'll have the most fun with this game if the mood of the melody contrasts with the topic. For example, with a very happy, upbeat tune like "Zippity Doo Da!" or "Tea for Two," suggest a morose topic, like public apathy, losing a baseball game, or two people meeting at a funeral. To a sad song, like "Eleanor Rigby" (All the Lonely People), you might suggest happy topics like Bugs Bunny or puppy dogs. You've got the idea. These unlikely matches will produce some likely laughs.

Some kids just won't stop. So you might anticipate this problem by putting a one- or two-minute time limit per song.

This game may not be suitable to kids under eight or nine, who generally know few songs.

Warnings:

Parents and kids: Since this is improv, parents should be prepared for a preponderance of references to nasal and other excretory matter. Don't worry, it's just a phase. Don't use the names of anyone in the car, since that could lead to hurt feelings.

Kids, I don't know what to warn you about. I don't know who your parents are.

In any case, don't be *judgmental*. That's the surest way to stifle creativity.

More Fun Ideas

1) To make it easier, you can "properly" associate the melody with the situation like an upbeat tune with an upbeat situation.

2) Give whoever is "It" a melody, and let them choose their own topic, or visa versa.

3) You might even want to record some of this. You might even generate a hit CD some day.

4) Have an improv Sing-Song at parties. Singles or couples could sing to or with each other using the melody/situation assigned.

Three Word Song Make-Up

Much like Combo Song, in a clockwise fashion, one family member throws out the name of a popular tune, but unlike Combo Song, she gives three "items," rather than a general topic or issue. The items can be nouns, verbs, adjectives, adverbs or a combination. They can be celebrities, other family members' names, etc. They need not be in the same category. The tune should be one that is known by almost everybody.

The person to the right must then spontaneously make up a song using the tune suggested and the three items. As soon as they are finished, they create the same challenge for the person to their right. A helpful hint with this variation is to use only one word if playing with younger children. As with Combo Song, the more contrast between the tune's mood and the items, the funnier the song will be.

Alphabetical Song Game

Benefits

1) Develops everyone's song repertoire.

2) Some of our best memories are the times we sang with our parents or kids.

3) Appropriate almost anytime: in the car, on a hike or walk, after dinner, during a party, etc. My wife and I often do this while cleaning the house.

4) Again, it beats much of what you hear on the radio.

How to Play:

This terrific travel game could get you across even Nebraska, singing all the way! All you have to do is take turns, going through the alphabet singing songs whose title begins with the needed letter (e.g. if your letter is S, you could sing "Summertime"). For a song to qualify, you must know at least the first line.

Helpful Hints:

Kids will often want to sing their song through to the end, which may be just fine for you, but also might drive the other kids or a non-family member nuts. So either be prepared, or establish a rule that sets a realistic limit (at the end of the egg timer, after two refrains, etc.)

Younger children know many fewer songs and therefore may need a little help or more leeway. For example, you could let them completely make up their own song. Or they could sing "Mary had a Little Lamb" for either M or L.

More Fun Ideas

1) If you like and know the song that someone has come up with, join in singing it.

2) You can put a time limit on how long each person can take to think of their song. The person who can't come up with a song within their allotted time loses a point.

3) You can make it easier by allowing use of either the first word or first noun mentioned in the song title or first line. For example: one could sing "Climb Every Mountain" if their letter was C or M. But they could not use this song for E.

4) You can make this competitive by simply announcing that you do not alternate and whoever gets to the end of the alphabet first, wins. Obviously, you cannot use a song

that your opponent has already used, and you can both agree to omit X and Z.

Stoplight Jokes

Benefits

1) Helps pass the time while in traffic jams.

2) Could develop new more humorous friends.

3) Great way to learn new jokes.

4) Gives you a great story to tell at dinner.

Equipment Needed:

Two or three short (under thirty seconds) tasteful jokes. Actually, I've used one great joke forever (all the others I know are too long.) Here's the joke: What do you get when you play country music backwards? You get your house back, your wife back, your dog back...

A bumper sticker is optional. If you have a stencil or can write or print exceptionally neatly, you need to merely cut and paste together a strip of white paper about five feet long and five or six inches high, on which you will write in large letters the following:

THIS DRIVER TELLS JOKES AT STOP SIGNS! or, THIS DRIVER TELL JOKES IN TRAFFIC JAMS.

Then glue it on to the bumper of your car. The letters should be at least three inches high in order to be easily read by a car twenty to forty feet behind you.

How to Play:

You simply roll down your window and tell a very short joke to the person next to you. If you have a bumper sticker that says This driver trades jokes at stop signs, then you can just wait until drivers roll their windows down and ask you for a joke.

I have this fantasy that if this kind of creativity were to catch on in a big way, traffic jams and long commutes could be as enriching as a poetry gathering and as funny as a stand-up comedy show on TV.

Warnings:

It is possible that certain localities might not allow such bumper stickers. I don't know. Check your with your local police to make sure. I first tested this in Los Angeles, and am now going on my sixth month of the writing of this and no police officer has ever said anything.

Needless to say, it would definitely be a danger to simply write, "trade jokes while driving." So please be sure you keep the

phrase "at stop signs" in your bumper sticker.

Helpful Hints:

1) You can just order our own professionally made THIS DRIVER TELLS JOKES AT STOP SIGNS! bumper sticker from us. See Chapter 20 for details how to order.

2) Put the sticker on your car door as well.

More Fun Ideas

1) I just know that any time now, car manufacturers will start putting thank-you horns (or more likely I'm-sorry horns) on cars, which we'll be able to sound at the appropriate times. When that happens, it will open up a whole new era of creative bumper stickers. You can start making bumper stickers that say stuff like, "If You're from Minneapolis, Honk Thank You", or "If You Want a Third Party, Honk Thank You, or If You Canoe, Honk Thank You" or whatever.

2) Whenever you think of your own new and fun "interactive" bumper stickers, let us know so that we can tell the world. See Chapter 20 for details.

> The voyage of discovery lies not in finding new landscapes but in having new eyes.
>
> —*Marcel Proust*

Zen Seeing

Thank You:
  Author John Bradshaw.

Benefits

1) There are few games I can think of that more powerfully allow one person to show another how the ordinary can be extraordinary and to help see the world more poetically.

2) Helps build or rebuild trust between partners, parent and child, or siblings.

3) This game develops a much deeper appreciation of nature.

4) A great way to just pass the time, if you're waiting around.

How to Play:

Get into pairs. Threesomes are possible, but a bit more dangerous, since the idea is to lead the other person(s) around with their eyes closed. The best situations are hikes in the woods, but your front or back yard, or even inside your home, will do just fine.

The idea is to carefully lead your partner by the hand, with his or her eyes closed, to visually interesting things, like a flower, a butterfly, the bark of a tree, a panoramic view of mountains or the sun coming through a tree, dew drops on a leaf, an apple, the silverware standing in your dish rack, etc. Usually something close up works best.

Situate your partner's head as if it was a camera in front of the object or view you've found. Your object is to align your partner's head so that when they open their eyes, they will be looking straight at the object you want them to see.

Then squeeze their hand, at which time they open their eyes for just an instant, then close them again. (When I am the leader, I usually tell the person to keep their eyes open only for as long as I squeeze.)

This gives the viewer both a wonderful surprise and a much more intense experience of the object or view than they would normally have. They see the reality, or essence, of that object more deeply than they would if it was just among everything else.

The viewer can request another "seeing" of the object or view by simply saying "again." Encourage your partner to ask for repeat viewings before moving on to the next discovery, since this experience is truly a wonderful joy they will usually want to have again and again.

Warnings:

This is to be done walking only.

Be sure not to do this on hilly or rocky terrain, in dilapidated condemned houses, in busy traffic.... Well, you get the idea.

Helpful Hints:

Be sure to use your free hand to further support the other person, especially if they have to step up or down.

Direct your partner verbally as well as by hand. Carefully watch the terrain and warn your partner ahead of time if they will need to step up or down, or duck their head, etc.

It's almost always fun to lead your partner to a close-up position on an object, since this is a point of view that is always new and surprising. However, some older people and people with poor eyesight may be less able to focus on close-up objects too close. In these cases, make sure they are at least a foot and a half away from the object in question.

More Fun Ideas

Do a five-minute blind walk in which you guide your partner around as above, but they feel the objects with their eyes closed the whole time.

Alliteration Road Game

Benefits

1) Develops love of language, verbal fluency, and vocabulary.

2) Encourages poetic abilities.

How to Play:

First I had better give examples of what I mean by alliteration. Alliteration is when words (in pairs or groups) start with the same letter, as in Peter Piper Picked a Peck of Pickled Peppers (the alliterating words can be separated by prepositions or articles like "a" and "an").

To play, see who can come up with ten alliterative travel-related adverb/verb or adjective/noun combinations first, either verbally or in writing. Some examples are: "maniacally moving," "whirling wheels," "magnificent mountain." Each player keeps their own score.

Handicaps:

If there is a big age or "talent" difference, handicap the better person by giving them a larger number of combinations to come up with.

Helpful Hints:

Keep notes in the car, so that you when you play again you can disallow combinations that have been used within the past two weeks.

It's probably a good idea to keep a dictionary in the car.

More Fun Ideas

1) Have the younger child call out a letter from the alphabet. Then, whoever comes up with an alliterative adverb/verb or adjective/noun pair first, gets the point. This is both a fun variation and also a way to involve a child who is too young to come up with alliterations.

2) The younger child can call out the travel-related noun or verb, such as "car," "driving," or "road," and again see which of the others can come up with the alliterative pair first.

3) Keep a chart of points won, and whoever gets the most over the course of a week gets to pick from your reward list.

4) For a more challenging version, require the players to provide their pairs in alphabetical order, either by alternating, or competing with each other to see who gets to the end of the alphabet first. Again, exclude X and Z, and perhaps Q as well.

Verb Travel Game

Thank You:
 Jackie

Benefits

Develops love of language, verbal fluency, and vocabulary.

How to Play:

The object of the game is to point out actions or verbs. Examples:

"Driving down the street I see people walking, the sun shining, people driving." The first person to find ten actions or verbs in their environment wins.

Helpful Hints:

Reduce the minimum number to win for younger children.

For anyone over the age of ten, the first person to come up with ten verbs wins.

If you're under twelve, your equivalent quota to win is the same number as your age.

Note: What children see and describe will no doubt vary from one section of the country to another. For instance, in a rural area you could see the grass growing (if you were in one place for a long time), the cows meandering, or the power lines swaying in the breeze.

In L.A.: See the robber lead the police on a high-speed chase, see the bank shootout; see the earth move without warning.

More Fun Ideas

1) Decide on a shape to look for in your environment (circle, square, etc.) For example: round wheel, round steering wheel, round face, etc. Double points if the description is alliterative!

2) A noncompetitive version would be to simply apply the alphabet game to this: When it's your turn, just name a verb describing an action you see that starts with the letter in the alphabet you have. If it's your turn, and your letter is J, you might say "grasshoppers jumping," or "the leaves are jiggling."

3) Decide on a time limit, say fifteen minutes. Whoever comes up with the longest written list in that time limit, wins (and gets to choose the next game).

Colors

Thank You:

Again to Bernie De Koven. Bernie, by the way, was one of the original founders of the New Games Movement, which developed new forms of physical games for groups.

Benefits

1) You might learn some new colors.

2) You get to shout a lot.

3) But most important, you start to feel that moment of perfect collaboration forming. It's disconcerting, particularly if the color you all yell is puce.

How to Play:

You need a leader. You could elect one, appoint one, or just allow one to naturally arise from the populace. Or you could just let the driver be the leader. The leader has to be able to count to three. So even a two- or three-year-old could be leader. After the leader reaches "three," everyone shouts out a color, any color: red, magenta, silver, yellow. No player may say the same color twice in a row. The game is over when all players say the same color at the same time.

Helpful Hints:

If you get into frequent arguments as to whether or not a color has already been said, take turns having someone be the secretary. That person can still play, of course.

For younger kids who know fewer colors, let one of the older whisper a color into their ear. Also let the younger kids know that many fruits are also the names of colors (e.g. tangerine, peach, orange.)

More Fun Ideas

1) If three or more are playing, and two people say the same color at the same time, those two get a point.

2) Let the game continue, even when all get the same color at the same

76

time. Let it end when no one, or only one person, can think of a new color.

3) You could also do this with the names of major-league baseball teams, or with vegetables, fruits, cars, writers, historical figures, etc. But colors do seem to work remarkably well. I tried doing it with the names of eighteenth-century German philosophers once, but it just lacked the same spirit. And, let's face it, if you've got a car load of people that could discuss German philosophers, you might want to play the colors game later.

Help Me Rhonda

Thank You:
   Karl Rohnke, the founder of Project Adventure and another one of the greatest game creators of all time.

Benefits:
Develops vocabulary and love of language.

Equipment Needs:

Each person must have a paper and pencil or pen. You also need an egg timer or stop watch.

How to Play:

Everyone takes turns being the leader. The leader calls out a name with no repeating letters, like Rhonda.

Each person, including the leader, then writes the name in bold letters at the top of their paper, letting each letter of the name be the heading of a column.

The leader then calls out the name of a category, like "animals." Each player must then list as many names of animals as possible within the time limit whose first letters match the letters at the head of each column. In this case, R-H-O-N-D-A might lead to "raccoon" under R, "halibut" and "horse" under H, and "owl" under O. One point is awarded for each acceptable answer and two points are given if the other players didn't think of it.

Use an egg timer or stopwatch to set whatever time limit you want. I recommend three to five minutes for short trips, and longer for long trips.

Helpful Hints:

If one child is much younger or another much more talented at this, require the older or more talented to come up with at least five, ten, or fifteen extra words or names, or give the older or more talented half the time you're giving the others.

The winner is whoever has the largest

grand total (if all players are fairly equal) or whoever has won the most games.

Handicaps:

You could require the more talented or older child to handle two names in the same time the others are handling one, for example if R-H-O-N-D-A is the first name, S-A-M-U-E-L could be the second. The driver or adult could come up with the second name. For the older to win, he or she would need to have at least ten items under both names.

Interview the Experts

Benefits:

1) Develops spontaneity.

2) Develops verbal fluency, one or more dramatic skills, and vocabulary.

3) Increases knowledge and/or interest in a topic.

4) Develops interviewing ability.

How to Play:

One person is the expert being interviewed. The other is the interviewer; there can be more than one interviewer, depending on how many people are playing.

The interviewer invites the interviewee—the expert—to select a topic they are expert in and to describe their title, the sillier the better. For example, the topic could be the increasing trend of dogs associating

with cats, with Dr. Schnauzer, a dogologist from Switzerland who has researched this growing problem in both Europe and the United States. Or the topic could be kids wearing beanie hats with propellers at school, and you would have a conversation with Dr. Bob Beanie, who has been studying beanie hats for the past thirty years.

The interviewer then proceeds to ask the expert questions about the topic, and the "expert" just makes up whatever answers they wish.

Helpful Hints:

1) Tell people not to try too hard or think ahead, but just to listen well and let whatever comes up come out.

2) Think up funny combinations of things in order to get an interesting topic. If you take the combination of "celery" and "hair," for example, the topic might be the recent discovery of hairy celery, or celery's possible ability to grow hair. Once you have the combinations, it's much easier to deduce the expert's field.

3) The interviewer should avoid asking "closed ended" questions, that is, questions that can simply be answered by a yes or no. In other words, avoid asking questions that start with phrases like " Would you ...," "Do you ...," "Are you ...,"

4) Try to relate your questions to issues of the day. This will add a lot of humor.

More Fun Ideas

If there are more than three of you, two or more can become the single expert, acting as if they are one person, by answering in sentences they make up together, one word at a time, going back and forth from person to person, either one word at a time, or whenever one pauses, the other continues. Of course two or more can be interviewers as well, taking turns asking questions.

Color Car Windows

Benefits

1) Develops artistic skills.

2) Reduces back-seat arguments.

3) Gives you the prettiest rear side windows in town.

Equipment Needed:

Driver's side rear car window and markers. Be sure to use washable color markers, which are available at any art supply establishment and most drug stores.

Even though you're using washable markers, you'll save yourself some grief by putting an old blanket over the back seat.

How to Play:

Decorate the driver's side rear window by letting your kids draw whatever they want. That's all there is to it.

If you have more than one kid in back, you'll just have to take turns., or divide the window in half, and have a time limit, unless you have some interesting alternative for the second child to do, like perhaps playing any of the above games with just you.

Warning:

Be sure to only use the back seat *side window* on the driver's side. Impairing vision out of any other *window could cause a serious accident!*

Wheel of Fortune

Thank You:

Dianne Smith, (Provo, Utah), one of the nation's leading experts on how play helps families.

Benefits

1) Adds extra suspense to a long trip.

2) Helps kids look forward more to trips.

3) Gives you cute-looking tires.

4) Avoids flat tires due to slow leaks (because you'll have people frequently checking your tires).

Equipment needed:

Chalk. Oh, and tires on your car.

How to Play:

This is best for long trips. Just have each player mark their initials on the side of a tire. Whenever you stop for gas or food, everyone gets out and looks at the tires. Whoever's initials are closest to the point where the tire meets the grounds gets to pick the snack or choose a particular seat in the car, or whatever reward you set out ahead of time.

Warning:

Be sure you always stop the car in a safe place far from the roadway itself, so that anyone standing on the driver's side is not dangerously close to traffic.

Make Up a Story

Benefits

In addition to those mentioned in Chapter 6, by playing this game with kids, it can help you discover concerns, anxieties, and dislikes your children have that perhaps they aren't even aware of themselves.

How to Play:

See "How to Play" instructions in Chapter 6. Since the Chapter 6 version is for two people only, be sure to agree on an order, clockwise or counterclockwise, if playing this game on a walk or in a car with three or more people.

Helpful Hints:

Tell the youngest child or whoever is having a hard time that they can always try the word "and," if they get stumped. It's good to give a three-second time limit, so the story moves, perhaps more time for young children.

Character in the Car

Benefits

1) If you choose a historical character, you can teach history.

2) Develops acting ability and verbal fluency.

How to Play:

Pretend you are someone else when you pick up your spouse or kid and see if they can guess who you are, or at least get into the act and play along by becoming a character themselves. Here's a list of possible characters for starters:

- Thomas Paine, Oprah Winfey, Ghandi, Fidel Castro, Martin Luther King etc.

- foreign agent meeting your contact in America to get the secret formula for "ze supermemory hormone;"

- chauffeur for a famous scientist like Albert Einstein;

- president of a new company picking

up a potential rich investor for your new invention for growing carrots and celery (or peanuts) at home and whom you must persuade to invest in your latest scheme (each time you have a new scheme to sell them);

• owner of a restaurant picking up a world-famous chef, who has invented a super new sandwich and you can't wait to hear about it.

Word Pairs

Benefits

Develops vocabulary and love of language.

How to Play:

This is a word-association game where the word that is associated must form a common compound word or phrase. For example, if I say white, you can say "White House." I can then say "houseboat." You can then say "boat cushion." If I then cannot come up with something that can pair with "cushion," within an agreed-upon time limit, say two minutes, you get a point and you get to start the game all over with whatever word you wish. If your wife wins, for example, she gets a massage. If your child wins, you could help her make something after dinner. In other words, be imaginative. (See Appendix A).

Helpful Hints:

You might want to have a good pocket dictionary in the car for this one, in order to verify words and usage.

Leaving and Coming Home

Maturity means reacquiring the seriousness one had as a child at play.
—*Friedrich Nietzsche*

Get Dressed Race

Clown Hug

Moment of Truth

New Neighbor (a.k.a. Neighbor from Hell)

Psychic Coming Home

Last Letter/First Letter

Who's Knocking at My Door?

Coming Home Tag

Coming Home Hide-and-Seek

Apeman/Apewoman for a Day

Shopping Spree

Dying to Get In

General Benefits

All of these activities are great ways to put you and your spouse or family into a good mood as you enter your home or leave it. Even if you're not in a good mood to start, the fake-it-'til-you-make-it approach, which I discussed in Chapter 5, will soon put you in one.

By starting your day off well, the leaving-home games help you improve your performance at work. Similarly, the coming-home games help you start the evening off well, and thereby improve your enjoyment of your family life at home. They also can act as a good shot in the arm or inspiration for the rest of the family, because most of these ideas are so energizing or so silly they are contagious. They give permission to everyone else in the family to be silly. I indicate under each game heading what situation they are best suited for—coming home, leaving home, or both.

Get Dressed Race (Leaving)

How to Play:

Whoever is dressed and ready at the door to leave first gets a reward, or whoever is first three out of five times in the week gets a grand reward.

No cheating by skipping the undershirt/underpants step. Couples might want to spot-check. Be aware that this could lead to a major delay in getting to work.

The winner must also have had to comb their hair and brush their teeth. If the person's head looks like they were struck by lightning, they probably haven't combed! If they breathe and you notice that the wallpaper begins to peel or if their heads are surrounded by flies, or if the EPA puts caution cones around the house, someone hasn't brushed!

Helpful Hints:

For children who find it difficult to fully function in the morning, Mom may want to number the child's clothing so that they may dress in the right order. No kid wants to ride the bus to school wearing his underpants on the outside! An accident like that could lead to serious trauma and cost you thousands of dollars in psychiatric fees.

Warning:

Use common sense. As a wise friend once warned me about haste: "Make haste slowly." Otherwise, you could fall, trip, or knock over something valuable.

Clown Hug (Leaving or coming home)

Thank You:
Phyllis Greenleaf, Grass Valley, CA.

Benefits

1) This is the best way to greet a family member or friend, or just to show them how much you care.

2) If you do this, you'll be memorable for your hugs.

How to Play:

Explain what to do to the person you are hugging—this must be a two-way thing. Grasp arms completely around each other and hold on tight. Then jump up and down while spinning around, making several 360-degree turns (agree on the direction beforehand).

More Fun Ideas

1) Take turns making up sounds, each imitating the other and joining in the other's creation.

2) Alternate your direction each 360-degree turn.

3) Take turns mentioning something you love about the other person or are grateful for.

Moment of Truth

(Leaving or coming home)

Benefit

1) Develops powers of memorization.

2) Increases everyone's knowledge and possibly wisdom.

How to Play:

It's very simple. Before you can leave, or before you can be let back home, you must recite at least a one-sentence saying by a famous person (many of the shorter quotes in this book would do). You cannot use a saying you've already used.

If someone has forgotten to learn a new saying, they get an "ignorance point." Whoever has the most ignorance points at the end of the week has to do some previously agreed-upon chore that nobody wants to do. Or conversely, whoever has the least such points gets a special reward.

Helpful Hint:

You can always get these short one-liners from good books of quotations, which are available at the library or any bookstore.

More Fun Ideas

Instead of a famous one-line saying, make it a joke.

New Neighbor (a.k.a. Neighbor from Hell) (Coming home)

Benefits

1) Develops dramatic ability.

2) Makes you look forward to coming home with more glee and anticipation.

3) Makes whoever is home look forward to your arrival with greater glee and anticipation.

4) Gives you exciting things to dream up while commuting.

How to Play:

Just knock at the door pretending to be the new neighbor, who's really quite a character. Warn your partner or kids ahead of time, since the suspense of waiting to see who you're going to be is half the fun.

The people answering the door should be nice and let the new neighbor in, so they can get into their act right away. Here's just a few ideas for how the new neighbor can be.

1) Agoraphobic, but having a breakthrough today, having worked up enough courage to finally come out. They're overwhelmed with joy at their breakthrough.

2) The advance person for the President, who's about to "pop" in on a "typical" American family. The advance person has to be sure nothing embarassing to the President will occur.

3) Overly zealous representative of the special interest group that you detest the most, who is intent on converting you to his cause.

4) Somebody from a particular ethnic group or part of the United States (a chance for you to practice this accent or dialect) who's either extremely curious about who you are, or just extremely friendly and wanting you to know who he is.

5) An expert at anything and everything—a real know-it-all.

6) The child of the new neighbor, who is unbelievably curious about everything in your life and in your home—he can never stop asking questions.

7) An out-of-control gossiper, who can't stop gossiping about other people in the neighborhood (the gossip is also made-up, of course).

Rules:

1) Be sure you knock on the door and truly do your best to act as if you are this made up person.

2) Whoever answers should do their best to neither completely oppose nor easily go along with the visitor. The most fun stance is usually that of being a very polite version of how you'd normally act in such a case. For example the advance persons, you'd casually reveal stuff about you

or your family (real or made up) that could embarrass the Pres. Whatever you do . . ., do not out-and-out oppose the new neighbor, otherwise the drama or action can't develop further.

Warning:

To be safe, you should always look through a window or peephole to make sure it's really family before letting the "stranger" in. In other words, be sure you exercise common sense.

Helpful Hints:

Try and do your new person with an accent or dialect. This will double the fun! You can get a book on doing accents or dialects at the library or at a drama book store (which might carry them used). This will make it much easier to learn accents and dialects, which is really much easier than most people think.

More Fun Ideas

1) Have someone tape record or even videotape your first minute or two. After a month of these characters, you'll have quite a humorous tape to play for the family or at parties.

2) When you leave home together, do this in reverse: Leave as an imaginary couple or family, with accents, new identities, imaginative mission. Stay in character for a few minutes while in the car or when you arrive at your destination.

3) Instead of being a neighbor, be other kinds of people with specific motives, for example:

• a police detective investigating a neighbor, family member, or relative;

• a contractor trying to convince you to get some part of your house repaired;

• an artist who is desperate to rent a room in your house, because he or she is in love with it;

• a door-to-door psychologist who offers to help people with their problems for free or trade, right then and there at the door;

• someone from a foreign country speaking in a language (actually made up gibberish) that the other person (and you yourself) can't understand. So you try to communicate a lot by gesture and facial expression, occasionally throwing in an English word;

• an infamous realtive you all know.

Psychic Coming Home
(Coming home)

Benefits

It's fun!

How to Play:

This game is especially for couples, or for kids who live in safe neighborhoods or

who can watch people approaching the door through peepholes or side windows.

Unless your kid or spouse has a great memory, warn them by phone just before coming home that you will be playing this game. The person who is home sees if they can open the door just before the person coming home actually touches the door handle. If you can, you should get some previously agreed upon reward.

Warning:

This game probably won't be much of a challenge if you have a dog—at least if he or she is like our dogs.

Last Letter/First Letter
(Coming Home)

Benefits

Same as above.

How to Play:

Warn the person at home just before coming home, that you will be playing this game. Whoever comes to the door must knock and say something like, "Hi! I'm home!" The person inside must then answer with a sentence starting with the last letter of the sentence that's just been said, in this case, the letter e in "home."

So let's say the person at home replies, "Even though you're home, is not reason for me to open the door according to this game's rules!" To which the person at the door must reply with a sentence starting with the letter S.

The person inside has to open up the door when they can't come up with a proper sentence within, say, ten seconds.

More Fun Ideas

If you don't want to be waiting at the door to get in, just agree you'll play as soon as you come in.

Who's Knocking at My Door?

(Coming home)

Benefits

Teaches history.

How to Play:

1) Decide on a famous historical figure you're going to be, living or dead, and when you knock, give a clue, for example, "Hello. Boy, am I glad to be home. What a rough day I've had conquering Europe today." (You're Napoleon).

2) The person answering the door has to guess who you are by asking yes- or no-questions (like in 20 Questions).

3) You can give another clue after three or four "no" answers, especially if you're anxious to get in.

4) Allow 10 questions, fewer for younger or slower kids, unless you don't mind waiting outside longer.

5) You can offer rewards if they get the right answer in less than six questions, or whatever you all decide.

Coming Home Tag (Coming home)

How to Play:

As soon as you're let in (or otherwise get in) and count to the agreed upon number, you can try and tag whomever is in the house. If you find the person, you get an award (also to be agreed upon).

Rules:

1) You must first count to 60 or 100 or whatever you've previously agreed upon.

2) If you let yourself in, you must of course announce sufficiently loudly that you are in and will be commencing your search within 60 or whatever seconds. You must also keep your eyes closed while counting, and ears plugged if possible (so

that you don't hear giveaway sounds).

Warning:

Be sure there's nothing on the floor that could cause you to slip.

Coming Home Hide-and-Seek
(Coming home)

How to Play:

First come and yell, "Hi, I'm home. Do you want to hide?" If your kid or spouse answers "yes," you then say, "Okay, sixty seconds to hide and then I'm coming back in to find you!" You then go back outside and close the door, leaving it unlocked so you can let yourself in. After sixty seconds go back in the house and try to find the other players.

More Fun Ideas

Whoever comes home can get to be the one who hides. And if they aren't found, they get to have a fifteen-minute back rub!

Apeman/Apewoman for a Day
(Leaving or coming home)

Benefits

I forgot the name of the psychologist who developed the theory behind this. His approach to therapy was rather controversial: Rather than encouraging couples who were having problems to talk more with each other, his approach was to have people act like apes and communicate their wants and emotions like apes would. I heard he actually got some good results with many couples.

How to Play:

Just agree at the start of the day who are to be the ape people, and try your best as you leave and return to act like one—a nice, helpful one, of course.

So, for example, if you want attention, go up and nuzzle against your mate, chile or parent, hug them, hug yourself, whatever, so he or she gets the idea. If you are angry, make angry ape sounds and bare your teeth. Jump around to get attention for table-setting and other activities and remember—even though you communicate like an ape, you do understand English!

Shopping Spree (Coming home)

Equipment Needed:

You have to have just gone to the grocery store and have a bunch of groceries.

How to Play:

First bring in all the groceries. Divide the bags amongst the kids as equally as you can. Decide the reward for the winner, who will be the person who can empty their bags first and put the food away properly.

This is a good game for other chores, too. Winner gets to pick the dessert.

Warning:

Adults should first put away anything you fear might get broken, like eggs.

More Fun Ideas

Put the bags together in the middle of the living room or kitchen and see who puts away the most number of items, by each person marking down their initials or putting a mark in a column they make on a big piece of paper headed with their name.

Dying to Get In (Coming home)

How to Play:

Call and warn whoever's home that you are going to play the game. The idea is to give a great "dying" performance speech at the door, pleading for entrance. You must pretend to be some stranger who has just become seriously ill or was attacked near the home or apartment.

Try to ham it up as much as possible with various moans and cries of pain. The party inside should act rightfully skeptical, ask numerous questions to ascertain the validity of the victim's claims, and make various excuses about why it would be dif-

ficult to let you in. Give the dying person three to five minutes, and then let them in; after all, you're a busy person with things to do.

Warning:

If you live in an apartment building, you might wish to keep your voice down a bit lest you cause undue alarm. And it is possible that this game might not work even in an apartment building with well-sound-proofed doors.

If you have discovered or invented your own leaving or coming home game. You'll be delighted and so will perhaps millions of others. Please see the end of Chapter 20 for details on how to send in your ideas and how we'll reward your effort and ingenuity.

CHAPTER 9

At Mealtimes

*Life is a great big canvas and you should splash all
the paint on it that you can.*

—*Carol Rae, artist*

Be Each Other

Who Am I?

Guess My Newspaper Song

Newspaper Cantata

Emotional Salad
(Family and Couple Versions)

Family Treasure Chest

Family Memories

Dinner in the Dark

Table Hide-and-Seek

Alliteration Supper

Poetic Dinner

Word Sparring

Concentration Supper

Whose Poem Is it Anyway?

I Never Have

True/False

Guess the Mess

General Benefits

One of the saddest sociological phenomena of the last two decades, aside from the fact that more than 25 percent of our children now live in poverty, is the disappearance of the family dinner. The immense value of these games and activities is that they can do much to help revitalize the tradition of the family dinner by making it a wonderful time of hilarity, sharing of tender special moments, of learning and nurturing of creativity in our children and in each other, of delightful surprises, and therefore of family bonding.

You can expand the number of games and activities you can do here by trying out many of the Riding-Walking-Biking games from Chapter 7. Most of those games work just as well during meals.

In our play we reveal what kind of people we are.
—*Ovid*

Be Each Other

Thank You:

Though I discovered this game all on my own, I feel it might have taken a lot longer had I not been reading the work of Viola Spolin, the mother of improvisational theater and author of *Improvisation for the Theater.* This book is a must for any of you who like dramatic games or role-playing forms of play.

Benefits

1) Few, if any, games in this book have the therapeutic power this one has. This game is incredibly powerful in helping children and adults see themselves as others see them, and therefore see their warts and other personality characteristics that need some correction.

2) Few if any games are as effective in releasing tension and creating an hysterically funny experience together.

3) Few, if any can make a dinner or any meal together as enjoyable as this one.

How to Play:

The basic idea is that partners pretend they're each other. For a family with children, the kid(s) get to become the parent(s) and the parent(s) get become the kid(s) (see below for odd-numbered families). Then you act like one another throughout dinner.

The role-playing should include much more than just how the other person eats. Urge people to think of the types of things the other person says, and how they say these things—their mannerisms and tone of voice. Now is when you find out that you constantly interrupt or complain or act morose, or give speeches with your mouth full. And you get to see what it looks like, probably in shades of green and brown. You play teeter-totter with your peas, or point at people with your fork, all quite unconsciously, no doubt.

And your daughter? What does she do to hide those vegetables? Does she blow bubbles in her milk? (Now is your chance to blast some fun at those gross, stinking, dirt-clod habits, *without lecturing.*)

Warning:

This game should definitely not be played if you suspect any of your family members to have any serious emotional problems, particularly if they are prone to depression, destructive (violent) or self-destructive behaviors, or if they are getting psychotherapeutic help. This is a very powerful game that can do as much harm as good, sort of like fire.

Rules:

1) Very important: Be sure to remind everyone to consider each other's feelings and be kind. Otherwise, people might feel uncomfortable in the extreme. This is very important. We don't want people to run away from the table crying or angry.

2) Be accepting of how others' limitations. Nothing will kill creativity and make people afraid of expressing themselves faster than judgmental remarks like "I'm NOT that way!" Know that almost everyone must exaggerate to get a laugh. Besides, if you can see the kernel of truth, instead of trying to deny it, you'll grow more.

3) If someone asks you to stop, please respect their wishes.

Helpful Hints:

1) It might help to announce the game some time beforehand. Maybe a few hours before supper or the night before, so that people can have a little time to think of the speech or eating characteristics they are going to imitate. (Of course too much time gives brothers or sisters time to think of ways to humiliate their siblings, which some think is basically their job, anyway.)

2) Suggest that people concentrate more on what people say or how they talk rather than how they eat.

3) Try not to interrupt anyone, unless that's the habit you're imitating.

4) Don't grandstand. Give other people a chance to perform.

More Fun Ideas

1) This is a wonderful game that couples can do alone.

2) Kids can do it among themselves during school lunch.

3) If there is an odd number of you, or only an odd number wish to play, each of you write your name on a slip of paper. Drop the slips into a cup, and then draw a slip. If you draw your own name, just put the slip back, and try again.

Be Each Other is a great game not just at mealtimes, but while doing chores, on long trips, short trips, or anywhere else where parents and kids get on each other's nerves. So what I'm saying is that this game can be played anytime, anyplace.

4) Be Each Other is a great office game you can do with your coworkers at lunch, meetings, or coffee breaks (see Chapter 12, "At School and Office").

5) You can also Be Someone Else: each member of the family picks a famous character from real life or the movies. You could be the first family or the Flintstones. There are innumerable possibilities. Once you've mastered your family's quirks, pick someone else's. Try relatives and friends!

6) Write down famous characters on slips of paper and everybody picks who they must be.

7) Or you can simply make up a character, by writing down three or four qualities or attributes of this character on a slip, and again everybody picks. The slips could say: "Southerner, slurps their soup, multimillionaire oil tycoon, extreme right-wing politics;" or "French, suave, famous artiste, who is likes to flirt and brag about their latest artistic accomplishments."

Who Am I?

Thank You:
    Mary Ann Spitzer of San Francisco, California.

Benefits

1) This game is great for building self-esteem and just helping family members get to know one another better.

2) This can also be very educational, especially with regard to history, science, politics, and the arts.

How to Play:

This is in a sense a version of Be Each Other. However, in this case you don't know who you are, and have to figure it out by how people react and treat you.

Each member writes down the name of an historical or famous figure, living or dead, on a slip of paper and puts the slip in a bowl. All participants then draw a name and without showing the name, put the slip on another family member's forehead for everyone to see, except for the person whose forehead it's stuck to. Just wet the blank side of the slip slightly with clean water (no licking!) and that should give you enough sticking power. The participants are then supposed to treat one another as if they were the person whose name they're displaying on their forehead. The behavior can be centered around a task such as setting the table, or just eating dinner. Age, personalities, gender, accomplishments, strengths, and weaknesses can all be factors affecting how people get treated.

Participants try to guess whose name they have on their forehead. The first person to guess who they are should get some reward (like getting out of a chore, choosing the next dinner game, or getting an extra dessert if appropriate. See the reward list in the appendix). A discussion about how they see each other and themselves should ensue.

More Fun Ideas

Each player receives about five small pieces of paper and each writes a personal preference, trait, or accomplishment of their own on each slip. Try and make it something the other players don't already know about you. All the papers are thrown into a bowl. The first player selects a paper and then reads it out loud and tries to guess which player it belongs to. (You may have to disguise your handwriting to play this.)

Guess My Newspaper Song

Benefits

1) Develops the ability to sing, especially to hold a tune.

2) Gives participants the pleasure of singing.

3) Develops reading ability.

4) Develops cultural breadth and depth (being able to recognize and start famous songs).

5) Develops enjoyment of words and reading.

6) Gets people to read the paper more.

[Dear *USA TODAY*: We'll change the title of the game to "Guess My *USA TODAY* Song", if you'll give the book a plug]

How to Play:

Just pick any article you wish and start singing it to whatever tune you can think of, and see who in your family can identify the tune first. For couples, just see if your partner can identify it at all.

Take turns at this. Or, to make it competitive, whoever identifies the song first gets a point. For couples, whoever identifies the song within an agreed-upon time limit, gets the point. Take turns, and whoever gets the most points first wins whatever reward you've chosen.

If the guesser still can't guess the song after a minute or so, you can slip a word or two from the actual lyrics into your singing of the newspaper article, which should give the guesser a clue.

When the guesser gets it right, they get to have a turn and do the same thing.

Newspaper Cantata

Benefits

Same as Guess My Newspaper Song.

Equipment Needed:

Any newspaper or magazine, old or new.

How to Play:

1) Choose a conductor who is in charge of pointing at people to sing, or go around clockwise whenever the conductor says "switch."

2) Go around the table and get some names of popular songs, the melody to which everyone present would know. (If you can't think of a tune

everyone knows, try "Happy Birthday to You," or "Three Blind Mice.") Go around the table again to get three or four articles from the newspaper to sing. The conductor or another volunteer should write down the song and article titles, and perhaps the page numbers for the articles, so that we don't get stalled later spending a lot of time looking for the article.

3) The conductor points at one singer, who starts singing the article operatically to the tune of the first song that you have chosen. The conductor can call on two or more at a time to sing together. Whenever the conductor calls upon the next person, the person(s) singing must immediately stop and the next person should continue the article and tune wherever the other(s) left off.

Helpful Hints:

Be sure to let the person singing finish their last sentence and phrase in their song before choosing someone else to continue.

The person who is least able to perform a singing role because of youth or shyness might best be given the conductor role.

More Fun Ideas

1) Do several articles, but keep the tune the same, so that you can perfect your ability to make the article fit the tune.

2) Try it with a worthwhile piece of literature or newspaper, so you might actually learn something of value.

3) Try using The National Enquirer or Star, or some other supermarket rag. (The absurdity of most of the articles in these publications will make this game even more fun).

4) Try it with a newspaper comic strip, assigning roles ahead of time. Sundays are best, because the comic strips are longer. Otherwise put several weekday strips together.

5) Try it with poetry!

> A first-rate soup is more creative than a second-rate painting.
>
> —*Abraham Maslow, psychologist*

Emotional Salad (Family and Couple Versions)

Benefits

1) Helps develop people's ability to express themselves and, in particular, their emotions.

2) The secretary or director role (see

below) helps people who seem shy at the dinner table to "come out" and participate more.

3) Develops vocabulary.

4) Adds a rich tapestry of emotions and vibrancy to the family dinner.

5) Teaches children that all emotions are valid.

Emotional Salad is great for families or couples whose emotional life is either too sad, too angry, too serious, or too blah. So if you are among the seventeen families in America reading this right now that don't fall into any of these categories, please go on to the next game.

How to Play:

As we all know, it's often not what you say, but how you say it that's funny! And that's the idea behind this game.

First, make a note of whatever topic (if any) you're discussing or arguing about at the time you decide to play this game, and who was last talking. (You'll want to pick up the discussion where it was left off.) This game is surprisingly good with arguments. If, like a lot of families, you spend much of the dinner in silence or not talking about anything of substance, consider the following suggestions or consult the discussion guide in Appendix B. Following are a few topics or questions to get you started.

For *families:* best things that happened to anyone during the day; biggest frustrations; something new you learned; doing

chores; watching TV; allowances; school work; extra-curricular activities; fantasy future trips; new interests or things you would like to do or learn; or any of the topics indicated under couples (below).

For *couples:* best things that happened to each of you during the day; biggest frustrations of the day; some special place or activity you would like to go to; advice about a work-related problem; a community or larger political issue you feel you should do something about; a health-related topic; some interpersonal communications habit or problem you are trying to work on; new interests or things you would like to explore.

For all sizes of groups, appoint a secretary-director. This person won't be as free to engage in discussion as the others, so you might want to choose someone who prefers not to talk much, or delegate this to the shyest or loudest family member. If there is an argument, you can just agree to take turns and keep track who is secretary each time.

Next, come up with a list of emotions or adverbs (like sadly, angry, lovingly, quickly, frightened, happy, awkwardly) while the secretary-director writes them down on a piece of paper; you should have at least fifteen or twenty. It's no big deal if the secretary-director mixes them up, since after all, this is Emotional Salad. You can use lots of great vocabulary here to develop your kids' and your own vocabulary as well. For example, try using words like lethargically, acrimoniously, or lasciviously, and then define the words. (If your family has problems coming up with a list of adverbs, maybe you should skip this game for now and concentrate on Kitchen Hockey or Slow Bike Race to warm up.)

Go ahead and discuss the topic you were discussing before you interrupted everything with this game, or pick a new topic. The more audience involved in the topic, the better. It should be something that everyone might have an opinion about.

At this point the secretary becomes the "director" and starts the game by announcing (and pointing to whomever is talking or was last talking before you started preparing for the game) the first emotion or adverb on the list. The secretary might say, for example, "Dad, 'quickly!'" Then Dad must suddenly change how he is talking and start talking very quickly, staying of course on the same subject.

After at least twenty seconds, but probably no more than a minute, the director (or tape recorder if you are doing the couple's version below) calls out the next adverb or emotion in the list, and Dad or whoever is now talking, must change instantly and talk in a manner that reflects that adverb or emotion.

Let's say you're about to ask your daughter about her new teacher, Ms. Jones, or maybe you're just going to ask her to pass the catsup. But the director has just called out "sadly!" So you now have to ask about Ms. Jones or request the catsup in the midst of a sobbing fit or on the verge of tears! And she must reply in kind, unless the director has called out another emotion.

Anyone can talk at any time, just as in normal conversation, but they must talk in the same emotion or adverb that governed the previous speaker.

Warning:

Do not play this game if you have a family member you have reason to believe is seriously emotionally disturbed, is addicted, or under psychiatric or psychotherapeutic care.

Helpful Hints:

When starting, the director should let the speaker talk at least twenty seconds before switching emotions. I know I already said this, but it's important.

The director can alternate back and forth between two emotions adjacent to each other on the list, at a rhythm that allows at least ten seconds on each emotion or adverb.

Once people are warmed up and have the hang of it, it's really fun to alternate back and forth between emotions for the same speaker, allowing only ten or fifteen seconds for each emotion. These emotions can be adjacent to each other on the list, or you can be creative and pick your own combinations.

Directors should be sure to announce the emotion or adverb loudly and clearly. Let the speaker finish a sentence, or at least a clause, before announcing the emotion or adverb. If a respondent freezes and is unable to come up with the emotion just named, the director should quickly call out the next word to keep the game moving.

If you're the one talking and then suddenly feel stuck when a new emotion is mentioned, or just want to get others involved, you can always look at someone else and ask them their opinion, asking of course in the proper emotion.

You can let the director do the entire list or pass it around to give other people a chance to be director.

Two-Person Emotional Salad

Couples or single parents with one child can try Two-Person Emotional Salad. The rules are the same as above, except that you use a tape recorder and take turns announcing your emotions into the recorder, remembering to leave at least twenty seconds between emotions or adverbs, but not more than a minute before mentioning another. Again list between twelve and twenty emotions, adverbs, and accents.

At the end of your list, rewind to the beginning, resume discussing the topic you were discussing, and hit "Play," being sure to set the tape recorder to playback loud enough to hear while talking. Allow the tape recorder to now be your director, and proceed as in steps four through six, above. You can both be the conductor, by just taking turns stopping the recorder for a few seconds before starting.

This is hysterically fun to do in a restaurant. You just need to keep your voice low, and your ears close enough to the tape recorder.

This is a great game to use while arguing.

More Fun Ideas

1) You can occasionally throw in pairs of emotions, giving people a choice, like "happy or sad," or "frightened or angry."

2) Once everyone feels comfortable with the game, the director can just yell "freeze" at the proper time, and the rest of the family can shout out an emotion, the first one shouted out being the one the speaker must use to continue.

3) The director can yell "freeze" in the middle of a sentence and then direct another member to finish it with a different emotion.

4) Try introducing accents and dialects as well, like German, French, English, Haitian, or Brooklynese, into your list of emotions and adverbs.

> Two of the oldest and most important ways for knitting communities together and passing on our deepest values are ritual and storytelling. We aren't sure why people stopped valuing their authentic stories and began to devalue ritual. All we know is that we want them back in our lives.
>
> —*Salli Raspberry* (*author,* Living Your Life Out Loud)

Family Treasure Chest

Thank You:
   Bernie Siegel, M.D.

Benefits

Celebrating birthdays, anniversaries, and holidays is fun, but why wait for special occasions that come only once a year to celebrate? Let family members know how much you love and appreciate them with little gifts every week.

What's more, these gifts cost no money. Now that we have your attention, read on.

Equipment Needed:

Paper, pens, and a small cardboard box, cookie tin, or giant glass jar to be your Family (or Couple) Treasure Chest. You may want to go shopping together and find a keepsake box that you all like. Garage sales are great places for this. Or just take any box and write Treasure Chest on it, or decorate the box with your family's name, pictures, or other family memorabilia.

How to Play:

During the week, pay attention when something happy, fun, warm, or otherwise moving happens to any of you, especially between you and another family member. Maybe Mom paid you a compliment. Maybe you got a real nice hug from Dad, or even from a sibling, or you did something especially fun with your partner. Maybe you just saw a beautiful sunset or puppy dog, got a promotion or good grade, or did something helpful for a fellow student or employee that made you feel good.

Write down the date that it happened and however many words you need to capture the essence of what made you feel so good. If you don't enjoy writing, just write enough to serve as a reminder (so that you can talk about it several days or a few weeks later). People too young to write can just draw a picture to remind themselves of the nice thing that happened. Fold up the slip of paper two or three times, and put it in the Treasure Chest.

Note: Renting out a sibling's room while they're at school doesn't count as a nice thing. Neither does having a sibling upholstered while they sleep. And no stuffing the chest with self-aggrandizing notes like: "The lady at the bank said she thought I was real cute and my parents should give me more money." Or, "The ice-cream man said I was very polite and well-behaved and he was surprised that I didn't get a bigger allowance." In fact, parents, disregard any notes that discuss money. The kid's running a scam and should not be encouraged.

The second part is to pick a night for your weekly Treasure Chest dinner, say Friday night (a good way to get the week-end started off on a high note). At that dinner, everyone takes a turn to pick a "treasure chest gift (note)" out of the box. The person whose "treasure" is chosen then reads their note. Proceed in this manner around the table at least two times. If your family likes this a lot and you're all writing at least three or four notes each per week, you could probably go three times around the table. It's best not to go too many times, so you can leave a few notes in the treasure chest unopened.

Helpful Hints:

1) If a player is too young to write, they can also bring home something small (that will fit into the treasure chest) that reminds them of the happy moment.

2) You could have a much larger container in which to keep the notes you've read throughout the year—sort of like a family diary.

3) Besides dating the note, it's a good idea to also mention the location where the event took place, especially if you ever want to have a special, once-a-year "Grand Treasure Chest Night," when you dip into a whole year's worth of notes.

More Fun Ideas

1) Have a Couples Treasure Chest for those intimate things you only want to share between the two of you. Combine this idea with the Gift Treasure Chest (following).

2) Gift Treasure Chest: Family members write down things they can do for other family members and sign their names. Each "gift" should be written on a separate piece of paper. Kisses and hugs are always welcome gifts. Other gifts might be: back-scratching; one free favor-to-be-determined (like a "love coupon"); freedom from one responsibility; an hour of time to do whatever the receiver wants; a handmade card; a certificate good for breakfast in bed. Homemade objects (crafts the kids may do in school),

drawings, candid photos, and offers to tell original bedtime stories are some other things you might want to include. When it is Treasure Chest Night, everyone draws something from the box (if you get yourself, put it back and keep drawing.)

3) You might want to eventually frame some of the best notes, or even paper your hallway or family room with them, covering them with clear lacquer. Sure, some people might think it's not very attractive. But, hey, it's your house. Do what you want. And if Martha Stewart doesn't like it . . . so what!

Family Memories

Thank You:
  Mary Ann Spitzer

Benefits

1) Just one of the greatest and simplest things you can do for the kids, and also for yourself.

2) If you try to ask about positive events that praise a family member, this game will help build self-esteem. It is especially good for the esteem the family or couple as an entity has for itself.

Equipment Needed:
Paper and pens.

How to Play (Family Version). See below for Couple Version:

Everyone writes down four questions on separate pieces of paper and numbers each question. Everyone must write the same number of questions; no two-part questions allowed—only one question per slip of paper. The answers are written on another piece of paper with corresponding numbers and kept by the creator. The questions must be about individual or family memories. For example, here are some possible questions:

- Where did we as a family get lost two years ago?

- What is Mother's favorite kind of movie?

- What cause did we all march for in 1994?

- What is Sara's most common dinner complaint?

- What is Billy's favorite expression giving approval to something?

- What is one of Dad's, Bobby's, Mary's or Mom's proudest accomplishments?

- Why did we not go on a family vacation last year?

If you have a sizable family, just shuffle the questions and have one person read the questions aloud. Then proceed clockwise or counterclockwise around the table.

The first family member to answer a question correctly gets a point. And the next person after him gets first shot at answering the next question.

The answers are verified through the written answer by the person who wrote the question. If there is a dispute as to the correctness of the answer, that is, if the creator's answer might be wrong, the person about whom the question concerns has the final say. If it involves the entire family, you all must take a vote. Whoever gets the most points gets a big reward or gets out of a chore.

How to Play (couples version):

If there are just two of you, ask the questions about yourself or the two of you, then trade questions, but keep your answers. Whoever gets the most correct answers gets a big reward or avoids a chore. Here are some examples of questions particularly suited to couples:

- What is one of the things Gary gets angriest about?

- What is one of Karen's favorite desserts?

- Where was the first place we ever went cross-country skiing?

- What was the date of our first meeting?

- What was our first playful activity or game?

- What causes did we write to the president and our representatives about last month?

Warnings:

Avoid bringing up memories that might be embarrassing to a family member (especially to a younger child or sensitive teen). If such a question is still contributed and anyone asks to skip that question, their wish should be respected and the question dropped.

If you disagree about something, just drop it until you can get definite proof. Don't get into a fight over it and wreck the game.

Helpful Hints:

Try to come up with questions that can lead to discussion or revive great memories.

The more the memory involves the entire family, the more family bonding this game will be.

All family members do not have to have been a participant in the memory for it to be a valid question.

More Fun Ideas:

This is a good travel game as well.

> Adults are obsolete children.
>
> —*Dr. Seuss*

Dinner in the Dark

Benefits

You really get to appreciate tastes and smells, and end up appreciating those aspects of food more.

Equipment Needed:

Newspapers and dinner, preferably food difficult to identify but fun to feel. Some food items that qualify are pasta salad, frozen grapes, mashed bananas, cold potatoes with a sauce, any vegetable or fruit cut into a weird shape, string cheese already torn, cream cheese, peanuts with shells.

How to Play:

1) Cover the table with newspaper. You might want to put some newspapers on the floor too! When dinner is ready, call everyone and have them sit down.

2) Lights out! Uncover the food and start eating with hands or silverware. (If the room is not dark enough, use blindfolds.) The object is to see if you can identify the food. Keep track of your own points, using the honor system. Whoever made the dinner verifies the answers and awards the points.

Helpful Hint:

The dinners should already be served on people's plates, so no one will have difficulty finding their food.

Don't monopolize. Give others a chance to guess.

Table Hide-and-Seek

How to Play:

Say you're eating at a restaurant, minding your own business. Suddenly you notice an annoying hum. You glance around to see if the local Kazoo Chapter is convening behind you. (We have a marketing agreement with ACME KAZOO, in Hibbing, Minnesota. We do a lot of these marketing agreements. We're poor. Okay?)

But no. These humming people are walking their fingers over saucers, around cups and glasses, along chair backs, even among the potted plastic petunia centerpiece. They are laughing with great glee. Who are these people? Finger-cramp sufferers, trying to get the kinks out? Tailors taking tablecloth measurements? Neither. They're a family playing a truly delightful round of Table Hide-and-Seek.

How to Play:

Seekers hide their eyes. The hider conceals a small object somewhere on or around the table. The objects you can use are endless (peas, raisins, sugar packets, olives) The places you can hide them are almost unlimited. ("I found it! The wet noodle was under Uncle Fritz's toupee!") More common places are under plates, in an empty cup, under a napkin, or under a spoon turned upside down. Your fingers do the walking as you search. (The Yellow Pages paid us to say that.) Be sure to limit the hiding place to the table itself. Meanwhile, the hider hums his favorite tune (good luck recognizing it), which gets louder as you get closer.

More Fun Ideas

1) If you are playing this in a restaurant and are too self-conscious to hum, you can simply use the old fashioned "cold, colder" and " warm, warmer, hot, very hot" technique, to tell people how close they are getting. Alternatively, shake your napkin faster and faster, the closer and closer they get.

2) Let there be two persons to hide the objects, two objects to hide, and at least two seekers. Those looking on, instead of humming, must say, "Bill, hot, hotter, cold," or "Judy, cold, warm, warmer," so the seekers will know who the comments are directed to. Yea verily, and let there be no objections. Try to "Name That Tune." Or, get your waiter/waitress to "Name that Tune." Or, if you're super daring, like no one we have come across, stand up in front of the restaurant and lead the whole place in a rousing guessing game which ends in a fulfilling sense of synchronicity for all—especially the Kazoo players.

3) Instead of "hot/cold," in the above variation, try more imaginative combinations like "oooh!/achhh!"

Alliteration Supper

Thank You:
Jackie

Benefits

Develops love of language and poetic ability.

How to Play:

In a given period of time between five and thirty minutes (you'll have to experiment to see what best suits you) see who can make up the most number of alliterative sentences about whatever is on the table, or anything else you wish to talk about.

The sentences must have at least three words in it, two of which alliterate, that is, start with the same sounds: I smell soup; Mom mashed the potatoes; Bobby, my brother. bites his beets (extra point here); Dad, I need your wise wit and artful advice (double points here). As indicated here, give extra points if someone gets three or more alliterative words in the same sentence.

This can be a bit challenging, even for adults, so consider some of the hints below.

Helpful Hints:

Allow younger kids to go by looser rules. For example, they can use items that are not on the table, and even make up fantasy people ("My friend Frieda flew to Florida today," could be complete fantasy, but allowable if the child is, say, under 10.)

If they are still having a hard time, suggest that they make up imaginary people with whatever name they wish and then alliterate to that name. For example: Sally saved her salad; Timmy tastes tomatoes.

To even out abilities, handicap the better kid or adult by giving extra points in advance to the younger or less advanced players. Another way to handle ability differences is to form teams, to balance things out, just as you would in doubles tennis, for example. Let the younger child suggest the nouns and the older come up with adjectives. If the game is still too challenging and therefore not fun for younger kids (or even an some adults), give such a person the scorekeeper role or simpler games to play.

More Fun Ideas

1) Only the food item has to be real. The rest of the words are altered to begin with the same first letter used by the food item: Blease bass the butter.

2 Just talk in rhyming couplets, either by saying two sentences yourself that rhyme, or by responding to the last sentence said by another family member with a single sentence that rhyme with it.

3) A more difficult variation would be to apply this throughout a conversation at dinner, but exempt articles (a, an, the). In other words, all sentences must either be alliterative or rhyme in couplets. Every time you say a correct sentence you get a point. Whoever has the most number of points gets a reward, gets out of washing dishes, or gets to choose tomorrow's dinner game.

Poetic Dinner

Benefits

Develops love of poetry in particular, and language in general.

How to Play:

This is perhaps the simplest yet most challenging mental game I have run across. There is only one rule: Everything that is said has to somehow include a reference to a food item, or way of eating, or a utensil that's on the table. The trick is to simply use simile and metaphor in every remark. For example:

Mom: I feel as worn out as the skin on that baked potato.
Son: You do? Was your boss acting real salty?

Mom: Yeah, she was beefing at me all day.

Daughter: I have a joke that could make you jiggle like this Jell-O (shakes it).

Helpful Hints:

If you say things you feel make no sense and are just plain gibberish, that's just fine. If you feel compelled to make excuses, you can always just blame your "inner child."

Word Sparring

Thank You:

Bradley Permentier of Alexandria, Virginia.

How to Play:

Hiiiiiiiii-ya! - iiieee, yoooo, HA! - woaaaa, heeee, cha! . . . No, not that kind of sparring. Those are just words that karate people use when they are kicking each other and throwing their kung-fu chops on each other. There isn't anything physical about Word Sparring, because you are only using words to combat with.

You can pick teams, play one-on-one, or if you think you are a truly accomplished Word sensei then you can take on everyone else like one of those guys in some B-rated martial arts movie who fights an entire city of people. Either way, study up on your vocabulary because this game is only for those who know how to say more than "Me Tarzan, you Jane."

To begin with, you need to think of a sentence that has one special word in it, something like: "I got in trouble at school today, so I had to *remain* after three to do some extra work." (The big word is in italics.) The actual length of the word depends on the age of the players. Hexadecimal is not a good word for a second-grader to play with. We don't want any tongue muscles to be sprained.

The other team or person then tries to come up with a sentence that uses a word in it that rhymes with that special word like: "So I hope you didn't *refrain* from doing that extra work."

To which the first team/person would reply something like: "I didn't and I can *retain* my lessons! No need to *retrain* me." The other team or person then might reply: "But will you *regain* your A average and again *reclaim* your right to go home on time?" Obviously, it isn't necessary to have the sentences make much sense, just as long as you properly use words that sound similar.

You should go back and forth for as long as you can. If you're able to say two rhyming words in one or two sentences, you get two points. The team that cannot come up with a comparable word loses the point to the other team/person. You can play to a set number of points, or just for fun. The great thing about this game is that you can start it up at any time, for any reason, when you hear one of those interesting words that sounds like so many others.

I don't want this to be a *hobby*.

No one said you had to change your name to *Robby* ... see, I just can't stop playing this game. It is so *fun!*
But I don't want to *run.*
Go on now, be a *hon....*

More Fun Ideas

This is a great car game.

Concentration Supper

Benefits

1) Improves our awareness of what surrounds us, at least during dinner. It's amazing how an entire pot roast can disappear and you don't notice it if you're not paying attention.

2) We will ignore the cowardly and dastardly benefit that you can steal someone's food while their eyes are closed.

How to Play:

This game comes from combining two favorite American pastimes: eating and watching game shows. Only in this case you create the game yourselves and thus save on your electric bill. (Tests in over thirty states and several other places have proven conclusively that people enjoy their food more when they're constantly looking to see if it's all still there. Thus, from a scientific point of view, you could call this game an appetizer.)

At the beginning or near the end of dinner, have someone at the table close his or her eyes. Keep them closed until given the "all clear." And no peeking! While that person is unable to see, move or hide one or more items on the table. No, not a pea or a hair, but something of weight and substance, like the bread, catsup bottle, butter, or the salad bowl.

Now, have the person open their eyes. They must determine what is missing or changed.

Helpful Hints:

If you have a much younger child, require them only to recall half as many objects as an older child or adult would have to recall. Or have an adult and child play as a team, where one of them closes their eyes and the other gives hints, like the first letter of the item that's missing.

More Fun Ideas

Make it competitive (males vs. females or children vs. parents) by giving five or ten points for each item discovered as missing and subtracting a point for each false guess. Whoever has the largest number of points gets the reward or gets out of a chore.

Whose Poem Is It Anyway?

Thank You:
Bradley Permentier of Alexandria, VA.

Benefits

1) Develops love of language in general and poetry in particular.

2) Adds a whole new dimension to the dinner experience.

3) Provides a wonderful way to learn more about your partner and/or kids.

We'd like to talk to you a little about poetry. Now don't turn your nose up. We aren't going to ask you to define iambic pentameter or discuss political metaphor in Dante's "Inferno". We think you'll like what we've come up with.

This is a game that has fun with poetry. It puts everyone in touch with their inner poet and laces the lyrical with laughter. I guarantee it'll make you laugh. It works best with a group of people, but two could make a go of it. Actually, if it's you and your special someone, you could have a great time playing the game where the poem has to have a love, sex, or romance theme.

Equipment Needed:

Paper, pens, and a good anthology of poetry (e.g. *Norton's Anthology of English Literature*. C'mon, you spent good money on it in the college bookstore. You might as well get some use of out of it.)

How to Play:

To begin Whose Poem Is It, you first need to pass out pens and paper to all players. Now, open a text that has a lot of famous poets and read just the first line of a poem. Hopefully, you get a bewildering look from the group after you've read the opening line.

If some cocky English Lit major begins to recite the rest of the poem the second you've finished reading the first line, pretend that person doesn't exist and read a new first line from another poem.

Once you have a first line that no one is familiar with, you're ready to move on to the next step. It's okay if a few players vaguely remember the poem. For example, if you read the first line from Poe's "The Raven," someone is sure to comment about "hearing it before," which was when they were daydreaming in freshman English, which is why, of course, they only vaguely remember it.

After the poem has been selected, the players write down the first line that was read. Participants now have ten minutes to complete the poem as best they can. If people don't know the poem at all (which is the case 99 percent of the time), they are to finish the poem with their own creation. In other words, they have poetic license to write whatever they want and be as absurd, wacky, creative, or silly as their muse moves them to be.

When the time limit has elapsed, players exchange papers with other poets and the poems are read aloud. After all the poems are read, players vote as to whom they think came closest to the correct version of the poem, or simple, whose poem they liked the most.

Warning:

Players impersonating Rod McKuen are disqualified and are not allowed to have dessert, either.

Seriously, it is important that no one make any negative remarks about anyone's writing, lest they hurt someone's feelings, and destroy a chance of ever learning to love poetry and to feel confident at this form of self-expression.

Helpful Hint:

If there's just two of you, the person finding the poem must be careful to use a piece of paper to keep all but the first lines of poems covered, so she doesn't know any more than the other person what the poem consists of.

More Fun Ideas

1) You may wish to give each round a theme. After a first line is selected, the person who reads the line might say that the poem has to be a love poem. Or, if it is someone's birthday, the poem has to be about that person. Or use a holiday theme. Or at

least one metaphor involving the dinner main dish. The possibilities are endless.

2) After each poem is read, the individual to the reader's left has to give a critique and interpretation of what the poem was trying to say. You won't believe what you hear!

I Never Have

Thank You:
Wonderful singer-songwriter Christine Lavin of New York City.

Benefits

1) This is a great way to get to know things about your family and friends that you never expected.

2) It's especially wonderful for extended family dinners and parties where you have several people around the same age.

How to Play:

This really should be played with a group in the same age bracket (kids alone or parents alone). In this game, the more the merrier, though two people could theoretically play.

There's only one rule for this fascinating game: You have to think of something quite common that you somehow never got around to doing that everyone else in your group has done.

Common examples for adults:

- I never have been to California.

- I haven't eaten a hamburger in the last five years.

- I never knew my grandparents.

- I've never ridden a horse.

- I've never had mustard on a hot dog.

- I've never broken a bone, etc.

- I never saw my parents dance.

For kids:

- I've never seen Mr. Rogers.

- I've never had a hot dog.

- I've never eaten a vanilla ice-cream cone.

- I've never swam.

- I've never met my grandmother (or grandfather).

If no one else in your group can honestly make the same claim, you get a point. If at least one other person has had the same absence of experience that you just announced, you win nothing. You can either play to a certain point limit or to a certain time limit.

Helpful Hint:

This game works well if you invite another household over for dinner. That way the adults would have enough adults to play among themselves, and if there are children, the kids will have enough people to play in their own circle, too.

True/False

How to Play:

This is best played by two people. One player makes a statement about themselves and the other must decide if the statement is true or false. This is a challenging game because it's hard to come up with a statement that the other can't immediately recognize as true or false.

Examples:

- I like butter better than cream cheese.

- I know several Italian expressions.

- I know a magic trick.

- I've never been lost in the woods.

- I was once robbed at knifepoint.

- I never dove off a diving board.

Warning:

Since this game could cause some hurt feelings, we think it would be prudent to first take the following test. Our advice is to skip this game if you answer "I don't know" to any of the following questions, which you should answer alone (without the presence of your partner). That's right. Get up slowly and close the door tightly, or just go get a flashlight and hide in a closet. Here are the test questions:

- Does your partner like sugar in their coffee?

- Does your partner wear underwear?

- Is your partner presently under care for a sexual disorder?

- Is your partner wanted in seven states for armed robbery?

- Did your partner ever play bass guitar for the Rolling Stones?

More Fun Ideas

This is also a great car or hiking game.

Guess the Mess

Benefits

1) Gets kids to finish their dinners!

2) Might develop some artistic skills. Who knows?

How to Play:

You get a point each time someone at the table can guess what you've created with your food (for example, a horse, a mouse, a bridge, etc.). Whoever gets two or three points first gets out of washing dishes, or an extra helping of dessert or some other reward.

Rules:

Whatever you create, you have to eat!

If you have discovered or invented your own at mealtime game. You'll be delighted and so will perhaps millions of others. Please see the end of Chapter 20 for details on how to send in your ideas and how we'll reward your effort and ingenuity.

Shopping and Eating Out

If life isn't a great adventure, it's nothing.
—Helen Keller

• • • •

Everything I ever did that was worthwhile in my life,
I always caught hell for.
—former Chief Justice Earl Warren

Bookstore Game	Public Opinion Poll
Take My Seat Please!	Compliment Competition
Full Monty	Supermarket Surprise Hunt
He took My Menu!	Alphabetical Shopping
Department Store Hide-and-Seek	Supermarket Race
Be Each Other in Public	Perfect Strangers

General Benefits

This is one of my personal favorite chapters, since being able to be playful in a public place is really something of a heroic act. After all, if you are over six or seven, you are often facing your fear of being a fool in public. Another reason I have a special spot in my heart for these sorts of games, is that they, by their very nature, can help free others to be more playful. This is why I hope if you ever invent any of your own public-place games, you will help us all find out about them by following the directions in Chapter 20.

All of these games and activities transform the common experiences of eating out, shopping, going on the bus or subway, etc. into unforgettably fun experiences. Because they are done in public, they require from most of us a slightly greater amount of courage, and therefore can become great adventures. Also, unlike the rest of the games in this book, these games benefit not only you and your partner, family, or friends, but in many cases members of the public who are watching and catch on to what you're doing, or as in the case of the Restaurant Joke Book game, actually get involved themselves.

Freedom can sometimes be frightening to people who are enslaved (by their job, traditions, social convention, prejudice, or all of these things). Not everyone will enjoy seeing you play and being free. Use common sense if you think you might be upsetting someone enough to threaten your own or others' safety. Those old enough to remember the movie *Easy Rider* should know what I mean.

Though it is probably obvious to most of you, I feel compelled to say that all of the games and activities in Chapter 7 (Riding in the Car, Walking, or Bicycling) can also be used on the way to and at the mall or eating out.

Bookstore Game

Benefits

1) Deeper appreciation of books.

2) Increased depth and breadth of one's knowledge.

3) A great couples game.

How to Play:

Each of you write down one or two of your favorite topics or questions on a slip of paper with your name on each slip. Fold and toss into a cup or hat and draw. If you get your own slip, put it back and draw again until you get someone else's. For the topic you get, you attempt within an agreed-upon time limit (I suggest at least twenty minutes) to find one or two of the best books you can find, and a paragraph or two within each book, that specifically address the topic or question. Then meet back and proceed to read and inform each other.

Helpful Hints:

It's best to do this in a book store that has a built-in coffee shop or at least a couch where you can sit down.

If your child might be a little too young to easily find the section where your favorite book would be, write in for him the names of the sections, and if possible suggested authors' names.

Since you might be in a book store right now, wondering whether or not to buy this book, why not try this game out now with your partner or kid.

If it works and you have fun, buy this book!

Use common sense and don't let your child wander on his own if he might get lost.

Feel free to ask a bookstore employee for help. (And tell them you got the idea from us.)

Take My Seat Please

Thank You:

Chris Prey and the late and talented writer Richard Brautigan, who invented this wonderful game. It first popped into their minds on a crowded San Francisco bus at rush hour.

Benefits

1) Helps make public transportation much more fun.

2) Develops quick thinking.

3) If the world had more games of kindness like this, we'd all be a lot better off.

4) Teens love this.

5) Helps people who are tired from standing up.

6) Might help develop friendships or at least create a little more community.

How to Play:

This game is best played with just two people.

The object of the game is very simple: see who can give up their seat to passengers the most number of times.

You can have a ball at this by just hamming it up. For example, when Chris and Richard first played it, and it got down to a situation where there was only one person standing, they would both offer their seat to that person. Chris would compete by saying things like, "You, sir, wouldn't want to sit next to a hippie (referring to Brautigan's long hair) would you? I think you'd much prefer my seat." And Brautigan might counter in kind or just change the subject by saying, "But sir, by sitting in my seat you will be able to see the famous San Francisco Pyramid Building and St. John's Cathedral."

More Fun Ideas

1) Take a walk around downtown when parking meters are enforced, and spend a few nickels to save people parking tickets by putting them in expired meters. See who can use up their nickels first, one nickel per meter.

2) See also the book *Random Acts of Kindness* and *Kids' Random Acts of Kindess* by Conari Press.

Full Monty

Thank you:

I got this idea from watching the movie *The Full Monty*.

Benefits

1) Develops choreographic skills and team work.

2) Makes waiting in lines one of the most fun experiences ever.

3) Develops new friendships.

4) Strengthens the bonds of existing family or friendship ties.

Why should you let the pop singing groups have all the fun and glory developing those rhythmic dance routines? Don't be a couch potatoes who just glares in envy. There's no reason you can't do the same with your friends, and have as much fun as, or more than, the big stars.

How To Play:

I particularly recommend this for groups of four or more people, either combinations of parents with young children (but old enough to keep a rhythm), perhaps seven to ten, or for teens to do on their own. Of course it could be a very romantic couple activity as well.

First, learn a simple routine together at home before going out. Pick a simple rhythmic pop hit that you all feel makes you want to tap your feet. Then develop a routine—a series of foot, leg, hand, and arm moves that you all do simultaneously. The key is to keep it simple. I recommend starting with something that's not too fast, say about sixty beats per minute. Make your movements fairly subtle, nothing too large or fast, starting with very small movements with your index fingers, or snapping on every other beat, or just tapping your right foot to every beat of the rhythm, placing it only a few inches out and to your right. Get together just three or four steps and put them together in a systematic routine in a specific order, for a certain number of beats per step, say eight beats for each step. So one routine might be as follows:

8 beats: Start with your right foot turned outward and tapping to each count.

8 beats: Add to this right foot action the shaking of your right index finger (as if saying "naughty, naughty!")

8 beats: Keep the right foot tapping and now replace the right finger routine with a choo-choo train movement, your right arm at a ninety degree angle, hands flat, thumbs up.

8 beats: Then just tap your right foot, without any finger or arm action, and repeat as above, over and over for as long as you wish.

If you have other young-at-hearts in the line, you might just get a few to join. And the more that join, the more likely more will follow.

When you get to the mall, deliberately find a big line to stand in. The longer the line, the better. Movies are great for this. Then try to space yourself, so that you allow at least one or two persons to get between each of you. Be sure to agree that whoever is closest to the head of the line is the leader and everyone must follow them.

When the leader starts, you all follow, but only one at time. Don't all start up at once. In fact, the idea here is to make it look to the others in the line that you are all getting into this routine independently, each deciding, after some hesitancy, to just start imitating the one who started it all. By your not being together, it will look spontaneous. In this atmosphere, you just might start getting others in line to join in; they'll be thinking that if all of you could be that spontaneous and unself-conscious, why can't they?

Helpful Hint:

Carry a boombox and play your tune, so it's not loud enough to annoy others in line.

He Took My Menu!

Thank You:
  Jack Lemmon, actor.

How to Play:

"Felicia [his wife] and I very often will improvise. The last time we did it, we were at Sardi's Restaurant. They thought we were a little crazy because we got carried away. We were sitting alone at a little table, and there was nobody at the table on either side. So I suddenly said, 'Pretend that a guy sat down next to you, we're both reading the menu, and I'm engrossed, and this guy suddenly takes your menu, and now you don't have a menu and he proceeds to read it, and order from it, and you can't get it back from him.' Well we got into this thing with an imaginary guy at the next table.... This went on for another five minutes. I know it sounds crazy, but the point is that you can have fun doing those things, making up things together."

Department Store Hide-and-Seek

(Macy's will love us for this one!)
Thank You:
  Pinky Zalkin for this one and so much more.

  This came to me one day when Pinky, my significant other at the time, wanted to take me shopping for some pants. I hate shopping, unless it's at thrift stores or garage sales. So I said I'd go only on the condition that if I thought of a game to make it fun, she'd play it with me. And I did. And she did. And it was a hoot! And I got a very nice pair of pants, which of course I managed to get an ink stain on three weeks later!

Benefits

1) Why should kids have all the fun in this world? You haven't lived until you've buried yourself in the center of a coat rack or lingered languidly in lingerie.

2) Makes shopping lots more fun for those of us who can't stand shopping.

3) Makes us really check out much more of a department store than we would otherwise see, and as a result, might actually lead to some additional unexpected purchases, theoretically at least.

How to Play:

Young children already play a version of this game when they get bored in large department stores. The game they play is more aptly named Which Clothes Rack Am I in the Middle of Now? And, of course, it is usually the clothes rack that has the most clothes on the floor around it.

When you play Department Store Hide-and-Seek, you are following in the foot-

steps of all the greats: Laurel and Hardy, The Three Stooges, the Marx Brothers in *The Big Store*. Our version may not be quite as madcap, but chances are you will garner a few strange looks from other shoppers. If this happens, simply continue to act like you're intently devoted to your secret mission, look at the shopper, and whisper "secret mission," or "looking for a missing person." Don't say, "looking for someone who's hiding," since they might get the wrong idea. Then slink away, casting furtive glances as you go.

First, before you begin, you need to establish the floor that the person hiding has to stay on. This creates a fair arena of play and one where the game can be completed in a reasonable amount of time. After all, you probably have to get up for work the next morning to make some money to come back to the store and actually buy something. Walk together around that floor a bit to decide where to hide (which of course you keep to yourself). If the floor is unusually large, you should further limit yourselves to a side of the floor, and agree on the landmarks that set the boundaries.

Second, as you walk around, think of a clue to give the seeker before they close their eyes and you go off to hide. For example, if you decide to hide in the bathroom showers department, you might whistle the melody to "My Favorite Things" (starts with "Raindrops on roses ...") or "Singing in the Rain." If your kids don't know these songs, you now have a great excuse to rent the videos of these great musicals those songs are in (*The Sound of Music* and *Singing in the Rain*).

Third, agree on what is to be the "safety" or "central" location, the place where the seeker closes their eyes and does the counting, and to where the "seekee" is supposed to return for safety before being tagged. Then set a time limit for the game, say five minutes.

If you are the one whose turn it is to hide, whistle your clue to the seeker, and the seeker then closes their eyes and counts to sixty while you immediately go and hide.

If five minutes go by and the seeker hasn't found you, you are safe to go back to the original starting place to meet the seeker again and give him or her one more clue, or you may use the"alpha wolf" variation below. The seeker again closes their eyes, and you again hide. Alternatively, the hider can declare themselves the winner and then take their turn being the seeker.

Warning:

Do not play this with children too young to get around a department store on their own without getting lost or in trouble. Exercise common sense. If the child is under twelve, have them accompanied by an older child or adult (or by another parent, if one is available). This "hiding together" can be very bonding. I think it's some sort of primeval thing.

Helpful Hints:

Be sure you both have watches.

If you are the sought, try to find a place from which you can see the seeker coming, so that you can have a chance to run back to the safety area without being tagged.

If you are the sought, try to avoid hiding in a place impossible to find. That way the challenge will be too great for the seeker, and therefore not fun for either of you.

More Fun Ideas:

1) Keep track of the time it takes to find the hidden person. Have something at stake, such as whoever takes the longest to find the other has to buy ice cream cones.

2) If, after three or four minutes the seeker is having problems, try the "alpha wolf" tracking method for giving clues. In a wolf pack, the alpha wolf is the leader. When a wolf gets lost, it howls, the alpha wolf answers, and the separated wolf knows what direction to head. The lost wolf howls and listens for the alpha wolf until reaching the pack. So the seeker, if frustrated, can give a wolf howl and listen for a response. The hidden person is required to howl back. The seeker then moves toward the direction of the hidden person, perhaps howling once or twice more. (Let us hope you will find your quarry before store security throws a net over you and you are

carted away.) If you prefer a more discreet signal, you might agree upon a simple whistle, or bring kazoos with you. There I go with the kazoos again.

Be Each Other in Public

Thank You:
To my wife, Karen Ehrlich.

Benefits

1) Develops empathy and dramatic abilities.

2) Makes shopping more much more fun.

3) Gives you greater self-knowledge.

How to Play:

On the way to the mall or wherever you are going to shop, each of you decide to be each other. If there is an odd number or arguments over who wants to be whom, just write your names on slips of paper, and draw from a cup or whatever, as you did in Be Each Other from Chapter 9.

When you are there, stay in character the entire time, until you leave. If for some reason you need to get out of character, just make an agreed-upon sign like the traditional T-shape, or time-out sign, with your hands, and quickly ask your question or make your comment.

Warnings:

Don't do anything that would get you arrested, and don't take this to such an extreme that you antagonize other patrons or store clerks.

Helpful Hints:

Don't be judgmental. If you don't like how someone is imitating you, just grin and bear it, and know that almost everyone will exaggerate to get a laugh. Besides, if you can see the kernel of truth, instead of trying to block it out, you'll probably grow more.

More Fun Ideas

Instead of being each other, just pick an age different from your own. One could take a parent role, and another a child or teenage role.

Public Opinion Poll

Thank you:
Karen Ehrlich, for adding the competition elements.

Benefits

1) Increases a person's self-confidence and speaking abilities.

2) Increases people's awareness about important matters.

3) Can lead to new friendships (teens might love this game) and therefore can be a great "alone" activity.

4) Can be used to satisfy school assignments.

Equipment Needed:

A clipboard, a few sheets of paper, and a pen.

How to Play:

First, the next time you go to the mall or movies think of an interesting topic to do a public opinion poll on and a reason for doing the poll. You can think of the topic on the way there or preferably come up with it the night before. Come up with a good and honest reason to be doing this poll (this will come in very handy later, as we shall see).

Kids, if you have to write papers for any of your classes at school (or if you are allowed to do extra-credit projects), ask if you can write up the results of your own public opinion poll you did (or plan to do).

Some other easy justifications follow. Don't say them unless you're going to follow through:

- You are getting the public's opinion for a letter you're writing to the president of the United States.

- You are writing an article for your school's newspaper or for letters to the editor of your city's major paper. (You aren't promising they will publish it. You're merely saying you're going to write it and send it in.)

- If you're an adult with a young child, you can say you're doing it just to teach your child about polling or interviewing.

- If you want to be daring, you can always just admit you are doing this for the fun of it.

Third, you should make sure to think of good questions, since you are taking up people's valuable time. A good question should ideally meet the following criteria:

1) It should give the person you are interviewing important information—ideally raise his or her awareness about things they should know (that are often ignored by mainstream media)

2) It should be easily understandable and brief, taking less than four minutes of the respondent's time.

3) It should require just a yes, no, or maybe response, or, if you want to get fancier, a strongly agree, agree, undecided, disagree, strongly disagree response.

Here are some good examples:

For interviewing adults. Let's say this week's hot news story was approval of the national budget by Congress. If it was anything like last year's budget, you could ask a question as follows:

"The current budget now being submitted to the president primarily benefits the top 5 percent of our population with its tax cuts, and balances the budget by removing healthcare benefits to the elderly. Which of the following best describes how you feel about this approach: approve wholeheartedly, approve, undecided, disapprove, or strongly disapprove?" If the respondent disapproves, you could ask a follow-up question about what they plan to do to register their disapproval.

If you are interviewing only kids, you might want to ask their opinion on a matter more familiar to them, like whether parents should be allowed to install screening devices on computers to make sure their kids don't visit any Web sites that the parents don't approve of.

Now that you've thought of some good questions, find a location where many people are passing by, or better yet, where they are just waiting in line. (If they aren't going somewhere, they probably have nothing better to do than to answer your interesting questions.)

Then approach people, introduce yourself and explain why and on what issue you are doing a poll, and ask if they don't mind giving you just a minute or two. If they agree, go ahead and ask the question(s) and take down their response. It's also a good idea to gather basic demographic data about your respondents, like their marital status, age (or apparent age, if you don't feel like asking), occupation, etc.

Warning:

If you interview on public streets, like in front of a store or movie theater, you shouldn't have any hassle. But if you are inside a mall, which is private property, you can legally be asked to leave. Your best defense is to tell the truth: explain you are doing an extra-credit assignment, or working on an poll to send in to a local newspaper, or just for "some educational fun." Show the person the questions you are asking, so that he can see they are intelligent and in no way taking business away from any of the businesses. Tell him that people are enjoying answering the questions, and ask the people, if they are still there, to vouch for that.

Helpful Hint:

If you are doing this for school, emphasize this in the first sentence, since it will elicit more sympathy and cooperation.

More Fun Ideas

1) This is a great activity for when you're alone, because it can also be a way to meet people.

2) If there are two or more of you playing this game, you can make it even more fun by betting on how people will respond to your questions. You could also compete to see who can ask the most number of people in a certain amount of time.

3) It could be a fun thing to do between classes in school.

4) You could ask respondents for their own suggestions as to what might be another question to ask people. You might come up with your next public opinion poll question this way. In fact, if you like it better than what you're using, you can always switch, unless you've made the first a class assignment.

Compliment Competition

Benefits

1) Helps build poise and self-confidence.

2) Makes people feel happier and better about themselves.

3) Develops your powers of observation.

4) Develops your gift for clear and precise self-expression.

5) Develops appreciation of the value of writing.

6) Might bring you new and wonderful friends.

How To Play:

Give yourself a time limit, say ten or fifteen minutes. Set a place to meet at the end of the time limit, and see who can compliment the most number of people in that time.

Rule:

To receive credit, you must compile a written list of the people's first names and what they were doing when you complimented them. If they were in a shop, you should write down the name of the shop.

When you see someone doing something nice, just go up and say something like, "Hi, I'm Gary, and I was watching how well you were . . . and I just want to compliment you for that. What's your name, by the way?"

Helpful Hints:

Look at common things, like the following:

1) How a mom or dad treats their kid;

2) How a couple treats each others;

3) How a sales clerk tries to be so completely helpful, patient, etc.;

4) How another clerk shows interest in her customer's background or interests;

5) How creatively someone dresses;

6) How kindly someone helps their elder parent or grandparent.

Supermarket Surprise Hunt

Benefits

1) You'll discover parts of a supermarket you never knew existed.

2) It gives kids something to do that will absorb their attention for quite a while.

3) Can be a very romantic couple game, especially if your gift is a flower or candle.

4) Makes shopping suspenseful.

5) Gives kids (and morally disabled adults) more experience knowing the joy that comes from giving.

How to Play:

Just spend ten or fifteen minutes (longer if you're doing major family shopping) to buy the other person a surprise gift for under a dollar. You can reduce this to fifty cents for younger children, or just subsidize the game.

You agree to meet on the other side of the counters, past the baggers. You can exchange surprise gifts right then and there or in the car. Be sure you select your gift without being seen and keep it well hidden while you are paying for it.

If there are three of more of you, write your name on slips of paper, and whomever you draw is whom you surprise. Since most families are odd size in number.

Helpful Hints:

As soon as you find your gift, put it immediately into a cart so no one else in your family will see what it is in case you cross paths.

Don't forget the possibilities with fruits or vegetables. You can write notes of

endearment on bananas too! Chocolate and flowers are usually safe bets.

More Fun Ideas

1) Add more suspense by inviting each other to stick their hand in the paper bag to see if they can guess what the gift is first.

2) Give people clues to see if they can guess what their gift will be.

Alphabetical Shopping

(best for supermarkets, but could work in a department store)

Benefits

1) Makes you much more aware of how much stuff there is in a supermarket or department store.

2) If you don't like going to the store, this game makes shopping time go faster.

How To Play:

As you're going down the aisles, see who can get to the end of the alphabet first by pointing out an item whose brand or generic name starts with the next letter in the alphabet that they have to name. For example, for A you could point out apple juice (if you in fact see it) or "Alfredo's Noodles." Now you have to find an item starting with B. Everyone else has the same task. Be sure you call your item out loud, so the other person knows you're being honest and fair, and most importantly, so they can't point to the same item and catch up to you.

If, by the time you've paid the bill, no one has got to Z, the winner shall be whoever got the farthest.

Helpful Hint:

You might want to agree to exclude Q and Z so that the game doesn't get bogged down.

Supermarket Race

Benefits

1) It's good, brisk exercise.

2) Helps get the shopping done faster, maybe.

3) Early readers learn to read faster.

4) People learn to not be afraid to ask questions (at least in supermarkets).

How to Play:

Call out one of the items you need, and on the count of three, the players race to see who can find the item first. "Finding" shall here be defined to mean "touching." And if you get there long before the other people, just stay there touching the item until they arrive. (Otherwise they won't know you were there first!) People keep track of their own points. Whoever gets the most

points by the end of the grocery list gets a reward. Be imaginative. See Rewards List, Appendix A.

Warning:

No running, since someone could accidentally bump into an elderly person or run over a little child. Just walk fast.

Feeling jaded, trite, run-down? Have I got an idea for you. One way to shake up the sand in the old bottle, get the sediment moving around is to take up two new identities. Get together and say you're going to meet at a certain place like a bar, a theatre or a restaurant, and casually, accidently bump into each other. Try to conduct a whole new relationship with each other. Like two new people becoming acquainted with each other. Resort to none of the tricks of the past, none of the known recognized factors of the past. Make yourself two new people. It's going to keep you busy, and who knows, you may fall in love with a new person.

—Ed Asner

Helpful Hints:

1) If there are more than three of you, divide into two teams, or just name one item per pair, since it gets too dangerous to have more than three people moving around quickly at once. If there are only two of you, you should still try to depart in opposite directions from your starting point. This will also add safety.

2) It's safest to play this game late at night or any time that's not a peak shopping time, so you have the least number of shoppers around.

3) If there are two of you, also depart in opposite directions from where you start. This will also add safety.

4) Whoever calls out the item must be as precise as possible, naming the brand as well as the specific type of thing, and size. Don't just say "apples," say "Granny Smith Apples, 3lb bag."

Warning:

No running! And look carefully where you are going.

Perfect Strangers

Thank you:
    Actor Ed Asner

Benefits

1) Renewed appreciation for the romantic places where you'll rendezvous—the bus terminal in front of the candy machine, the bell pepper bin at the supermarket produce section, the longest line at the DMV.

2) This is a great way to enliven and make your relationship new again. "Recreation," you know, looks suspiciously like re-create.

How to Play:

This is a couples game for those times when you and your partner/spouse/significant other have slid into a "Degree of Normalcy" in your relationship—that is, boredom—and nude bungie-jumping is out of the question. This game is GUARANTEED to bring results. (Notice we don't say what results.)

The first thing to do is to agree to play. If agreeing is difficult, try using the timeless Three B's of Successful Negotiation: Badgering, Begging and Bribing.

Then choose a place to meet, somewhere you'll always remember: The front steps of the local precinct building? The zoo? That little crepe restaurant in Paris?

Now, mentally travel to that place in your mind where you store all the happy characters you've ever imagined. That's right, your happy place. Now choose a character to portray.

Dress to fit that character, and don't worry if you end up wearing something very different from your normal attire: if you run into anyone you know, you can always claim to be your own evil twin.

Keep your appointment at the designated location. Now, here's the fun part: you and your mate will act like you don't know each other. Yes, sometimes you may do this anyway, but this time it's for the best of reasons. Glance at one another and begin conversation as you would with a stranger. ("Say, have you tried the bean soufflé?") Inevitably, you will be smitten by the charm of your partner's new guise. (Don't blow this part!)

Don't say a word about the life you already know with your partner. Treat every fact like a totally new discovery—you will not find this hard to do when your mild-mannered CPA mate makes up wild stories about jungle expeditions in Zaire and asks you to come along. (Say yes.)

The great thing about this game is you can really let your imagination go. Meet like this weekly if you desire or monthly, annually, tri-election-yearly, semi-autumn-equinoxically....

We would love to hear about your own inventions of new and free ways to have fun in public places, for our new book on 'mall games,' and our website, (SimpleFun.com). Let's teach the world to play. For details on how to submit your ideas and how we'll reward your effort and ingenuity, please see the end of Chapter 20

CHAPTER 11

Watching TV

*I suspect that normal human brains are built to be challenged
and that it is only in the face of an adequate challenge that normal
bihemispheric brain operations are engaged.*

—*Dr. J. Levy*

TV Karaoke™

Commercial Socks

Clothes Encounters

Tower Race

Learn a TV Scene

Penny Football

Over the past few years there has been a growing amount of terrifying research, (See Appendix D) that strongly suggests that, during the approximate fifteen years the human brain takes to complete the wiring or programming of its billions of "uncommitted neurons" (those neurons responsible for all the higher functions, like thinking, creating, imagining, or problem-solving), the end result is very much affected for the worse by television.

So I feel uncomfortable suggesting people do anything with a TV set, even playing games around it. In addition to the direct neural damage and its effects on our ability to imagine, create, and solve problems, there is a huge amount of sociological evidence demonstrating the extremely destructive effects of television on marriage and family cohesion. As I mentioned earlier, I am confident that we'll be talking about television a few years from now in the same way that we're talking about cigarettes today.

Though I have made a Simple Fun set of videos, as well as this book, to communicate my ideas more vividly on how to make ordinary situations extraordinary, and have even worked for years to develop a TV series based on the same concept of this book, if I had my way, I'd prefer a society without televisions. For now, though, I hope to fight fire with fire. The games in this chapter can, I feel, reduce the damaging effects of television, and if played may even prevent such effects during the television-watching experience.

General Benefits

All the games here convert the dangerous mind-numbing drug of TV into something that can at least stimulate creative interaction between spouses and all other family members, and at best, as in TV Karaoke™ (below), actually stretch, exercise and probably enhance your brain's powers.

All of these activities will provide far more memorable fun and bonding experiences than anything you've ever seen on television.

Interestingly, when I made the rounds to try and get my book on television, I discovered that those in power would never ever want to put these TV games in the show, because if people played them, they might not pay attention to the commercials.

TV Karaoke™

Benefits

1) Why play this game? Because, to paraphrase Chevy Chase, television is pretty mindless and you're not. And this game can prove it to you and your family and friends.

2) Develops spontaneity, acting and improvisational abilities, verbal fluency, and imagination.

3) Unlike TV itself, TV Karaoke™ provides an incentive to get some kids (those too shy in this situation) to read and see the value of reading.

I'd also like to say that this game is worth special attention as the most powerful of all the games in this chapter in transforming the otherwise deadly medium of television into an artistic medium. You'll be able to use TV like improv actors use fellow actors to create their art.

How to Play:

First, find the worst movie or television show you can possibly find on the air. This will be a piece of exhaustive research requiring at least a minute of frantic channel surfing. As a matter of fact, almost anything works, including the news (as we can see when we watch the *Saturday Night Live* news announcer give satirical interpretations of various pictures in the news). Soap operas are a gold mine of painful facial expressions and longing gazes. Videotape a soap opera to use for later, or rent a video.

Decide which characters you will play. You can do this with as few as two people, by just waiting for a two-person scene to begin. Alternatively, each of you could take on two or more characters, which will really keep you on your toes.

If there is a bunch of you, and you can't easily agree who is to take whom, just write the characters down on slips of paper and draw. If there are more of you than parts, just take turns. Whoever doesn't get to go first, can have the advantage of learning by watching the mistakes of his predecessors. Whoever doesn't get to play on a given round can also be given an "alternate" status, to provide lines for anyone who takes too long to talk. Classic family shows, which you can often find on NICK at Night, will usually have enough characters if you have a classic-sized family.

Remember, the first time you do this may be a bit awkward. Just assume that the first show you pick won't be as good as later ones. As with many games, the more you play, the more fun it will be.

Before you begin, have the players announce their choices of character. Otherwise you might end up with a real jumble when that first line comes up.

Watch the program for five minutes or so to allow players to come to some understanding of their characters. Ignore the plot: it won't be half as much fun as yours anyway.

Now, turn off the sound and begin to speak for the characters as they move their mouths. It usually takes a minute or two to find a thread and get a plot moving, so give it some time. The sillier you are the better.

Rules:

1) Don't plan or think. Just listen carefully to what was said before you, and to the expression of your character on the screen, so that the content of your response will connect with your Family member's, and the emotion will fit that of the character on the screen.

2) No judgment. There are no right or wrong, good or bad words in this game; whatever anyone says is just fine. Parents should be prepared to be a bit shocked at times about language, but not let that spoil the fun of the moment.

3) Alternates must wait a few seconds before filling in with a line.

Helpful Hints:

1) If someone is feeling very reluctant to play this game, let them have the role of director or tell them they can just use the *generic expressions* below. The director can either announce who is "on," at least at the start (until everyone has done it at least once) and then later announce the emotion being shown by the character on the screen if and only if it isn't being demonstrated by the speaker.

2) If you prefer, you can just pick something from the suggested list of "generic expressions" that follows; they go with almost any remark anyone might say. You'll eventually start feeling comfortable enough to move from the generic lines to the *ad-lib lines* (also below), where you only need to add one or two missing words. After a few of these, you can start making up complete lines all on your own.

3) If you don't want to direct or use the "generic expressions," you can always help by making up additional generic expressions or ad-lib lines yourself for the next game.

4) The best way to help family members and friends to overcome their inhibitions is to get our two-volume **Simple Fun Home Videos**, which contains a special version of **TV Karaoke**™ specifically designed to enable families to easily get into playing this game. In particular, I have developed a special technique which enables a child or adult who is feeling shy or reluctant to ad-lib, to

slowly ease into participation with the rest of the family. (See page 241 for ordering instructions).

This TV Karaoke™ video offers various prompts on the screen, enabling you to eventually speak the actors' parts in a slow step-by-step progression that you control at your own pace. Please see end of Chapter 20 for ordering information.

More Fun Ideas

1) For a much simpler version (really the warm-up phase) of TV Karaoke™, just have each person pick someone in the show and try their best to parrot whatever they are saying as they are saying it, as closely in synch as possible. You obviously need to have the TV sound up for this. Allow yourself a few minutes of bungling to get into it.

2) If you have a room full of uncured hams, try turning the television sound off completely until almost the end of the show.Then tune in to the real ending and compare it with your own. You'll be amazed at how much more imaginative you've been than those Hollywood hacks. What do they know anyway?

3) With three or more players, one can be director. Whenever the director says "switch," actors trade roles.

4) The director can also call out emotions (different from those on the

screen) for the other players. "Cliffie—sad! Bertha—angry!" Then the actors must act with those emotions. It's a welcome challenge to your acting ability.

TV Karaoke™ Generic Lines:

These are for those feeling a bit shy and in need of warm-up lines like these to get into the swing of things. After you've played with these for a while, move up to the ad-lib lines which follow.

- I think I see what you mean.

- Could you repeat that again? I can't believe you said that!

- Excuse me for changing the subject, but could I talk to you about your hair?

- Gee, do you really mean that? That's fantastic.

- Oops, forgive me. But I forgot I left the stove on, and I have to go.

- I forgot I have to make a phone call too!

- You really believe that, don't you!

- Your eyes sparkle so much when you talk like that.

- This is just too much. I need some relief.

Ad-Libs Lines:

After you're warmed up using some of the above lines, you're now ready for these.

Just fill in the blank as it calls for, with whatever pops into your mind. Remember, don't think. Your first impulse is always best in this game.

- Excuse me, but could I see that (noun) in your pocket?

- Is that a (noun) crawling on your (nose)?

- You have a very (adjective) point there!

- How can you talk this (adjective) way to me?

- You're making me feel so (adjective).

- Excuse me for changing the subject, but I must go to (noun) right now.

- That's a very impressive (noun) you just (verb).

- You know, I love the way you (verb)!

- I don't know if what you're saying is a (noun) or a (noun).

- You're so (adjective), the way you (verb) with your (noun)...

Commercial Socks

Benefits

1) Develops balance.

2) Gives you something much more fun and beneficial for the family to do than watch commercials.

3) Gives you a wonderful and deeper appreciation of socks (and flat heads!)

Equipment Needed:

Socks or toilet paper rolls, paper cups, etc.

How to Play:

Before turning on the television, place in your lap a pile of socks or whatever other items you decide to use.

Then, whenever a commercial break appears, the family competes to see who can balance the most number of socks on their head and shoulders by the end of the commercials. Non-playing onlookers are invited to get involved by cheering on the underdog or lightly tickling the winning player—just to even things out. This game can be played in teams, with parents against kids, males against females.

Helpful hints:

Squeeze the sock to flatten it out more, to make it easier to balance.

Handicaps:

Tickling; wearing football helmets; shaving heads (just kidding).

More Fun Ideas

Dishwashing or Room Cleanup Variation: See who can get their respective chore done before the commercials end. Players gets to inspect one another's allegedly completed tasks.

Clothes Encounters

Benefits

1) Shelters you a bit from the negative conditioning effects of commercials.

2) Is especially bonding between family members.

Equipment Needed:

Old clothes that two or more people can fit into.

How to Play:

As with Commercial Socks, viewers pair off and when the commercial breaks come on (usually there are three or four commercials in a row, lasting for a total of 90 seconds to two minutes), one team gets up and tries to see how many pieces of clothes they can put on together. Each piece of clothing must connect both people somehow.

You can pair off guys vs. gals or parents vs. kids, or just compete against your self, trying to beat your previous record.

Helpful Hints:

If you want to be more precise, use a stop watch or egg timer. Also, the bigger the pieces of clothing, the easier it is to play.

Warning:

Do not use nice clothes that you'd be depressed about tearing.

More Fun Ideas

Forget the TV and just use a stopwatch or three-minute egg timer.

Tower Race

Benefits

Gives you the natural joy of creating something tangible.

Equipment Needed:

A pile of old newspapers and a roll of masking tape. Two rolls of masking tape would be better.

How to Play:

The idea is to compete with other players to see who can build the highest tower within the span of one, two, three, or four commercials, or over the span of an entire program, working during the commercial breaks. Build your tower by curling the papers into tubes, and tape the tubes together end to end and/or along the seam.

We hear that Donald Trump has even played this game, which resulted shortly thereafter in a chain of newspaper towers appearing across the country, financing several major corporate takeovers yet to be investigated by the IRS. But this could be just a rumor.

Helpful Hints:

Handicap the faster or more dexterous by having them use mittens. Or pair off in teams to balance out the competition.

More Fun Ideas

1) Give a prize for the most creative tower.

2) You can build towers at your desk at work, but we don't recommend doing this unless your employment contract guarantees your right to impulsive and silly behavior at odd moments. Everyone should have such a contract.

Learn a TV Scene

Benefits

1) Develops verbal fluency, poise and vocabulary.

2) Develops acting and observation abilities.

3) Develops memory.

How to Play:

From a TV movie or a favorite TV show, pick a scene that contains the same number of actors as there are of people wanting to play. Audiotape the scene and then transcribe the dialogue onto paper. Each of you then pick your character, learn their lines, and then perform the scene together.

More Fun Ideas

A great romantic couple version is to pick a romantic scene, like the closing scene in Casablanca,and do that together.

Penny Football

Thank You again:
  "Guru of Play" Bernie DeKoven

Benefits

1) Develops ear-hand coordination and reflexes.

2) Teaches you the value of a penny.

Equipment Needed:

Twenty-two pennies, nail polish and/or liquid paper.

How To Play:

Tune in to a football game on television (or even on the radio!). Prepare your "teams" by painting the players' numbers on pennies with nail polish or liquid paper. Now, line up your team of eleven "players" against your partner's eleven-penny team

The rest is simple, but challenging: just move your players according to the announcer's directions.

Helpful Hint:

Play on a smooth title or wooden floor.

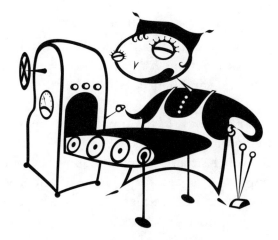

CHAPTER 12

At Work

When work is a pleasure, life is a joy!
When work is a duty, life is slavery.
—*Maxim Gorky*

Be Each Other at the Office

Five-Minute Fun Break

Rooftop Party

Joke Exchange

Biggest Mistake Award

The Groucho Glasses Routine

Best Lines Rewards

DiBono's Six-Hats-Thinking

Executive Chair Race

Be Someone Else Office Calls

Compliment Calls

Office Art Wall

Pretend Caller

Creative Phone Answers

Office Kidnapping

Intercom Game

Elevator Game

Elevator Roulette

General Benefits

As most management consultants will tell you, adding an atmosphere of playfulness to the office leads to increased employee morale and hence greater retention.

Adding playfulness to the office can increase creativity, and hence problem-solving effectiveness. And since adding play to the office situation creates happier employees, and happy employees are more productive (and get sick less often), these play ideas can lead to greater worker productivity. If your office has outside customer contact, you might end up attracting more customers, since playfulness is to people as honey is to flies.

One of the most important incentives for employees is the chance to be creative. Creative opportunity leads to greater employee retention.

And since playfulness is incompatible with anger, these games can lessen the likelihood of people stressing out and becoming angry with each other or with customers. They also simply provide an outlet for stress.

"Dare to be stupid"
(sign over computer of
Ron Grossman, head geologist
at NASA).

You can further expand the number of these office games by applying many of the games from Chapter 7 "Riding in the Car" and Chapter 9 "Mealtimes" to the office situation, especially to the Five-Minute Fun Breaks (see below). Lunches, coffee breaks, and even office meetings will benefit from these games.

Introductory Warning:

Obviously, use common sense. If your boss hasn't already read this book, you should first give it to them, perhaps along with a management book or article extolling the values of playfulness and creativity. Otherwise any of these games and activities could lead to reprimands or worse. And that wouldn't be fun. I recommend you first schedule a discussion on the whole idea of making the office more playful, perhaps over an office lunch, where you could demonstrate by using Be Each Other, for example.

In other words, DO NOT play these games without permission and active involvement on the part of those in power. You should also try to reach some consensus on the value of such play on the part of your coworkers, or at least get them to agree to experiment for a week or a month.

Be Each Other at the Office

Benefits

1) Can do much to help employees see themselves as others see them, which can be especially useful to management.

2) Can add more humor to the office milieu.

How to Play:

This goes just like the Be Each Other dinner game (see Chapter 9) except you'll play it during lunch or coffee break.

Everyone writes his or her first and last name (in case two people have the same first name) on a slip of paper, folds it small, throws it in a cup, shakes them all up, and draw. If you draw your own, put it back and draws again.

Rules:

Again, don't be mean, and don't be judgmental. Be sensitive to others feelings—if someone is uncomfortable and asks you to stop, do it. See additional rules, p95.

The trouble with the rat race is that even if you win, you're still a rat.

—Lily Tomlin

Five-Minute Fun Break

Thank you:
Michelle Berger of San Francisco.

Benefits

This is a great way to reduce office stress and thereby improve efficiency. When things get just too stressful, declare a five-minute fun break.

How to Play:

The idea of this game is to simply take a five-minute fun break to do anything that's fun.

Agree ahead of time where everyone is supposed to go on these breaks (usually the lunch room, but it can also be a hallway or a conference room). Agree ahead of time that whoever calls the break gets to suggest the activity—one that can be done in five minutes or less.

It's best to assign an order, giving each person in the office a particular day of the week, or part of a day, that's theirs to announce the break.

Activities could be exchanging jokes, cackling like chickens or roosters, or meowing like kittens, or pairing off into thumb hat wrestling matches, using those office coffee sugar packets.... You can have fun however you want, as long as it's just for five minutes at a time. (See more examples below.)

Warning:

Again, don't be judgmental. For example, don't accuse any activity of being "stupid," or "silly." As long as it's physically safe, it's legitimate.

Helpful Hints:

If you notice one person tending to call for the Fun Breaks too often, you can limit the breaks to two per person per week.

Five Minute Fun Break Ideas

Here are lots more Five-Minute Fun Break (FMFB) ideas. Remember the possibilities are as limitless as the combined imaginations of everyone in your office.

1) Everybody give one another compliments or give a collective neck and shoulder massage around a circle.

2) Prepare a wonderful snack as a surprise for your fellow employees.

3) Have a boom box at work and bring some favorite music to lift people's spirits (Afro-Haitian or polka should work), and just all of you dance for five minutes.

4) Have some topics ready to announce and have everyone write a poem on their own and then read it at the next FMFB, or alternatively write a group poem, passing it around, letting each person write a line.

5) Write a poem or silly limerick. Remember, you don't have to show it to anyone, so let loose.The point is to have fun.

6) Try out almost any of the games from Chapters 7 or 9. Have a five minute Alphabetical Discussion; a quick version of Be Each Other; play Alphabetical Song or Kvetch.

7) Play a game I call Psychic Nonsense: get into pairs or three-person teams. Stand back to back and then count to three. And on the count of three, you both simultaneously spin around to face each other, and simultaneously combine a nonsensical body movement with a nonsensical sound. Don't think. This is pure improv. Let it all be left brain.

8) Read a short story from a good book of short stories you keep at the office for such occasions.

9) Create your own office (or floor) secret handshake or salute.

10) Give a quick dance lesson.

11) Bring copies of the words to a song you think everyone would like to sing together and do it!

12) Agree the day before to bring surprise gifts, nothing over one dollar to exchange during the FMFB. The gifts are all put into a big bag and people take turns drawing from the bag. Rule: The first thing they touch, they must pull out.

13) Have on hand humorous books of jokes, or cartoons clipped from the newspaper.

14) Put on some relaxing music, loosen your clothing, close your eyes, and have a bona fide daydream. You can obviously also do this alone as well. Then agree during the next FMFB to share whatever daydreams came up.

15) Bring along some outrageous clothing to put on for your FMFB.Put on the wildest clothing combo you can find. If you feel especially brave, spend the day that way.

In the nine months that followed a workshop conducted by C. W. Metcalf (humor and fun consultant) at Digital Equipment Corp in Colorado Springs, twenty middle managers increased their productivity 15% and reduced their sick days by half.

—HR Focus, February 1993

16) Bring tennis shoes to work and have short races in the nearest sufficiently wide and long space you can find. (Alleys in back of your building often work well. But station lookouts to warn you of occasional cars or trucks.) If you have a simple square perimeter office corridor on your floor, you can race in pairs. To avoid bumping into each other, start at the same point, but run in opposite directions. Whoever gets back first, wins! If you don't want your boss to see this game, just pick a different floor. Or try the roof.

17) For a quick show-and-tell, have everyone bring one of the funniest pictures they have from their own scrapbook. The search for such a photo could be painful: you might discover you haven't done anything outrageous in the last ten years! Given such a danger, be sure to announce in advance that if people can't find anything, they can bring a couple of ideas that they've thought of doing. Then maybe all of you who haven't done much can get together some evening or at a "Silly Sunday"brunch to do some. Don't forget to bring your cameras.

Rooftop Party

Benefit

A party, or an experience of serenity, is an easy way to end your day on a good note.

How to play:

If you work in a sufficiently tall office building, during the winter time you can often catch a beautiful sunset from your rooftop. Watch it alone (bring along a folding chair from home you can bring up there to sit on). Or make it a party, and tell everyone to bring drinks and snacks. You could even bring your favorite "music to watch sunsets by."

Helpful hint:

If you don't work in a sufficiently tall building, scout the tallest ones closest to you. If your rooftop access is locked, you can usually arrange to get it opened if you are an employee in the building.

More Fun Ideas

Don't wait till sunset. Use your rooftop for lunches, Five Minute Fun Breaks, or coffee breaks.

> The first time I ever participated in a skit as a manager during a company meeting, I realized the power of acting silly, or real, in front of a group. The response, the attitude, even the ultimate respect was overwhelming.
>
> —*Cynthia House*
> (*quoted in* At Work,
> *November/December 1996*)

Joke Exchange

Equipment Needed: A large can or box. Label it "joke exchange can: If you take one, put one back. Please don't offend anyone's race, religion, or sex."

How to Play:

Place your joke exchange can in the lunch room or at the receptionist desk. Place jokes in and take 'em out!

Biggest Mistake Award

Thank You:
  Ram Dass and Ben Cohen

Benefits

1) Encourages individual responsibility.

2) Improves employee morale.

Equipment Needed:

A large coffee can labeled "Biggest Mistakes," as in Joke Exchange.

How to Play:

Set the Biggest Mistakes box in the lunch room or somewhere easily accessible by all employees. Once a week, the staff gets together and gives a reward to the employee who owns up to making the biggest or most stupid mistake.

Helpful Hints:

Obviously, you want to have the full support of management on this one, lest you cut your own throat.

The Groucho Glasses Routine

Thank You:

Wavy Gravy and again Ram Dass. These two wonderful men both sit on the Board of the Seva Foundation, which is dedicated to eradicating preventable blindness in third world countries.

Benefits

This game is powerful in preventing board and other serious meetings from getting overly serious and stiff.

How to Play:

In meetings, whenever someone says the word, "serious," everyone must immediately put on Groucho Marx glasses (those glasses with a big nose and furry mustache attached to them). Again, management must be in support of such fun.

Best Lines Awards

How to Play:

This is for meetings. Decide on a variety of award categories and judges for each category. (This also increases everyone's attention to each and every sentence.) Here are some categories:

- Give a reward for the funniest one liner
- Give a reward for the most poetic one liner

- Give a reward for the most insightful one liner
- Give a reward for the best use of a metaphor
- Give a reward for the best question

DiBono's Six-Hats-Thinking

Thank you:

Edward DiBono, the originator of this fun problem-solving approach.

Benefits

1) Gives people permission to be much freer in contributing ideas and information, which will lead to the best solution to a problem.

2) Makes it much easier for people to confront those with opposite points of view, and for the latter to take in such opposing information.

How To Play:

Everyone bring six hats, each of a different color: blue, green, red, white, yellow, and black. If you don't have hats of all those colors, a big colored sock, T-shirt, or scarf will do. Then try wearing these at various points during your meetings, according to the scheme that follows.

- blue: when discussing how you are talking (meta-communication statements, statements or questions about your process)

- green: when generating creative ideas

- white: when brainstorming all the positive reasons why something is a good idea

- black: when brainstorming all the negative reasons why something might not work

- red: when sharing emotions, whatever they may be

- yellow: when providing relevant data and facts

It probably is best if all wear the same color at a time, and switch at the same times.

> We are under a lot of pressure, and toys are our comfort. We need them like Linus needs his blanket.
>
> —*Mary Owen, Oracle Corp.*
> *(quoted by Mark Leibovich,*
> San Jose Mercury News,
> *Aug. 4, 1996)*

Executive Chair Race

Equipment needed:

Two chairs with wheels.

How to Play:

You can only play this with two people at a

time, but everyone else will want to watch. Just find a wide enough hallway, sit on your chair facing away from the direction you're heading, and on the count of three, race each other the length of the hallway.

Warning:

Don't do this if you have any physical problems or your boss doesn't approve. Also be sure to station people along the route to make sure no innocent pedestrians get in the way.

Be Someone Else Office Calls

Benefits

1) Develops your poise and dramatic abilities.

2) Develops your ability to talk to almost anyone.

3) Makes your working life much more enjoyable.

4) Gives some joy to those you call.

How to Play:

Pretend you're someone else and put on an accent when you make a phone call. Or, answer your phone as someone. Here are some possibilities, some best done as the caller, and some best done when answering:

- Your new English or French personal assistant or secretary (calling or answering)

- A Brooklyn-accented plumber or maintenance head reporting a major leak in the building of the person you're calling.

- A fast-talking New Yorker who claims to be a long-lost relative of whomever you're calling.

- A flower-delivery service representative trying to persuade whomever you're calling to buy a bouquet of flowers for the president of your company.

- The security cop who guards the building of whomever you're calling.

Warning:

Be culturally sensitive. Imitating an accent associated with a particular race or ethnic-group could be experienced as offensive, especially in a work situation where you don't always know everybody well. If in doubt, ask first. Unless you have anyone from France, Britain, or Germany working in your office, you're always safe with these.

> We feel a fun atmosphere builds a strong sense of community. It also counterbalances the stress of hard work and competition.
>
> —*Elizabeth Pedrick Sartain, Southwest Airlines*

Compliment Calls

Benefits

1) Develops your poise and ability to talk to almost anyone.

2) Makes people feel appreciated and strengthens your relations with them.

How to Play:

One of the great tragedies of life is that most people wait until someone dies before saying all the things they liked about them. So today, out of the blue, why not call someone you like and tell them why you like them? The more specific you can be the better. Just say you were thinking about them today and you felt a need to let them know how much you appreciate them.

Office Art Wall

How to Play:

First of all, the boss or office manager must like this idea. Or forget it.

The idea is to find a wall that employees can paint on in any way they wish.

Paints, water, brushes, etc. should always be available near this wall for anyone to use any time they need the break. People may paint alone or with friends whenever they are on break. It should be a rule that one may not paint over someone else's painting.

Helpful Hint:

Agree in an office meeting how often the wall can be covered over to allow for new paintings, or agree on some solution to what to do next when the wall is fully covered.

Warning:

Be sure to use water-soluble latex paints, so people don't ruin their clothes.

More Fun Ideas

See if your office manager or boss would allow each person who has their own office to paint one of their own walls.

Pretend Caller

How to Play:

This is a version of Be Someone Else, but it's worth a separate mention. The idea here is to call a coworker—someone who you know can take a joke—and pretend to be a major business client or the secretary or administrative assistant of that person. You obviously need to disguise your voice. An accent would probably be the easiest way to do that.

Then you might go on to either wax eloquently about how impressed you are with the presentation or letter you received from the person you're calling, or if you feel particularly daring, tear into that person about some made-up bumble or affront to your company.

Warning:

Be sure you let your coworker know it's a gag before their ulcer starts to act up! And don't go on too long, since you are probably talking to someone whose time is very valuable.

Creative Phone Answers

Thank You:

Eleanor Cousins, wife of the late Norman Cousins, who pioneered the exploration of the vital importance of humor and laughter to health.

> When fun is part of your culture, people are more relaxed and open to thinking about new, creative, or innovative ideas—a trait that always has been and always will be a competitive advantage.
>
> —*Cathy Miller, PacifiCorp*

Benefits

1) Makes your working life much more enjoyable.

2) Gives amusement to those you call.

How to Play:

There are an infinite number of variations, but one of the most common answers that Norman gave when he received a call during the day was to answer, "Beverly Hills Emergency Hot Line. If you wish emergency legal help, press 1. If you need the suicide crisis hot line press 2. If you wish to report domestic violence, press 3. And if you are just bored, you can talk to me." If he heard the caller press a button, he would immediately give them the actual number they would need to call for help with that problem. Besides giving people a laugh, he also performed a genuine informative service.

More Fun Ideas

Obviously you could vary the above in endless ways. One of my favorites is to pick three of my favorite causes (which may vary from week to week), and use them in place of the above, giving people the appropriate phone numbers. This can also include an important piece of legislation in Congress, for which I give people the number of Congress to call to get their representative's number. (202-224-3121).

Office Kidnapping

How to Play:

Hide an office item belonging to a coworker, such as a stapler, and leave an obvious ransom note.

Warning:

Be sure not to hide something likely to be extremely necessary and without which your colleague might miss a deadline.

Intercom Game

Equipment Needed:

A portable radio that can be put up against the intercom microphone. You could also bring your tape recorder with prerecorded music.

How to Play:

This is really in the category of practical jokes, so be sure you read the warning below before attempting this.

When you are about to take your break and leave, just find an interesting music station (heavy metal or Spanish-only, maybe polka, if you're lucky), or turn on your tape recorder to play whatever tape you brought. Set the radio or tape player close enough to the intercom microphone, so that it will be clearly audible on everyone's speaker, and turn it on. Hit all the intercom extensions in rapid succession and then run, leaving everyone in the office to "enjoy" your musical interlude, or be racing around to find where it's coming from and turn it off!

Helpful Hint:

You'll be most able to get away with this without upsetting people if your office has a "practical joke day" once a week, where everyone agrees ahead of time that it's considered okay for people to try out practical jokes.

Warning:

Be sure you are sufficiently well liked and that your office mates have a sufficient love for practical jokes!

Elevator Game

Thank You:

Alfred Hitchcock, the famous film director. He called this his "elevator story."

Benefits

1) Develops your story telling abilities.

2) Could be a great way to meet new people in your building.

3) Adds healthy level of suspense to elevator trips.

How To Play:

The idea is to enter into an elevator with a friend or coworker, preferably on your way out of the building, so that you're going down, and preferably at the end of the work day, so that the elevator will be full of people, who will all exit on the ground floor.

You simply start talking thusly in tones of shock and horror: "You'll never believe what happened! When I came into his

office, he was crawling on the floor ..." (pause a few seconds between each installment to add more and more suspense) "And there was blood every where...! (more pausing) "I couldn't believe my eyes. He then motioned me to come close to him ..." You want to say enough, or pause enough, to drag out the story so that just before getting to ground level you say the following: "And then he whispered to me ..."

As the elevator doors open, you simply wait and enjoy everyone in the elevator somehow trying to hang around you as long as possible without seeming too conspicuous, and then you exit the elevator without completing the story!

When Hitchcock did this gag with an unwitting friend, the friend anxiously asked Hitchcock, "Well what did he say?" And Hitchcock simply replied, "I don't know. That's just my elevator story."

Elevator Roulette

How to Play:

At least two people are needed to play this game. You all get into an elevator, close the door, hit the buttons for all the floors, and then swing into a song you've all agreed upon. As the doors open, you can either be bold and continue singing, or act "normal" and pretend that you don't know the other nut(s) in the elevator.

We'd love to hear your own inventions of new and free ways to have fun in the office. You'll be delighted and so will perhaps millions of others. Please see the end of Chapter 20 for details on how to send in your ideas and how we'll reward your effort and ingenuity.

CHAPTER 13

Waiting and Hanging Around

The one quality joyful people share is that they know how to express their uniqueness, they sing their own song.

—Salli Rasberry

General Benefits

All of these games turn "dead" time into creative and fun time, into opportunities for flow (see Balancing Act or Sticky Fingers), or closeness (Balloon Hug), sheer hilarity (Messy Comedian) or developing new skills (Top 7 Standards, Make My Doodle, or Messy Comedian). And by keeping kids occupied in these ways, you also reduce incidences of fighting and other forms of destructiveness that happen out of boredom.

If you are waiting or hanging around alone, you can also do any of the activities mentioned in Chapter 16 "Being Alone". In fact, I'd recommend them.

Balloon Hug

(samurai wrestling in the comfort of your own home)

Benefits

1) Well, how many chances do you get to really ram someone? This is like safe sumo wrestling for people who weigh under 600 pounds. And most of the time, you end up getting a big hug—a really big hug—at the end. Can't beat that for emotional connection.

2) Balloon Hug helps release aggressions in a safe atmosphere; it's good for your lungs and it's a great way to decrease an unwanted domestic balloon surplus.

3) It's a fun way to get people who normally haven't been hugging much to get back into it in a way that's a lot of fun.

Equipment Needed:

At least two people and at least two large (eight inches in diameter, minimum) balloons. Only the weapons die in this game, so you'll need more balloons the more times you play.

How to Play:

I don't know if I should be telling you about this game because of its purely aggressive roots. It's just that it's also so darn affectionate. This game begins as a combination of a duel and a joust and ends in a big, explosive hug. Think of it as what would happen if they filled all the weapons in the world with air.

Each of you blows up a balloon. (Be considerate. Not everyone blows as hard as everyone else, so allow the other person to finish, please.) Make the balloons as big as you can without popping them.

Be sure you aren't wearing shirts with sharp pins or buttons in front. Then hold your balloon in front of you against your chest and stomach. Next, either stand back to back at the center of the living room or face each other at the corners of the living room, depending on how ticklish your backside is. Outdoors, a big yard that allows you at least twenty-five feet of distance from each other is also fine.

Next, count to ten, pacing away from each other as you count. Then turn and, yelling whatever war cry seems appropriate—"Death To All Tyrants!" "Nationalized Health Care or Bust!" "Long Live Mr. Rogers!"—you fly at one another head-on, using your balloon as your cushion at the point of impact. The balloon that bursts belongs to the loser, or winner. You decide. Usually, neither balloon bursts, at which point the combatants hug one another as hard as they can, with the balloons between them, until one of the balloons does burst.

Warnings:

1) Pick up your balloon shreds after each round, as they can cause chok-

ing and suffocation in curious infants and birds.

2) Also, be sure you've moved any breakable or sharp objects from the playing area.

More Fun Ideas

1) If you're going to be outside, play on a nice soft lawn, since people have been known to fall down, usually giggling like fools.

2) You can also play in the rain. (Yes, wear old clothes. Or not. They're not our clothes. We don't care. Use your own judgment.)

Butt Bump

Thank You:

This game wasn't really invented. It was discovered in a discotheque in Martinique in 1963 by two anthropology graduate students on leave from the University of Chicago. Unfortunately, they never published their findings, and so the game has only recently surfaced due to incredibly intense research on our parts. Really intense research. In the field. True story. Really intense. We had to go to Martinique.

Seriously speaking, I want to thank the Inuit Native American tribe for this one. The Inuits have an enormously playful culture. *We* should be so civilized!

Benefits

Of course, there's the sheer aesthetic pleasure of the bump itself.

Then there's the cardiovascular benefit, the muscle toning for those often-neglected parts of the body, and the definite ego satisfaction for people who have low centers of gravity (a real virtue in this particular instance). But we won't lie to you. The best part is the profound enjoyment of the bump.

Equipment Needed:

Well, you should probably wear pants. We're not being judgmental about this, but you probably should.

How to Play:

You need players in multiples of two for this. It helps if partners are close to the same height, although that is not a necessity. It's kind of like dancing, you see.

The two people squat down back to back. How far apart are they? There is an official *Simple Fun* measurement for this purpose. One of the players places a thumb on their own behind and stretches out the index finger of that hand. If it touches the other person's behind, it means they're much more intimate than they were two minutes before. It also means that they're the right distance apart. Move close together if the distance is too great.

Now, without looking or moving their feet, these two players attempt to nudge, cajole, push, or in some cases smash their rear ends until someone's feet move. If you move your feet, you've been officially (and we can't over emphasize the significance of this too much) butt-bumped.

Warning:

Be sure that everyone understands that the point is just to get the other person to move their feet, not to knock them over.

More Fun Ideas

The truly adventuresome can try this game in the dark. Make sure you move all the furniture out of the way first.

Nose to Nose

Thank You:

No one really knows the exact origins of this game. Some scholars of leisurology say it can be traced to Cyrano de Bergerac, who may have used a version of the game as a method of foreplay. But that might be too easy an answer. At any rate most experts agree that France is the likely source of the game due to the fascination of the French with anything nasal or nasal sounding.

Benefits

1) Easy morning energizer to get you going.

2) Great way for couples to experience romance and suspense at the same time.

How to Play:

This is a very simple game in that no surplus equipment is necessary, only your own personal nose and the nose of the player(s) of your choice, which may be your child (before 9:00 P.M.) or your partner (after 9:00 P.M.—actually the early morning is pretty interesting too). It's a kinder, gentler version of Pin the Tail on the Donkey, with your partner being the you-know-what.

Participants begin by standing back-to-back as if commencing a duel. (If you are just lying in bed with your partner, start out facing each other about an arm's length and a half apart. The more practice you have, the farther apart you can start.) Both players should close their eyes, open their nostrils, and take two steps forward. Now turn around, and one of you move slowly toward your partner. Only one person should be moving, while the other stays perfectly still. Don't open your eyes! You don't really want to see this, believe me.

Be very careful not to move or to emit any sounds. The object is to tenderly touch tips of noses. If you end up nose-to-chin or nose-to-cheek or nose-to-lamp shade, start over.

And just remember: In this game, you can pick your partner, but you can't pick your partner's nose. (Sorry, but I just couldn't resist that one.)

Handicaps:

If your partner is too adept, have them spin around once or twice before commencing.

More Fun Ideas

1) Both players close their eyes and move toward each other simultaneously.

2) Match other body parts in addition to your noses, like palms.

3) Try other combinations: nose-to-ear, nose-to-hand, etc.

4) With a little imagination, couples may create an avant-garde version of Twister by adding more intimate body parts and removing those confining colored circles. To add further humor, the partner waiting to be touched could give directional hints by using honks, moans, whistles, kisses or names of White House Cabinet members, or whatever to indicate left, right, up, down, back, etc.

Top 7 Standards List

Benefits

These activities are very intellectually rich. None of them are original to me, but I believe they are often forgotten and for this reason worth at least a quick mention, particularly since they are much more valuable than the others in this chapter for the development of various skills.

1) Read to each other from a favorite novel or book on a subject of mutual interest.

2) Write a letter together to a friend, or in protest to the president or your representative (see Chapter 19 for more details on this).

3) Compose a poem together.

4) Compose a song together (best to have a guitar or piano around, and music paper or a tape recorder).

5) Invent a new dance step together. If you don't have a radio or other source of music with you, you can just set the beat and sort of la-di-da a song together while going through your steps.

6) Write a play or screenplay together.

7) Act out famous scenes from the movies. You can get books of scenes at the library or any bookstore.

Balancing Act

Thank You:
Penny Warner

Benefits

1) Develops balance.

2) Beats watching television.

Equipment Needed:

A pile of equally-sized objects—pencils, books, plastic bowls—enough for each player to have one of each.

How to Play:

All players create a pile for themselves of the same objects (that is, everyone has a pencil, a book and a bowl) and a start and finish line. On "go," everyone walks with one object on their head from the start to the finish line and then back to the starting line to carry the next object. If the object drops, the player must go back to the finish line and start again. Whoever races with the most objects within the set time limit (during a commercial break or using an egg timer) wins. (Be imaginative, See Reward List, p245).

More Fun Ideas

1) Have players balance the object on a tablespoon.

2) If you have enough people, you can make this a relay.

Sticky Fingers

Thank You:
Jackie Kzczynski, San Francisco.

Benefits

1) Develops good hand-eye coordination.

2) Develops patience, at least with toothpicks.

Equipment Needed:

Toothpicks and Scotch tape.

How to Play:

Scatter some toothpicks on the floor or table. Everyone puts a little rolled-up tape on the end of their fingers, then, using one finger at a time, attempts to pick up the most number of toothpicks without dropping any. The first one to lose a toothpick is out. The person with the most toothpicks stuck to their hand by the time all are picked up is the winner.

Handicap ideas:

Have the best person use their nondominant hand.

More Fun Ideas

If you want to be really silly, you could apply tape to your toes or nose and go after the toothpicks that way.

Make My Doodle

Thank you:
Penny Werner of San Francisco.

Benefits

1) Develops drawing abilities.

2) Develops visualization abilities.

3) Offers a completely nonverbal, non-competitive, low-stress method of communicating with one another.

Equipment needed:

Each person should have a small pad of paper or a few sheets of larger paper, along with pens or pencils. Crayons are even more fun. And water colors and paints are incredible.

How to Play:

The first player draws a spontaneous doodle, then gives it to the next person to complete or elaborate any way they wish. That person then passes the doodle to the next player (if there are more than two playing) or just passes it back to the first player to continue or to keep. Now the second player makes their doodle from scratch and lets the first person complete it.

Helpful Hint:

Sit side by side so that the initiator can see what the other person is making out of their drawing.

Touchy Toes

Thank You:
Two unknown lovers I once saw doing this while waiting for the subway in Manhattan.

How to Play:

Just face each other so that your toes are facing directly toward each other about one to two feet apart. Then try to gently tap the tip of the other person's shoe with your own shoe. Gently, now.

You can keep score to add more drama and let the winner kiss the loser, or get out of paying for dinner, or choose a movie.

Ice Cube Swimmers Challenge Cup

Thank You:
Philip Vahovich for this great kitchen Olympic event.

Benefits

Develops lung capacity.

Equipment Needed:

A large glass or aluminum rectangular cake pan, one large rubber band, two small glasses, two straws, and two big ice cubes.

How to Play:

So you thought ice cubes were only for drinks, black eyes, a fullback's knees, and that Spike Lee deal in *Do the Right Thing*?

Well, crack the trays, all you couch-potato Mark Spitzes, and but gather family and friends for the great Ice Cube Swimmers Challenge Cup. But hurry. The players are melting.

First, take a wide rubber band and stretch it lengthwise around the center of a large rectangular cake pan. From an aerial view, the pan would look like a swimming pool with the rubber band creating two swimming lanes. Then fill the pan with water almost to the top

Invert the glasses and set them in the cake pan at one end. Place your ice cube "swimmers" on top of the glasses. On the count of "three" you and your opponent, using your straws, blow your ice cubes off the glasses and into the cake-pan pool. The object is to get your ice cube down the pool and back using only the straw and your hot air to propel it.

Rules:

Stay in your own lane! If you pilot your ice cube like the Exxon Valdez, and it enters the forbidden waters of your opponent's lane, you must go back to the starting block, or set the cube back one straw-length, or whatever you all decide. (You may use your hands to restart your cube in this situation.)

Helpful Hints:

Put a colored rubber band around your ice cube to give it a Speedo swimsuit.

If your ice cube melts before the race is over, it is either too slow, or you are play-ing outside in July.

But if you get yourself a fast cube, put it back in the freezer and use it again! (Just kidding.)

Headline Guess

Thank you:
Jackie Kaczynski of San Francisco.

Benefits

1) Develops memory.

2) Develops reading abilities.

How to Play:

Everybody except "It," looks at a page of the newspaper, usually the front page to start, and tries to memorize as many of the headlines as possible. You can allow five to ten minutes. Experiment.

Then "It" starts to read from an article (from the beginning) until the other person(s) can guess the headline for the article. Then the players switch, so that "It" must now guess the headline of the article being read.

A perfectly correct guess gets 15 points. Whoever guesses the most headlines at the end wins.

For every word wrong in the guessed headline, 3 points are subtracted from the guesser's score.

Helpful hints:

1) Use pneumonic devices to remember the titles (including a visualization of a picture that would represent key words in the newspaper titles).

2) Repeat to yourself over and over the elements of the picture, or the headlines themselves.

Slapsie

Thank You:

Bernie De Koven, Palo Alto, CA, who's also one of the best playshop leaders in the country.

Benefits

1) Develops hand-eye coordination.

2) Sharpens one's attention.

How to Play:

Remember that game you used to play, or perhaps still do, where you place your palms down onto your opponent's hand which are face up and then they try to suddenly move one or both of their hands and slap the tops of yours?

Well this is the same game, but played with three people, each of you sort of facing into the center of an imaginary triangle and no more than two arm's lengths apart from each other. Each of you has your right hand palm down on top of the palm-up left hand of the person on your right and your left hand palm up with the right

palm-down hand of the person on your left.

Warning:

Be sure to warn everyone that some slapping is involved and warn the older ones not to hit the young ones too hard. This is supposed to be fun, not painful.

Messy Comedian

Thank You:

Penny Warner

Benefits

1) Encourages self-control.

2) It's a great incentive to get shy members of the family to act more comedic.

How to Play:

Whoever volunteers to be the comedian tries to make the others laugh. The trick is that the listeners' mouths are all filled with water. Whoever spits it out laughing is then the comedian. Having your mouth filled with water makes even the dullest comedian seem hysterical.

Warning:

Obviously you should play this game outside, or be sure you have covered the table with a waterproof table cloth. Be sure to play in clothes that can get wet.

Collaborative Kitchen Sculpture

Benefits

1) Develops spatial and artistic abilities.

2) Develops interests and abilities in construction and in structures and materials.

Equipment Needed:

Whatever you can find in the kitchen: spoons, forks, string, plastic bottles and glasses, tupperware, tooth picks, straws, fruit, vegetables (celery makes great beams!), tin foil, corks, baggies, spatulas, etc.

How to Play:

Just create a sculpture.

Warning:

Avoid using breakable or sharp objects.

Helpful Hints:

Work in separate rooms where you can't see each other, so that you avoid that terrible hobgoblin of creativity: comparison.

There's lots more ideas like this with common household items in a wonderful book by Barbara Sher called *Extraordinary Play with Ordinary Things.*

Follow My Finger

Benefits

This is a great way to introduce someone to the joys and surprises of drawing.

Materials needed: Several pieces of paper (at least 8½-by-11 inches) and a pen or pencil.

How to Play:

This game is played by two people at a time. One of you closes your eyes and offers your nondominant hand, in the fully open position, to the other person, who proceeds to take it, palm down, and guide it gently over an object, while the person with closed eyes proceeds to use his free hand to draw the object.

More Fun Ideas

The second person uses his or her own face as the object.

Kitchen Band

Not a terribly original idea, I know. But I couldn't resist. Some games are so wonderful, yet surprisingly forgotten.

How to Play:

Just use common kitchen items as musical instruments: pots, pans, glasses, bottles, cartons, etc. Use anything from chop sticks to knives, forks and spatulas as your drum sticks. A barbecue-sauce brush or hand-held egg beaters make a pleasant, softer sound.

Helpful Hint:

Try playing along with music from the radio until you get comfortable and more self-assured. Then you can proceed without the backup.

Decide who among you will be responsible for providing the bass, or the lowest beat. This person is necessary to set the basic beat and rhythm. He or she should use a large plastic or Tupperware bucket to make a sufficiently deep sound.

If you have the time and can get a big metal washtub, you can make a washtub base, using a broomstick handle and a clothesline. But I guess I'm getting carried away here.

Playing Popular Sports

If you obey all the rules, you miss all the fun.
—*Katherine Hepburn*

Paperball Tennis

Two New Ways to Play Baseball

Three-Team Basketball

Two-Ball Basketball

Tackle the Person with the Ball

Kitchen Hockey

Three Kinds of Tag

Hide-and-Seek with Your Pet

General Benefits:

These games all provide some physical exercise. The football and baseball variations provide even more exercise than the traditional sports themselves. This chapter teaches all of us that you can always make a new and sometimes better game out of an old one.

All the games also have the special distinction of teaching kids and parents that any game can be changed and improved simply by applying one's imagination, that there is nothing set in stone about any game. Most importantly, this chapter teaches us that rules and games exist for the benefit of humans and not the other way around. Therefore if only a few are receiving the benefit, it's probably time to change the rules. This is a principle that we apply to government and other important human endeavors whenever we make a significant social advance, like establishing of democracy itself, granting women the right to vote, or creating laws protecting children and the environment.

Paperball Tennis

Benefits

1) Develops hand-eye coordination.

2) Can be used to get your kid to pick up their junk paper off the floor (if you require that only that kind of paper may be used).

Equipment Needed:

Paper

How to Play:

This is a game that can be played on any sidewalk with cracks.

Just take a piece of paper and wad it up. This is now your ball. Your hand is the racket. The crack is the net. Serve underhand by hitting the paper ball with your hand. The returns are swatted back and forth across the crack. Score can be kept tennis-style or just by points. Out-of-bound calls are optional.

Two New Ways To Play Baseball

Version One

Thank You:
    Wavy Gravy of Berkeley, California

Benefits

1) Everyone in the infield and outfield gets much more excitement and experience catching and throwing the ball.

2) Everyone gets much more practice hitting the ball.

3) Everyone laughs more.

How to Play:

Feel free to use any or all of these variations, or make up your own. It's the regular game of baseball except:

1) everybody plays with their opposite hands;

2) everybody gets at least six strikes; all infielders and outfielders must handle the ball once before throwing it to make an out;

3) You must hop from second to third base, not run.

More Fun Ideas

1) Players who are really in shape can situate second or third base somewhat near a tree that has a firm outstretched limb, strong enough to easily support the heaviest player, with a rope tied to it. Before being allowed to touch the base, the runner must climb up the rope, touch the tree limb, and then climb down (careful not to burn your hands).

2) This one is for rural areas, where you're playing on your own land or parks without any restrictions. Roll an old jalopy or a big bus up to second base. In order to get to second base, you need to go in the rear door (or whatever door is farthest from the pitcher), run through to the front and then outside the front door (or whatever door is closest to the pitcher).

3) Immediately upon reaching home base, the player gets a neck and shoulder massage. Adults, if you want further reward for getting to home base, wait till you get home … there are kids in the field! What's wrong with you?

Version Two: Dictionary Man/Woman Baseball

Benefits

1) The players learn some vocabulary; it's educational for a change.

2) Other benefits are the same as version one above.

Equipment Needed:

Beyond the regular stuff for baseball, you need a dictionary.

How to Play:

In addition to the rules in version one, you designate one player from each team the "dictionary person."

The dictionary person should have a list of "challenge words" (ranging from easy to difficult, depending on the abilities of the players) to give players throughout the game who seek to get to first base.

The dictionary people from both teams should consult with each other before starting the game to make sure that their lists are comparable. Better yet, have an adult umpire or referee perform this judicial task.

The dictionary person stands midway between home and first base. In order to run to first base, the player must correctly define whatever word they are given by the dictionary person. If the runner cannot give the correct definition by the time the first baseman gets the ball, they're out.

Warning:

Be sure to warn the dictionary person to be watching the batter so they do not accidentally get hit.

Helpful Hints:

It is important that all the infielders handle the ball at least once, so that the runner has enough time to define the word.

Start out with words that are fairly easy, to avoid undue frustration. Tell the dictionary people to take into account the runners' ages and language abilities. Try to give very hard words to those kids you never cared for! This will discourage them and maybe they'll go home!

More Fun Ideas

1) Require the runner to mount a tricycle or bicycle at second base and ride to third base.

2) Require the runner to run backwards between first and second base.

3) Require the runner to hop on one leg between bases.

Three-Team Basketball

Thank You:

Ron Jones, of San Francisco, California, who's done more than anyone else I know to help physically- and mentally-challenged kids through the use of imaginative games.

It was pouring down rain one summer night in Philadelphia, and my lady and I went out to get something to eat, and we played hide n' seek in a park, in the pouring down rain for about almost two hours, and we had a ball. It was a lot of fun, and it didn't cost any money. We got wet, but you'll dry off.

—Stan Shaw, actor

How to Play:

Simple. Just use three teams instead of two. The third team's basket can be either one of the two baskets. Just decide ahead of time.

Helpful hint:

Remind players playing this for the first time that they have to be able to enjoy chaos for this to be a truly fun experience.

Two-Ball Basketball

How to Play:

Just use two balls instead of one. You might not have much practice with defense, but you'll have a lot more practice throwing and dribbling. Play just as you would regular basketball, trying to get some defense in whenever you don't have the ball yourself.

Helpful Hints:

To keep the chaos within bounds, you should invent whatever rules you need. For example, if one team fouls, all action stops, and the other team gets both balls for free throws (two attempts per ball as usual) or to rebound from the sideline.

You'll probably need to give someone the job of scoring, given how chaotic this game can become.

Tackle the Person with the Ball

Benefits

This game gives you about ten times more exercise than normal football.

How to Play:

The name of the game says it all. Forget all the other rules associated with football. You don't even need teams. If you don't feel like getting tackled, just throw it to the player nearest you.

Warning:

Be sure not to allow more than one tackler, so you don't end up with several people on top of one.

This is even more dangerous than regular football, since there will inevitably be more tackling. So wear proper protective

equipment on the face, head, and knees, and play on soft ground.

More Fun Ideas

A much safer version is to just tag the person with the ball.

Kitchen Hockey

Benefits

1) Great indoor exercise on a rainy day.

2) Another way to make decisions.

3) Creates a whole new dimension of food appreciation.

Equipment needed:

Two spatulas (preferably plastic), a thick (one-inch) slice of cucumber, zucchini, orange or lemon or other round fruit or vegetable. Don't use a fruit that is too heavy.

How to Play:

Yearning for excitement from the world of Sports? Longing for the roar of the crowd, the fever of competition, the smell of sweat (coming from the big guy in the bleachers sitting next to you)? Dream no more. Here's a sporting event that brings you not only the thrill of victory, but nostalgic charming memories of your childhood as well. In this game, you will use ordinary, unsuspecting, innocent kitchen tools to perform magnificent athletic feats.

Picture yourself, clad in T-shirt, jeans and protective tennies, feet spread, poised ready to strike, a determined look on your face as you deftly wield your hockey stick. (No, it's not just a rubber spatula. Where's your imagination?) Now, carefully eye your goal at the other end of the arena (between the dishwasher and the garbage pail). Pucks ready? (No, that puck isn't a mere slice of zucchini. Where are your visualization skills?)

Now begin your game. As you and your opponent swoop to and fro across the floor, the air crackling with excitement, think of this: right this moment, you're playing with a vegetable. Yes, that's right. Just like when you were a kid throwing Frisbees with burned oatmeal cookies. Now doesn't that bring back nostalgic, charming memories of your childhood?

Warning:

Use only plastic spatulas, as opposed to metal ones or cake servers. If possible, wear boots or some form of protection over the feet and ankle area, since you're liable to get hit there. Do not play this game with bare feet or in socks, or you'll soon be bleeding.

Helpful Hints:

If your kitchen isn't long enough to play in, choose the biggest room you can, but be sure you've moved any furniture and fragile objects. If you end up playing on a carpeted area, you will have to use a round fruit that can roll.

Door openings can be the goal areas. If you don't have doors at each end, then use pillows or liter-size soda bottles, filled with water and set about two feet apart.

More Fun Ideas

1) Play with straws and a Ping-Pong ball on a big table. Establish goal areas (between two salt shakers or two plastic glasses) and try to blow the ball into your opponent's goal.

2) You can also use an ice cube if you're a strong blower.

Three Kinds of Tag

Version One: Hug Tag

Thank you:
Rose Farrington, Santa Fe, New Mexico.

Benefits

1) There's hardly any better exercise than tag. Just try it. And you'll soon find out that even if you're a jogger, you'll be winded in no time. This version, however, is fairly mild, so it can be played even by older folks.

2) This is a great way to give people more affection. A wise person once said, "Everyone needs four good hugs a day, and if everyone got that we wouldn't have any wars!"

3) It's a great icebreaker for parties, if you have a large enough yard.

How To Play:

You need at least four people, though the more the merrier. Like any other game of tag, the object is to tag someone, so that they're It and you aren't. The new It then goes on to tag someone else.

Rules:

1) In this version, a person is safe from being tagged as long as they're hugging another person. But, you can only hug the same person for five seconds at a time.

2) Whoever is It should hold or wear a brightly-colored handkerchief or towel, so everyone knows who they are.

3) Some girls and women may not feel comfortable, so remind the boys and men to only hug around the waist; you should demonstrate this hug to be sure that it's clear.

4) "Tag-backs" are not allowed. This means you cannot tag back the person who just tagged you.

Warnings

(And these go for all the tag games): Be sure no holes, cliffs, railings, sharp objects, trees, cables, etc. are in the vicinity. Also be sure, if you're playing inside, do not play on a slippery floor, and remove all fragile items or furniture.

Helpful Hint:

If small children are playing with adults or larger children, have the larger people run backwards (or just speed-walk rather than run) to catch the younger players.

Version Two: Backwards Tag

How to Play:

This is really meant for when someone is much faster than others. That person must simply always run backwards, whether or not they're "It".

More Fun Ideas

The person being handicapped must hop on one foot, skip, or jump.

Version Three: Mirror Tag

Thank You:
    Karl Rohnke of Project Adventure, Hamilton, Massachusetts.

Equipment Needed:

Each person must have a small mirror, but not too small, measuring about 6 by 8 inches. Very small mirrors are much harder to work with and be seen when their sun reflection zaps you.

How to Play:

You play tag as usual, tagging not with your hand, but with reflected sunlight. If a flash from a mirror is seen by one of the fleeing players, that person must freeze for two minutes. You'll know when you've been tagged; the retinal alarm set off by the reflection of the sun in your eyes will be impossible to ignore.

Obviously, everyone must agree to be honest and to freeze when hit. A pre-game joint decision that makes the game even more fun is to agree that anyone hit by a light flash must dramatize their retinal surprise by falling down and yelling.

To avoid being tagged, you can try not to look at a player who's trying to flash you, or you can stay "downsun" as much as possible. But don't, or you won't be able to play!

This game still needs some experimentation. So we'd much appreciate any helpful hints you can send in, as well as your own tag versions.

Warnings:

1) Pick a mirror with dull or smooth edges.

2) Be sure not to carry a mirror larger than that noted above, because it becomes unwieldy.

3) Do not stare at the reflection or the sun, since this could cause permanent injury.

4) As with the other tag games, be sure there are no dangerous obstacles around.

Helpful Hints:

1) Wear sunglasses that block ultraviolet rays and that cut glare (though you should make sure that they don't cut the glare so much that you don't know when you've been hit.) You should still be able to see the flash but don't look at it longer than an instant. Even with sunglasses you should never stare at the sun.

2) Whoever is "It" should wear a red hat or something bright on his head that can clearly be seen from a distance, since this game is best played in a large wide open area, like a sandy beach.

Hide-and-Seek with Your Pet

Equipment needed:

A pet dog or cat. Okay, they're not equipment, more like additional players.

How to Play:

Just hide and see if your dog or cat can find you. This doesn't work with every dog or cat, but I hear it works with many. Let us know your results.

Helpful hint:

Have another player hold the pet long
enough for you to hide.

Warning:

This is a house game. Do not di ti outside
where your pet might run away or get
lost.enough for you to hide.

Dealing with Chores

And every task you undertake becomes a piece of cake,
a lark, a spree...It's very clear to see! That a spoonful of sugar helps the
medicine go down... in the most delightful way!

—*Mary Poppins*

Wash 'n' Clean to the Music

Room Clean Race #1

Room Clean Race #2

Read 'n' Clean

Setting the Table Race

Secret Buddies

Beat the Clock

Auction-It-Off Box

Job Swap

Folds and Flowers

Spin a Job

General Benefits

These activities and games are ways to make chores fun, or at least make it easier for the "medicine to go down." Your children will grow up realizing that work and play are not inherently contradictory, that they don't have to be segregated and alienated from each other as they are now in our society, and that all you need to make work exciting is creativity and, as we talked about in Chapter 3, the conditions for "flow:" a balance between our abilities and the challenges of the chore situation.

Of course the great utilitarian value of these games is that when work can be made fun and exciting, children are more willing to do their chores, and as a result parent-child conflicts become much less frequent, and parent-child bonds become much stronger.

Wash 'n' Clean to the Music

Benefits

1) Gets kids' rooms cleaned.

2) Develops positive association in children with cleaning their rooms.

3) Provides some exercise, and who knows, you might invent a new dance step or two.

How to Play:

Do you remember hearing such a rhythmic and happy piece of music while you were washing the dishes or cleaning your room or sweeping the floor, that you couldn't help but choreograph your cleaning actions to the music? That's what this is, more an attitude than a game.

Now when I say to do the chore to the music, I don't mean just with the music on. I mean to really move your hands, arms, legs, head, and neck to fit the music and words of the song.

It's almost always easier and more fun to do chores like the dishes with two people. Just try and pick music that you both really like. This might take some doing at first, but is well worth the trouble. Happy Brazilian or Afro-Haitian usually works very well regardless of age.

You can exclaim and banter back and forth to the music like this (imagining both to be finger snapping in rhythm as they say the following):

Dad (pulling out the sock drawer to the music): "Throw me those socks, bump bump!"
Child: "And hand me those towels! Yeah, yeah."
Dad: (grabbing his ends of sheet): "Now you take your end..."
Child: (grabbing his ends of sheet): "And I'll take mine!" (as they pull and tuck to the accents of the music)

More Fun Ideas

If you put on a little rap music for inspiration, you can take turns making up couplets. But if you prefer your children to get their room(s) cleaned up on their own, tell them to think up their own music before dinner, and if the room is ready by dinner time, they can perform the rap song they made up during the cleaning operation.

Room Clean Race #1

How to Play:

Since parents and children often enjoy competing with each other, try having weekly competitions; for example, the child and one parent could compete to see who can get their room cleaned up first, and the other parent (or another child!) could be the referee. The reward could be to let the winner choose dessert that evening, or the game you'll play at dinner or even a short family trip destination.

Helpful Hint:

If one room is far worse than the other, the person with the dirtiest room should get a head start until the referee feels both rooms are about the same.

More Fun Ideas:

Pit kids against adults rather than males against females.

Room Clean Race #2

Thank You:

Valerie Cambanes and Annike Lane of Brooklyn Park, Minnesota.

Equipment Needed:

Pencil, pad of paper, and dirty rooms. (You got kids, you got dirty rooms. Once my friend Joe cleaned his son's room and found he had another kid!)

How to Play:

You need two people to play this game. This can be either two kids (or an adult and a child), or an adult who's as messy as a child, or two kids who occupy the same room, or you can invite a best friend you're willing to show your room to and show where things go, and who's willing to do the same for you at their home.

Each player has a piece of paper, or better yet, tablet, with their name on top. On the word, "go," they both start picking up the room or rooms, but each must pick up items in twos, threes, or fours. If you pick up two shirts, you mark on your sheet two marks or checks; three socks, three marks; four pencils, four marks.

Note:

A bag of fruit or a dozen eggs only count as one item! Of course if you only have single items left, then go for it and give yourself a mark each time.

Whoever has the most number of marks by the time the first room is clean gets a reward. (As if living like a decent human being isn't enough of a reward.) You can agree, for example, that whoever wins gets to wear the other's clothes for the day. Or whoever loses has to buy the other an ice cream. Or whoever wins gets to choose the next game you play together.

Warning:

If you're in the same room, be careful not to run into each other. This game really can lead to a lot of manic movement! If you have separate rooms and you're still running into each other, you've got problems of biblical proportions, and I can't help you.

Be careful to place fragile items so they do not fall or get stepped on.

Read 'n' Clean

Benefits

1) Encourages reading.

2) Makes your child more knowledgeable (if the reading material is informative).

How to Play:

If you have two or more kids who can read, have them first sit down and make a list of the books or stories they'd like someone to read to them. Then, when it's room-cleaning time, one child can read to the other who's cleaning, and then reverse roles. It's one way to make room cleaning a much more enjoyable experience. With a very young child, use the same method, but you read to them.

Helpful Hint:

Readers should be ready to occasionally reread sentences, even paragraphs, if the child who is cleaning has a lapse of attention trying to figure out where to put things or where to find a missing shoe or shirt.

Parents may intermittently leave surprises under pillows or sheets, but only when the bed (or entire room) is clean. That old principle of intermittent reinforcement (rewards some of the times) is perhaps one of the most important things a parent should know.

More Fun Ideas

1) Have the two kids make up a story together, where the one who isn't cleaning becomes the secretary-writer. They then can read this at dinner time as a reward.

2) Add this interesting variation: The cleaner has to put one thing away to get a paragraph read to him or her.

Setting the Table Race

Equipment Needed:

A kitchen timer.

How to Play:

Just use the timer or stopwatch each night and see which family member or child can set the table most quickly. For example, one child sets it Monday and Tuesday, the other sets it Wednesday and Thursday, and you set it Friday. Keep track of the times for each evening, and whoever has the shortest time at the end of the week, gets a reward.

If you have an even number in your family, divide the table in half and have two players compete with each other, each taking a half.

Warning:

Not to be done with fragile glassware.

Secret Buddies

Thank You:
    Denise and Mark Weston, authors of *Playful Parenting*.

Benefits

Like many of our games, this game is a good way to develop empathy and altruistic values. In particular, this game helps children focus on other family members and experience the joy of doing things for that person anonymously!

How to Play:

All you have to do is each put your name in a hat and then each draw a name secretly. Whomever you draw is your "secret buddy." You are now to find little things you can do for your buddy anonymously (from carefully disguised anonymous notes, to little gifts, fixing things, or even cleaning up their room or doing some of their other chores.)
    At the end of the week you can give prizes for best deeds and for "best secrecy."

Warning:

Since people get pretty territorial about

their rooms, be sure to discuss in advance who will allow a "secret buddy" to clean their room!

Beat the Clock

Thank You:
    Lee Canter

Benefits
Reduces parental nagging.

Equipment Needed:
 A kitchen timer.

How to Play:

Set a timer for ten minutes or however long it takes to complete a particular chore. If your children can complete it by the time limit, they get a special reward.

Helpful Hints:

Be sure to mutually agree on the time limit. Compete among yourselves and reward the grand winner each week.

More Fun Ideas

1) Break the chores down into shorter jobs and challenge your child or parent to complete the job before the end of a favorite song. Alternatively, if you don't want to bother dealing with short chores, use the duration of an entire album.

2) Another timer available to us nowadays is the TV commercial break (usually three or four commercials lasting almost two minutes).

3) Try this same game to motivate the kids to get dressed in the morning. If they do it in time, they get a star put on a "good morning chart." What's a good morning chart? Read Lee Canter's *Winning the Chore Wars* for details on this and lots of other good tips for systematically rewarding your kids for doing their chores. (See also, Appendix D.)

Auction-It-Off Box

Thank You:
Denise and Mark Weston, authors of *Playful Parenting*.

Benefits

1) Teaches people quickly to put things away.

2) Teaches consequences for not putting things away. This is most applicable to dealing with stuff left out that belongs to particular individuals.

Materials Needed:

Medium-sized cardboard box.

How to Play:

Write "Auction-It-Off Box" on the box and name someone the Auctioneer.

Explain at a family meeting or at dinner that every time a family member uses something and doesn't put it away in its proper place, anyone who finds that something can put it in the box.

At the end of the day, everyone looks inside the box, sees if anything belongs to them, removes their things, and puts them where they belong. If you don't put away your things at the end of the day, the Auctioneer may claim the items and hold an auction two or three days later. At that time, the owners of the item need to buy back the item by offering services, like extra chores.

Helpful Hints:

Imitate a real auctioneer by saying "going, going, gone to the boy who's offered to wash dishes tonight in exchange for getting his Walkman™ back."

Job Swap

Benefits

1) Family members get to better understand each other's burdens and responsibilities.

2) Adds variety to one's chores.

3) May provide an opportunity to learn new things, like administrative ability if you take on the chore of organizing the job swap.

How to Play:

Each family member makes a list of their own household tasks, and then you all decide to "swap a job," meaning you each trade a chore, and agree on a time you will do that chore. For example, you might swap taking out the trash for setting the dinner table.

Be sure after all this to create a family chart showing the swapped jobs and the dates they will be done. Post the chart, so all can see their new jobs. You may do this for a day, a week, or however long the two parties agree. They may even decide to swap those chores permanently.

Helpful Hints:

For a child, the job of making this all happen—getting people to sit down and swap jobs—can be a job itself. So this coordinating is a legitimate task to trade for another chore or two.

Folds And Flowers

Thank You:

Valerie Cambanes and Annike Lane, Brooklyn Park, Minnesota.

How to Play:

Fold some clothes with your partner and, when you're both finished, make flower designs out of the folded clothes. For example, use a folded sock to form the middle of the flower. Then place three folded shirts around the outside to form the petals of the blossom. Whoever makes the most flowers wins.

You can only use the clothes you have folded, so there is an incentive to fold the most clothes.

Helpful Hint:

To avoid flowers that are too "quick and dirty," it might be best to require that a flower must involve at least four pieces of clothing.

Spin-A-Job

Thank You:
  Lee and Marlene Canter

Benefits

1) Eliminates most arguments about which chores to do and by whom.

2) Avoids favoritism.

Materials Needed:

A spinner. You will need to cut out the spinner and the jobs wheel on page 189 (please see directions), and make yourself a Spin-A-Job wheel like the one on the next page. Fill out the chores on the wheel together with your child naming all the jobs that must be done and can be done by your child. Be sure the chores are age-appropriate. (Note: If you decide to use this game for adult chores, make a separate Spin-A-Job wheel, since there might be some chores adults can do that young children cannot. Just photocopy page 189— make several copies.)

How to Play:

Have your child spin the wheel several times (however many chores you agree on ahead of time). Whichever the spinner lands on become your child's chores that week. You can do the same for yourself and for others in the family.

Helpful Hint:

Let the child know that if he or she gets the same job twice in a row the second week, they can spin again, till they get something different.

If you have discovered or invented your own Chore Game, please let us know. You'll be delighted and so will perhaps millions of others. Please see end of Chapter 20 for details on how to send in your ideas and how we'll reward your effort and ingenuity.

SPIN-A-JOB WHEEL DIRECTIONS

Cut out and glue the Job Wheel template on the next page onto a thick piece of cardboard.

Note: If you want to make additional Spin-A-Job wheels, for just the adults, or for a future time, photocopy page 189 first.

Fill in whatever chores need to be done, as below.

Cut out the spinner or arrow on the next page, and glue it on a piece of cardboard. Then cut again, using the outline of the spinner to guide your cuts.

Attach the spinner or arrow to the center of the finished wheel with a tack or metal brad so that it can spin freely.

SAMPLE SPIN-A-JOB WHEEL

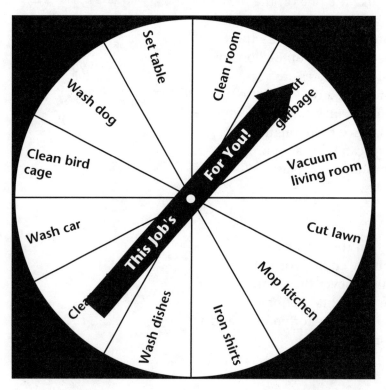

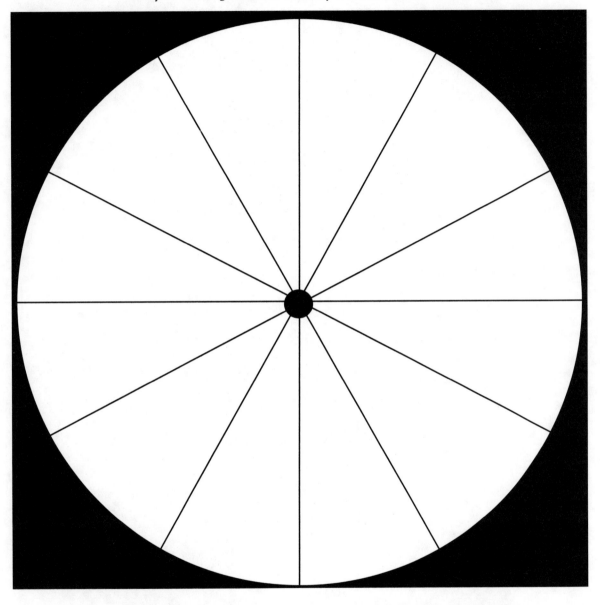

cut this out ·············· This Job's ● For You!

Being Alone

General Benefits

All of these activities turn "aloneness" into an exciting and creative condition, helping the time pass quickly preventing boredom and the unpleasant experience of loneliness. These activities will help children's brains to develop to their fullest creative potential. The verbal activities will, of course, further increase your verbal skills, and the artistic (those done with materials or musical instruments) will enhance your artistic abilities. All of these activities, then, are much better for your brain than TV. Since almost all of these activities develop certain skills, they will also increase your self-esteem.

•　　•　　•　　•

"Creativity is the best
antidote to loneliness."

—*the Author*

The Value of Aloneness

I was, in effect, an only child. My brother was almost twelve years older than me and my parents both worked. It's also taken me longer than most folks to get married, so I have spent much of my life alone.

One thing that I strongly believe about being alone is that it is the best situation in which to become creative (except perhaps when you are trying to creatively entertain another person).

When you enter this creative space, your loneliness disappears. I am fond of saying that creativity is the best antidote to loneliness. In other words, it seems impossible to feel lonely and creative simultaneously. So perhaps the best thing you can do when you are alone is to create!

The activities in this chapter all have one trait in common, besides being able to be done alone: they let you use your creativity.

Imagination Stretchers

Background:

Probably the worst but most common thing people do alone is watch TV. Recent neurological research (see, for example, *Endangered Minds* by Jane Healey) has demonstrated that children's brains essentially program themselves up to about age fifteen. The brain does this through its interaction with the environment, and one of the poorest sources of environmental stimuli for the brain is television. One experiment shows that the brain is actually less active watching TV than it is when the person is simply staring at a blank wall. This is probably because when you are staring at a blank wall, you soon start to daydream, and create your own stories, ideas, fantasies, visions, questions, etc. That process of creativity is in fact creating many more neural connections than the passive act of watching TV.

So what are some far healthier alternatives? Far more stimulating than either TV or the blank wall are any of the games and activities below, which involve the brain in direct interaction with the environment through the creative act. I know I'm only supposed to talk about new ideas in this book. But I feel compelled, just once, to provide a list of not only some new suggestions, but some of the best standard ideas to get you started.

Music:

- Memorize a favorite song, or just listen to music and lip-sync.

- Make up your own song, using a tape recorder if you don't know how to write music yet. Give yourself some limits to start with. For example, choose a genre like country western or rap, and a topic like "how my boyfriend or girlfriend was not a friend," or how you feel about someone, or about some made-up character with unusual characteristics.

- Practice a musical instrument. It's usually best to do this a few short times a day than to make yourself do it for a time so long that it gets to be unpleasant.

- Put on some favorite dance music and invent a new step or whole new dance.

Words:

- Read a book or magazine. Comic books are fine for young readers (and older ones, too!). Whenever you're out shopping go visit a used book store (if there is one in your area) so you can get books cheap. Garage sales are also a good source of cheap books. Otherwise get them from the library.

- Write a poem or new lyrics to a popular song.

- Write a short story or make up a parable.

- Make up your own secret code or language to use for secret messages to a friend. You could use numbers to stand for letters, or letters to stand for other letters (z could equal a, y could equal b, and so on).

- Think of characters with various problems that you could be when your parent(s) or partners comes home from work or that you could play at dinner.

- Imagine you are stranded on a desert island and a genie comes and tells you she can't help you escape, but she can give you one thing to have with you. What would it be? Try and think of other interesting questions like this to ask a friend or family members, and write them down.

- Make a list of all the good books and movies you've seen and try to figure out why you liked each one. Is there one thing they all have in common?

- Visit the local library and explore not only books, but the magazine rack, the Internet, etc.

- Write a pen pal (you can find them on the Internet).

- Learn two new words to surprise your folks with at dinner.

- Write a play, commercial, or skit to perform for your family at dinner or instead of watching TV.

Athletics

(exercise is highly effective at preventing you from becoming depressed):

- Work out with weights

- Practice certain techniques needed for a sport you wish to master (e.g. shooting baskets, batting a ball, hitting a tennis ball against a wall). Many sports can be played alone, like skateboarding, running, surfing, swimming, karate, etc.

Creating things:

- Paint or draw a picture of a place you would like to live.

- Build something out of glue and pieces of wood, clay, cans, wads of paper, tin foil, pieces of cloth, or papier-mâché.

- If your parent/partner will allow it, paint a landscape, flower, animal, or whatever you wish on your wall. If not the wall, see if they'll let you paint a white T-shirt.

- Sew a design onto blue jeans or a shirt.

- Plant and grow a garden of flowers and/or vegetables. Plant a fruit tree.

- Pick some flowers from your yard.

Combinations

(word play plus materials):

- Play with dolls and a doll house (you're never too old).

- Bring out the toy soldiers, tanks, planes, etc. I'm partial to this myself, having spent years playing with these, constantly stretching my imagination by concocting every imaginable challenge for my heroes to surmount, and utilizing every conceivable physical

obstacle in the basement for my battle terrain. I was also busily creating dialogue as well for the soldiers and pilots. Far more exciting stuff than what I see people doing on computers.

- (For five to ten year olds) Make a giant box (the refrigerator and oven boxes you can get from appliance stores are ideal) or two such boxes into a fantasy interstellar starship.

- Experiment with combinations of any two or more items from the above list (e.g. paint a poem on your wall or shirt).

Make a "Good Reasons to Be Alone" List

Benefits

This activity can do wonders for one's spirit, self-confidence, and self-esteem.

How to Play:

Since you may often be alone, pretend the universe has several very good reasons for you to be alone (which it may in fact have), and make a list of all the wonderful one-sentence reasons you can think of to explain why you frequently have opportunities to be alone.

To get started, begin each thought with one of these phrases: "To be able to discover . . ." or "Because I might become a famous . . ." For example, your list might read:

- to discover and develop a special talent for writing music;

- because I am to become a famous singer-composer;

- to discover at the library a new friend I would otherwise not have met;

- to discover and develop a special talent for writing;

- because I am to become a famous political leader or filmmaker;

- to discover and develop a special athletic ability.

When you finish your list, post it on your wall in a very visible place, look at it whenever you start to feel lonely, and add to it whenever you get other ideas.

Preparing for Other Games in the Book

Benefits

1) Helps make the other games that much more successful for everyone.

2) Increases your chances of being the winner, if the games are competitive.

3) Sharpens your skills in the game for which you are preparing.

How to Play:

Now that you have a whole book of new ways to have fun, you can spend some of your alone time preparing for some of these games and inventing your own. For example:

- Think of characters you could be at dinner and write down their brief descriptions on separate pieces of paper for everyone to draw out of a bowl and act out. (This is for a variation of the Be Each Other dinner game.)

- Make up a list of fun adverbs to use for the Emotional Salad dinner game.

- Write some notes for the Family Treasure Chest dinner game.

- Memorize some song titles and first lines for songs you could use in the Alphabetical Song car game.

- Think of funny ways you and your family could answer the phone at home or work.

- Make up your own new games for situations you are often in, like doing chores, eating in the school cafeteria, playing popular sports, eating dinner, hanging out at the mall, or watching TV. (see Chapter 20).

- Think of ways you could help those less fortunate than you (see Chapter 19) and act upon your ideas. You could write letters to your senator, representative, the president, or the

CEO of an irresponsible corporation). You can even write letters for your family to sign and send, though if you handwrote them, other people will at least type the letters up themselves or rewrite them in their own handwriting.

Yellow Page Race

Benefits

1) Helps you learn to use the yellow pages in your phone book, to network, and to do research in general.

2) You learn fascinating facts.

Equipment Needed:

A phone and a timer for each player (a watch indicating seconds will do) and the yellow pages.

How to Play:

Call up a friend and agree on a question you both will try to answer. Then on the count of three, each of you hang up, hit your timers, and see who can get the answer first using the yellow pages and common sense to call someone who might know the answer. When you've got the answer, record your time and call your friend back. Whoever did it the fastest, wins.

Rules:

It cannot be a historical question, and you can call anyone but a librarian.

Practice Talking in Accents

Benefits

1) Enables you to play many other games much better.

2) Helps you be more playful and funny and thereby to make friends more easily.

3) Develops a new dramatic ability.

How to Play:

Just listen to, or better yet record with an audio tape recorder or the VCR, any character off the television whose accent you want to learn. Then parrot him as he speaks until you get the hang of it. After you're comfortable with this, try applying it to your own made-up sentences, first using the words you've already been hearing, but in new combinations.

Helpful Hint:

1) Most libraries have some books or audio tapes on learning accents.

2) If you know someone with an accent you'd like to learn, tell them what you're doing and ask if you can tape them talking.

I've been acting for a while so I would strongly recommend the tools of acting for people to investigate their surroundings and each other in order to find ways to amuse themselves. One way I would suggest is that in almost any large city and any good bookstore you'll find several good books on accents for the actor. They carry phonetic guides as to how to "shape" your speech. They'll also be accent books on American accents. An enjoyable past time would be for an individual or couple to get one of these books to work on....

They could work up an ability to use these accents with each other to the point of going out on the street, to conducting a life of their own as people bearing those accents.

I strongly recommend it.

—*Ed Asner, actor*

Accent Phone Calls

Benefits

1) Develops your poise and dramatic abilities.

2) Develops your ability to talk to almost anyone.

3) Gives joy to those you call.

How to Play:

Technically, this and the telephone games that follow require a second person. However, since you can do them alone from home, I am including them here.

Put on an accent when you call someone and pretend you're someone else (see example below). Be sure you are calling a friend (or parent), since calling a stranger would most likely be considered harassment.

Accent Phone Answers

Benefits

Same as above.

How to play:

Answer the phone as someone else in an accent or dialect. Here are some possibilities:

• an exchange student from Germany;

• a cousin visiting from Russia;

- a fast-talking niece or nephew visiting from New York;

- a slow-talking relative from Mississippi;

- a famous child celebrity who is supposedly your friend (just answer with the first name, and if they ask for the last, tell them the celebrity's last name)

- a French chef hired to cook for a special party tonight;

- the new English butler of your household;

- an English or French nanny;

- the Brooklynese (e.g. 'Rocky Balboa') plumber working on a leak;

- a psychologist relative staying with the family (you might toss out a few active listening responses to the caller, like "sounds like you're feeling a bit stressed today").

Warning:

Be sure to tell the caller that you are just kidding before they hang up, lest you somehow get your parents or yourself in trouble, for example, by leading the caller to think you are doing much better financially than you really are, or that someone in your family is having psychological problems.

Meditation

Of course I realize this is not a particularly new idea—millions today meditate. However, it is still rare to teach it to kids, and for whole families to do it together.

Benefits

1) Improves subsequent concentration.

2) Improves subsequent creativity. I get many of my best ideas while meditating—while trying to have no ideas!

3) Reduces anxiety level.

4) Helps one feel at ease about being alone.

5) Lowers blood pressure. This is especially good for older adults.

How to Play:

First, get into a comfortable sitting posture (e.g. sitting in a straight-backed chair) with your arms to the side, feet flat on the ground, back against the chair. Take several deep breaths, filling the lower area of your lungs first (by extending your abdomen), and then filling your chest. Now close your eyes.

You can repeat a word or sound over and over throughout the exercise, or just focus on inhaling and exhaling. Now imagine all of your anxieties—about school, work, your body, family life, whatever—as clouds or bubbles, and just tell yourself that you are letting these concerns float away. Whenever new thoughts arise, that's okay; just let them drift away, too.

Thoughts will almost always keep coming. It's impossible to keep the mind empty for longer than a minute or two when starting to meditate. But that is fine, because as mentioned above, these later ideas that pop into your consciousness often are the best ideas that will ever occur to you.

Start doing this just 5-10 minutes per day, and work up gradually to a half-hour or longer, if you can.

Helpful Hints:

1) In explaining this to a child, you might try pointing out payoffs that will have special attractiveness to kids, like being smarter or feeling good about themselves. Kids see little virtue in being relaxed.

2) Let the child do this alone sometimes.

Find a Mentor

Benefits

1) Provides one of the best ways to learn a useful skill.

2) Can develop a close and deep friend.

3) Teaches you networking skills and self-confidence.

How to Play:

Figure out what craft or skill you wish to learn. Think of any one you already know who has this skill, or who might know someone who has this skill. Expand the possibilities by asking relatives and friends who they know. When you find possible leads that don't pan out, be sure to always thank them and ask them for suggestions for whom else you could contact.

Visit your potential mentor at times that are slowest and most convenient for them, tell them how much you're interested in learning their craft, and ask the mentor what they would want in return. (Figure out in advance what you could offer in return, like cleaning up their studio or weeding their garden.)

Guess the Sound

Thank You:
Karen Ehrlich

Benefits

Wiles away the time and entertains someone else.

How to Play:

Get a utensil or any appliance that makes a distinctive sound. Then call someone you know, make that sound in the receiver, tell him or her what room you're in (to be using that appliance), and ask him or her to guess what you're doing based on the sound.

More Fun Ideas

1) Put the receiver up to the television for just five seconds at a time and see if the listener can guess within three "strikes" what program it is.

2) Read the first line from a famous novel or poem and see if the

other person can guess where it's from. They get three guesses, After each guess a new line (or paragraph) is read.

Name Search

Thank You:
   Karen Ehrlich

Benefits

1) Develops word fluency, spelling and vocabulary.

2) Develops love of language.

How to Play:

Make up your own "name search" grid that you will present to the other player. Skip this game if you don't have a family member or friend who likes word games.

First, take a piece of lined notebook paper, and turn it into a grid by using a ruler and making vertical lines about a half-inch apart (the same distance that separates the horizontal lines) so that you are creating little squares. A grid that's fifteen squares by fifteen squares is sufficient.

Then pick a category, like animals or cars, and write down underneath or above the grid the names of twelve to fifteen animals or cars (more if you want to make it easier, less if you want to make it harder). These will tell the person who is doing the search what words to look for.

Next, place these words anywhere you wish throughout the grid. Be sure to mix up how you write the words, writing some horizontally, some vertically, and some diagonally. If you are an adult making this for your partner, you might want the words to make a sentence that expresses a nice sentiment toward your partner. Finally, fill in all the empty grid squares with letters or letter combinations that do not spell real words.

Helpful Hints:

You can try and trick the searcher by using letter combinations that start with the first two or three letters of a word on the list.

More Fun Ideas

If you have more than one person searching for the words, make it a competition to see who can find the most number of words on the same grid. Each person can put a distinctive border or color around the words they find.

Name That Tune

Benefits

Same as above.

How to Play:

You and your friend each get your favorite (different) radio stations on, then take turns calling each other and seeing how many seconds it takes each of you to guess the tune.

You can devise all sorts of scoring methods. For example, whoever guesses within thirty seconds gets a point. Whoever gets ten points first gets to wear the other person's clothes for a day or has to be bought an ice cream cone of their choice. Or you can score as in Guess the Sound above, giving the receiver three "balls," a ball being a five-second listen to the tune. If you don't guess within three balls, you lose a point.

CHAPTER 17

Making Decisions

I find that people, even when I tell them they have six
months to live, they're still afraid to have fun, even though
they only have 180 days. Whether it's a year or ten years,
or fifty years, we still have a limited time here. So allow
for the child in you to come out, allow the child in
you to be liberated. Give yourself the freedom.
You have a limited period of time here.
—*Bernie Siegel, M.D.*

Thumb-Hat Wrestling

Onion Jousting

Paperball Basketball

Paper-Rock-Scissors Variations

Earth-Water-Fire

Sad-Mad-Glad

One Potato, Two Potato

Whaddaya See

General Benefits

All of these games take the pain out of decision making and conflict resolution, and turn those problems into opportunities for more fun. These games are certainly more rational and fun methods for settling conflicts than having a fight. If you're a parent trying to make a decision for a child, these also avoid all the time lost trying to make a difficult decision by yourself.

Just think what our day-to-day life would be like if we made almost every relatively unimportant or ambiguous decision by playing a game. The more decisions we made, the more fun we'd have each day!

In addition to the more novel approaches to decision making that I'm going to present, you should not forget that you can always resort to such common and quick techniques as: breaking tooth picks or twigs and drawing lots (or straws); putting names or outcomes on slips of paper, putting them into a jar, and drawing them out. These methods are also good if you need to make a decision by yourself. No matter what method you use, it's even more important to notice your gut reaction or feeling when the choice is presented using these random methods or the flip of a coin. If you suddenly have a negative gut feeling to the result, that's a strong sign that you should be choosing the other choice. Conversely if you are a bit relieved about the result, then you probably have in front of you the best choice.

If you have to select a person, as opposed to making a more intangible choice, you can fall back on the old standbys:

- Whoever can leap the farthest, gets the ball into the basket first, memorizes the poem first.

- Whoever flicks the coin closest to the wall or edge of the table without it falling over.

- Whoever draws highest-ranking card from a deck of cards.

- When in doubt, just remember the rule we all learned in kindergarten: just take turns!

Dozens of New Decision-Making Games

Besides the ones we focus on in this chapter, you can pick almost any other game in this book, and let whoever wins gets to do choice A or whoever loses gets choice B. For example, let's say you're trying to decide who washes and who wipes the dishes. You can just play Alphabetical Song (from Chapter 7) and whoever gets stuck and can't think of a song for more than sixty seconds has to wash. Or you can play Knock Your Socks Off, from Chapter 6, and agree that whoever loses that game has to take out the garbage.

For all games that are being used to make a decision, be sure that those playing are well matched. If not, handicap the advantaged.

Thumb-Hat™ Wrestling

Thank You:

Fred Schildmeyer and Bernie De Koven. I forget which of you mentioned this one to me first.

Benefits

1) Doubles as a great waiting game at restaurants. (Using sugar packets).

2) Transcends intimacy barriers by allowing physical contact that's non-threatening, which makes it especially useful for stepparents trying to blend in.

3) Ideal for unaccomplished athletes, those who are all thumbs. It's not for everyone, just thumb people. (Sorry. I couldn't resist!)

Equipment Needed:

Gum wrappers, tin foil, sugar packets, the little creamers you often get in restaurants, or our own special fitting *Simple Fun* (thumb-hats which you can order by following the directions in Chapter 20).

How to Play:

Following are the guidelines from the Official Rule Book of the International Thumb-Hat Wrestling League.

Before beginning, players are to outfit their thumbs with a cup or helmet, or, as I call them, "thumb-hats™." (By the way, if you're thinking about capitalizing on our invention with your own line of thumb-hats for the fall, forget it. We've already thought of it and have signed deals with Michael Jackson and several other famous "hand celebrities.")

To fashion a helmet for your battling thumb, I have two recommendations. One is to use the outside foil wrapper of a five-stick packet of gum. It is the perfect size, can be molded to look like an army helmet or armor of a Spanish conquistador, depending on your mood that day, and you can chew the gum, which helps calm the nerves before going off to thumb war.

The other item that works great is an empty sugar packet. These make really cool hats and the thumbs look like a couple of popes slugging it out.

Once you have a hat, assuming you are both right-handed, grab each other's right hand in thumb wrestling position [see illustration], keeping your elbows on the table. The first person to knock off the other player's thumb-hat is the champ, and gets to make the decision.

Helpful Hints:

1) Hat design and engineering are important factors to consider. Your basic cone has striking power but is easily flipped. The tinfoil sombrero, while stylish and ethnic, poses definite problems with balance. Of course, the most important factor is the thumb in the hat.

2) Be creative in your countdown. Instead of saying "ready, get set, go!," you could say "one, two, three, four, if you lose, you sweep the floor!," or "one, two, three, kaboom, if you lose, you clean your room," depending on what task the decision concerns.

3) You may decide to play best two out of three, but you should always allow a few trials for warming up.

Handicaps:

Seasoned athletes may be asked to wrestle while being tickled or while standing on one foot. Someone who's winning too often should tear off a quarter inch or more from the bottom of their sugar packet or gum wrapper so that it will come off more easily.

More Fun Ideas

1) The Olympic version of this game requires that wrestlers give out a samurai cry when knocking off a hat. (This rule is designed to simultaneously distract your opponent and vent your warrior alter-ego.)

2) If you have four people to play, try tag teams, whereby two others can get their hands somehow involved. I've never actually done this. But theoretically it sounds possible. You'll just have to experiment and have patience.

3) Play with opposite hands by interlocking your fingers. Whoever has their index finger closest to the wrestling arena (in other words, the uppermost hand) will have the advantage, because their thumb will be able to extend farther away from the action. So whoever has the largest hand should probably not be

the one whose index finger is upper-most.

4) This next one is a variation of thumb wrestling, not thumb-hat wrestling: Take a five-by-seven-inch piece of heavy cardboard and place a line down the middle. Make two holes for your thumbs about one and one-half inch away from the line on both sides of the line. Then make two short lines as indicated in the illustration, on either side of the line connecting the thumb holes.

Onion Jousting

Thank You:
    Karl Rhonke, Project Adventure, Hamilton, Massachusetts.

How to Play:

Outline or otherwise mark out an area five or six feet in diameter. You can spread out a sheet, or just use chairs to create a fence.

The players stand in the area, each armed with two teaspoons (tablespoons for the less adept) and one small onion. Place the onion in the spoon of the nondomi-nant hand. The contest is to try and dis-lodge the onion from the spoon of your opponent.

Rules:

1) A player cannot step out of the circle. You are allowed to hit your oppo-nent's onion or spoon with your free spoon. Any other contact can result in forfeit. If an onion is dropped, the player who had the onion loses. If both onions are dropped simultane-ously, the first to hit the ground loses.

2) Combat begins by both players eye-balling each other and ritualistically clicking the bowls of their free spoons against one another twice before any offensive action is allowed.

Warning:

Be careful where you do this so that knick-knacks don't get broken and other people don't get annoyed.

Helpful Hints:

Allow a few trials for warming up.

More Fun Ideas:

1) Joust with just the one spoon that is holding the onion.

2) Joust with other utensils and other vegetables or fruits.

3) See Kitchen Hockey in Chapter 14. This could also be used to make deci-sions.

4) You could have a whole series of Kitchen Olympic Events, a "Kitchen-cathalon!"

Paperball Basketball

Benefits

1) Develops manual dexterity and hand-eye coordination.

2) Makes decisions fast.

How to Play:

This game is best used for deciding who of two or more people gets to do something or gets to get out of doing something.It's the old wastebasket routine. But many forget that it can be used to make decisions, especially for kids old enough to toss with some accuracy.

Wad up some paper into a ball and find a waste basket seven to twelve feet away, farther if everyone is good. Whoever gets the highest score out of seven shots gets their way as to whatever the decision is about.

Paper-Rock-Scissors

Benefits

Offers a new spin on an old game.

How to Play:

First, a refresher course for those who have forgotten or never knew how play Paper-Rock-Scissors. This works between two people. On the count of three, the two put their hands into the center either as a clenched fist (Rock), open hand (Paper) or with two fingers sticking out (Scissors).

If both people play the same hand—if they both put out a Rock—then you throw again. But if the two players make different hands, the winner of the throw is decided according to the following principles:

- Paper vs. Scissors: Scissors is the winner because scissors cut paper.

- Rock vs. Paper: Paper is winner because paper covers rock.

- Rock vs. Scissors: Rock is winner because rock smashes scissors.

Now for our cute alternatives:

Version One: Fire-Earth-Water

The symbol for Fire is one hand upward, fingers apart, like flames going up. Water is your hand cupped (to hold water), and Earth is your hand cupped downward with your fingers pointing down and wiggling, sort of like a jellyfish. Water douses Fire, Fire burns up Earth, and Earth soaks up Water.

Whoever wins two out of three gets to make the decision. If neither wants to make the decision, then just assign one possible outcome to each person. And if that person wins, that's your decision.

Version Two: Sad-Mad-Glad

This version gives you further mastery over your dramatic skills and helps you learn to have fun with your emotional expressions.

Here, Glad beats Mad, Mad beats Sad, Sad beats Glad. Or just make up your own rules; I have no deep psychological principles behind this formulation.

More Fun Ideas

Make up your own combinations and symbols.

Instead of hands, use your mouths: sticking out of the tongue, blowing hard, and a big growl. You decide which expression beats the other. I bet you could do a lot with that.

One Potato, Two Potato

Thank you:

Irene Ehrlich, who gave me this in memory of all those who grew up in Brooklyn and played this game. Because I think most of us who didn't come from Brooklyn might not know this wonderful game, and anyone else probably has forgotten it, it is worth suggesting here.

Benefits

1) A fun way to decide between two or more people who want to do something.

2) It will delight any parents or grandparents who grew up in New York.

How to Play:

Everybody stands in a circle and makes

fists out of both of their hands and holds them out in front, thumbs up. One person is the caller, who starts the game by deciding which fist to hit first. The caller then lightly taps one of their fists atop all of the other players' fists, going around the circle, to the beat of the following rhyme:

> One potato, two potato
> three potato, four.
> Five potato, six potato,
> seven potato, more

Since the caller can't hit their own fist that's doing the tapping, they should just touch the tapping fist to their own chin or mouth. The fist that gets tapped with the final word "more" is eliminated from the next rounds, and the eliminated fist is put behind your back. The caller continues repeating the above rhyme, until all fists but one are eliminated. Whoever is left with the remaining fist is the winner. Each time you start the rhyme, be sure to start it on the next fist clockwise to the one that was just eliminated.

Helpful Hint:

If you are worried that the caller has a pre-arranged strategy, you decide which fist is the first to be tapped.

More Fun Ideas

If you are deciding between choices of action or places to go, rather than choosing a person to do something, just assign the actions or places to the players.

Whaddaya See
(for one person only)

Benefits

1) Saves time lost vacillating.

2) Might give you some insights from your unconscious or right brain you might otherwise not have thought of.

This way of decision making is only for a situation where one person is trying to make up their mind what to do. It is not for deciding between two or more people.It also only works for people who are fairly good at visualizing.

How to Play:

I don't recommend you play this unless you've first tried the more rational pros-and-cons approach. However, once you've done that and still are undecided, I figure you've got nothing to lose by trying this approach. The important thing is that once you've made, or in this case "discovered," your choice, you then proceed to do what-ever you can to make the most of it. Just announce to yourself that you're going to close your eyes, and whatever image is the first to pop up on the screen behind your eyelids, that image will determine your choice. For example, it is my turn to decide where to go for a hike. One choice is in the mountains with a stream, the other overlooks the ocean part of the way, and is closer. Thinking about the pros and cons still leaves me undecided. So I close

my eyes, and what do I see but a gurgling stream. There's my decision.

Helpful Hint:

Pay careful attention to how you feel when you think your choice has been given to you. Do you feel disappointed, or do you feel almost eager to begin? If the former, then this is not the right choice. Choose the other.

CHAPTER 18

Dealing with Anger and Conflict

Anger is a tool, not a master. Anger is meant to be tapped into and drawn upon. Used properly, anger is useful. Sloth, apathy, and despair are the enemy. Anger is not. Anger is our friend. Not a nice friend, not a gentle friend, but a very loyal friend. It will always tell us when we have been betrayed. It will always tell us when we have betrayed ourselves. It will always tell us that it is time to act in our own best interests. Anger is not the action itself. It is action's invitation.

—*Julia Cameron*
The Artist's Way

Guess My Anger	Make Up an Excuse
Resentment Chest	The Feeling Board
Conflict in Accents	Core Scene Scripting
Alphabetical Kvetch	Clown Nose Arbitration
Spin Away Anger	Bully Defense

General Benefits

Next to some of the dinner games like Treasure Chest and Be Each Other, I feel the games in this section are the most powerful in developing cohesion or closeness between partners and between parents and kids. Additionally, these games are perhaps the most useful of all the games in this book for developing emotional maturity, with a repertoire of constructive responses for dealing with anger and frustration.

• • • •

Important Warning

These games are in no way suggested as a substitute for psychotherapy or medical treatment for people with serious psychopathology.

These games should not be used with people who have serious psychopathology or are being treated for depression or rage attacks.

These games are not intended to be used in the heat of anger.

I am a strong believer in the wisdom of our grandparents in this respect: Keep it to yourself for a while, until you cool down. I don't mean to stuff it or sit on it, or deny it. I mean to process it. Behind all anger is fear, hurt, or sadness, or some combination thereof. So figure out what you might be afraid of or what is hurtful to you in what the person said or did. Once you've done that, you're probably ready to play these games.

For a far more sophisticated discussion about anger, I highly recommend *Anger: The Misunderstood Emotion* by Carol Tavris (see the Resource Guide at the end of this book).

Guess My Anger

Benefits

1) Gives the angry one (called here the "angeree") some relief just seeing the person they're mad at (the "angerer") working hard having to guess.

2) The angerer has to review all the things they do that can trigger anger in others.

3) Forces the angeree to sit on her anger and not immediately express it.

4) Something about this process can sometimes actually bring up laughter in the angeree. Don't count on it, though. It really depends on how serious an offense has been committed.

How to Play:

The angeree must announce that they are angry and then ask the angerer to guess what they are angry about. The angeree *cannot* start spouting off.

The angerer must start guessing, for example delimiting it as to time and place: Was it something I did in the past half hour? Past fifteen minutes? Past five minutes? Did it happen during this walk? Did it happen back at the house? In the kitchen? Did it concern the radio? Angeree's option: perhaps provide a reward if the angeree can guess within four guesses?

Resentment Chest

Benefits

1) Creates a ritual for the mature handling of anger, so that rather than being immediately vented or completely suppressed, it gets expressed, but only after an interval of time to allow the angered person to hopefully better understand its source, cool off, and get some distance. (They didn't conceive the seven-day gun law out of thin air, you know!)

2) Can be an important family ritual that is especially powerful in creating a very deep level of trust, and therefore honesty and cohesion.

3) Develops an enjoyment of writing (because you discover its use as a vent, microscope, sorter etc.) and improves one's writing ability.

4) Enables people to get in touch with and describe their feelings, and deal with anger in mature and constructive ways.

5) Teaches adults and kids to listen to one another.

How to Play:

1) Before the next flare-up, when things are fairly calm, introduce the idea of finding or creating a special box that you'll call the Resentment or Anger Chest. Kids could decorate a shoe box, or scour the neighborhood for

what's being thrown away, or perhaps they could go with you to garage sales to buy a metal cookie box.

2) Explain that whenever any of us gets upset with each other, with anyone else in our lives, or even with an impersonal situation, we will write down an "I message." An "I message" always has this form:

When 1)_____ (describe as objectively as possible the words said or physical objects and actions that occurred), I thought 2)_____ (however you interpreted the aforementioned remark or situation), and that made me feel 3)_____ (describe your underlying feeling that's underneath the anger).

For example, "When 1) *I came home and saw that you left your toys in the hallway*, I thought that 2) *my chances of tripping and getting hurt some day soon would be high*, and I became 3) *afraid*." For example: "When you forgot to stop at the store and pick up the potatoes, it made me think that I wouldn't be able to depend on you, and I would therefore have to do most of the work for both of us, and that thought made me feel both afraid and hurt." Then you sign your name and put the note into the Resentment Chest.

3) Agree upon one dinnertime a week to share the contents of the

Resentment Chest. Some couples without much conflict may choose to do this only once a month. Other families, on the other hand, might decide at this point to go looking for a larger box!

4) At the appointed time, the resentment box is brought out, and everyone gets a chance, going around the room, perhaps once or twice, to randomly pick a resentment and give it to its writer to read aloud. I recommend only reading one the first time, to let people get used to the game. In fact, if you have a big family (bigger than four), you might want to divide this ritual into two halves. One half of the family gets to do it one evening, and the other half gets another evening.

Procedure for sharing and responding to resentments:

1) Whoever is reading must first ask permission from the object of the resentment if they can share the resentment; the reader must respect the other person if they say they are not willing at this time to hear the resentment. I recommend no more than two "not willings". If you are the object and you agree to hear the resentment, you must politely listen to the resentment note. No defense or interruption allowed.

2) You must then try to paraphrase back what the writer said. This must be done until the writer feels they have been heard and understood. You are not being asked to agree here, just to paraphrase.

3) You then must do your best to convey your sense of the feelings of hurt or fear the writer feels.

4) The writer then asks if they have the facts correct, at which time you can offer any correction you would like to give.

5) If you have in fact caused the hurt or fear by your action, you will admit to this, apologize, and ask the writer for forgiveness. You might also want to ask those at the table for advice on how to solve the problem that gave rise to the resentment.

6) If the writer forgives you, fine. If not, you should ask at least two more times at separate occasions. After that, you have done all you can do.

7) To avoid anyone feeling too picked upon, if someone is the receiver of more than two resentments, the person who drew the resentment should put it back and draw another until they draw a resentment against someone or something else.

Warning:

1) Again, you should not play this game if anyone in the family is under any

psychotherapeutic care or even under any unusual emotional stress.

2) For this to work constructively, it is extremely important that the resentments be shared as "I messages."

3) Again, do not force someone to hear a resentment if they have not given you permission. In fact, you should respect anyone's wish to stop at any time. You can always discuss the resentment at a later date. I recommend deciding as a family the maximum number of "not willings" to allow.

Helpful Hints:

1) You might prefer doing this over dessert. (You might also prefer doing this over the phone, but too bad!)

2) I recommend doing this on a different day from the day you do the Treasure Chest dinner activity (see Chapter 9).

Note:

If you play all these dinner games that I've suggested throughout the book, you'll probably never have a chance to eat . . . and I will have written the greatest diet book since Deal-A-Meal! Move over, Richard Simmons . . . I mean it! Move over!

3) Just as with the "Couple Treasure Chest," you might want to have two resentment boxes, one for parents only, and one for the whole family.

In any case, if you play this game well, you should be able to resolve most resentments by the end of the evening. If you don't play this game well, be sure you don't have any sharp knives or expensive china on the table.

Conflict in Accents

Thank You:

Carolyn Permentier, for letting me practice this with you and your encouraging feedback.

Benefits

1) This game is especially good for taking the edge off anger, because it forces you to get outside of yourself, to gain enough objectivity to talk in an accent—as if you were another person—about what is upsetting you.

2) As a result of this "depersonalization," both parties become calmer, and therefore less defensive.

3) The more the person who is the object of the anger is being amused, the more their fear level goes down. And when fear is reduced, so is defensiveness, and they are better able to hear your hurt, and understand why you are angry.

4) This is especially good for handling sensitive issues between a couple.

And as we all know, even in the happiest of times, couples often don't see eye to eye.

5) Develops dramatic imagination and abilities.

6) Teaches yet another anger management tool (that will also have great payoffs if your child goes into management).

7) Improves your office climate, if you're already in management.

How to Play:

When you're ready to communicate your anger, ask the person you need to talk to if it's okay to make a little game about it, where you talk in an accent and so does he or she. You each pick whatever accent or dialect you each prefer.

Try as best you can to speak in "I messages " and to *actively listen* to the other person: paraphrase back to them what you understand they are saying and try your best to identify both their surface and underlying feelings. (One excellent book on active listening is Thomas Gordon's *Parent Effectiveness Training*.)

Here's an example of a husband using a proper British dialect to deal with an issue with his wife: "My dearest darling Diana. This is quite difficult for me to say to you, because I love you more than words can say; however, there are times of late when you say things in jest about me in front of our friends that really hurt my feelings, quite. I know it is not your intention, my sweet, but I should like you to know how it really destroys me when you behave in such a manner."

The wife then replies in her own choice of character, which might be that of a proper British lady, or it might be a taxi driver from the Bronx or a recent Chinese immigrant. Perhaps in the end, when you're both laughing, you can explore ways that you both agree may help clear up the underlying causes.

Warnings:

Remember, be sure you've given yourself enough time to process your anger and calm down before attempting this. Do not pick an accent or dialect that you've already associated with an angry or defensive character, since this will only make matters worse.

Helpful Hints:

For some reason I find the characters of French, British, and "Southern gentleman or gentlewoman" to work extremely well in this game. This is probably because they draw you into a posture or attitude of being "cool and suave," "precise and in control," or "extremely calm, sharp and witty" respectively, and all of these attitudes are pretty much incompatible with an angry tone.

At the risk of belaboring the point, I can't stress enough the importance of trying to listen and help the other player discover the underlying fear, hurt, or sadness at the core of their anger, and to let them

know that you hear it. This game is not a substitute for the art of active listening, but rather a way to perhaps make it easier and more fun.

I would strongly encourage to your visiting your library, bookstore, or a a drama bookstore if you have one in your city, to find a book on accents and dialects. This will help you greatly in learning a rich variety of voices that can be used in many other games as well. Short of that, record dialogue from a rental movie or television with a character speaking in the accent you want to learn and just practice imitating their speech.

Alphabetical Kvetch

Benefits

1) Shows by example how we can channel anger into more fun emotions, and that we have more control over our emotions than we may have thought.

2) Especially useful for a long trip that's having its share of problems, but also great for short trips (to school, shopping, eating out or the movies), after-work walks, and of course, hikes.

How to Play:

There are so many wonderful ways to kvetch, it's hard to narrow down the possibilities, but I'll try. (Oh my God, this is hard! How can I even do this, I don't know. But never mind me, I'll do it!)

The rule here is simply to go through the alphabet in turns, complaining about whatever you can dream up—real or imagined—that starts with the letter you get on your turn. For example, if it's your turn and your letter is B, you might have the following kvetch: "I wish I had more *b*ucks in my pocket today," or "*B*ill at work (or school) sure gave me a hard time."

The idea is to not only have fun with complaints, but to give vent to real gripes and frustrations in a way that's more fun and easier to hear. Chances are, just being heard in a spirit of good fun will allow the other person to feel safe and ready to consider adjusting their behavior.

Here's an example from one of my adventures canoeing with my wife one day on a river in Wisconsin. We had gotten lost entering a big lake and couldn't see where the river continued on the other side. To make matters worse, a major headwind had come up, making paddling very difficult. We were already tired from paddling several hours and it was even a bit cold and rain was imminent. So we said:

Me: My *a*rms are hurting with all this paddling!
She: This *b*oat is going nowhere with this wind against us.
Me: *C*anoeing is not exactly fun right now.
She: *D*arn it! I wish we had gotten better directions.

More Fun Ideas

1) Make it more competitive by racing with each other to see who can get to the end of the alphabet first, agreeing upon a reward at the beginning.

2) Give extra points if you can also start your sentence with a word that starts with your letter, as well as have the thing about which you are complaining start with that letter. The last sentence above ("Darn it! I wish ...") is an example of a double points sentence.

3) The listener can point out a good thing about whatever is being said to be bad, and then go on to name his or her own kvetch. For example, if the kvetcher complains (for *F*): "My *f*eet start to really get sore hiking on these rocks," the listener might reply, "That's what makes it nice to get a foot massage when you get back."

Spin Away Anger

Benefits

1) Shows how physical exercise can often affect our emotions for the better.

2) Show us how we can really be the masters of our feelings.

3) Allows us to transform anger into

laughter, or at least lessen it enough so that we can get some perspective, understand it better, and then communicate it more effectively to another.

How to Play:

Agree ahead of time, just as an experiment, that the next time any of you gets angry at the other at home, you (or both of you) will face each other and then begin spinning in circles, like we all did when we were little. Remember?

Warning:

Don't spin so much that you get so dizzy you might fall and hurt yourself. But just in case, be sure to move all furniture and sharp or fragile objects from the vicinity. Be especially careful to leave plenty of distance if two of you are spinning at the same time.

Helpful Hints:

We're not at all sure what the best age is for kids to do this one. So please share with us how this works with your kids, and any ways you discover to improve upon it that we can share next time around with our readers and right away on our Web site at www.SimpleFun.com.

Make Up an Excuse

Thank You:

Fred Schildmeyer and your wife, wherever you are. They were running very late, to get to a wedding reception two hundred miles away, and were beginning to blame each other, saying, "If you had done this" or "You should have done that." Then they suddenly got this great idea for a game.

Benefits

This one is a big help in evaporating conflict, especially marital conflict, when you are running late for an event or visit, and can also transform anger into hysterical laughter. This is probably best left to adults, since children might misconstrue it as condoning lying.

How to Play:

As I was saying, Fred and his wife were running very late and suddenly realized, why not just make up the most heartwrenching story they could think of, about all sorts of misfortunes that had suddenly hit them, so that rather than be mad, their friends would be happy just to see them alive, and then laugh, when they realized Fred and his wife were putting them on.

As I recall, the story they invented—which had to account for being more than three hours late—started out something like this: "Just as we were leaving, there was actually a small earthquake, but it was enough to shake loose an electric live wire off the electric pole, which fell on our wet lawn where our dog was lying, which caused him to fly about six feet into the air! We managed to drag him out without getting electrocuted ourselves, and then we had to give him CPR. You should have seen Kathy doing mouth-to-mouth. Tell 'em, Kathy, what it was like."

Kathy then continued the story with details about her mouth-to-mouth with her dog, and the two alternated relating the harrowing adventure until they had fully explained their tardiness. You'll probably go into hysterics just trying to rehearse your story with a straight face.

Helpful Hints:

As usual, take turns. And try and be as straight-faced as possible.

Warning:

Your story should be as preposterous as possible, so that the people you are talking to eventually realize you're making it up. Otherwise you're lying, and I am obviously against condoning or encouraging lying unless it's to save an innocent person's life. If for some reason your friends believe you, you had better let them in on the fact you're storytelling. They should have gotten such a kick out of the story itself that they won't mind you were late and that you made up the story. If they do, let us know right away (SimpleFun.com), so we can add further warnings to this section.

More Fun Ideas

Each of you take turns accepting the blame, rather than blaming the other, again by making up extravagant stories, or perhaps believable stories. The fun is in each of you interrupting and trying to outdo the other by saying, for example, "Kathy is just trying to protect me. It was really all my fault, because what happened was . . ." and then Kathy says, "No, Fred is just trying to protect me. It really happened the way I said. In fact, . . ."

The Feeling Board

Thank You:
　　Fred Schildmeyer, again.

Benefits

Pretty much the same as those cited for the Resentment Chest.

Materials Needed:

String, felt-tip pen, tape, large poster board. For the last, you can take a big cardboard box, open it up and flatten it out, covering it with butcher paper. You want to end up with a writing area roughly three feet by three feet.

Attach two pieces of string to the board at the upper right- and left-hand corners. The strings should be long enough to reach anywhere on the board. To the ends of the strings, attach a felt-tip pen and a roll of tape. Hang the board in a place accessible to all family members.

The purpose of the tape is to make it easy for any family member to simply tape to the board anything they may have already written, drawn, or cut out from the newspaper.

How to Play:

This is an ongoing activity, like the Resentment Box or Family Treasure Chest. The idea is to generate a weekly or monthly record of the family members' thoughts, triumphs, and troubles, and to insure that all family members know it's okay to have and express any feeling they wish.

1) Write the beginning and end dates of the week (or month) on top of the board.

2) Explain to everyone at dinner or at a family meeting that they can write any feeling they want, and if they don't want to share a feeling, they can write some thought that's important to them. (Some people feel more comfortable sharing feelings if you call them "thoughts.") You can open the field of eligible materials to anything—photographs, objects, drawings—as long as it's something that evoked some strong feelings in you.

3) At the end of the week, take the board down, and look at it together. Talk about its content; laugh at its humor. The board can be saved for memory's sake.

Rules:

No one can make fun of, disagree with, or otherwise judge another person's comments. And no one should be mean to another family member. Criticisms must be written in the form of "I messages" as above in the Resentment Chest activity.

Helpful Hints:

Keep your boards. Someday one of the kids or one of you adults might be inspired to write a play, screenplay, story for school, novel, or self-help book, and those boards could come in handy.

Core Scene Scripting

Thank You:
   Harville Hendrix and Helen Hunt, authors of *The Couples' Companion*.

Benefits

As Hendrix and Hunt put it so nicely, "Most couples have a 'here we go again' argument in which the same scene is played out each time, with the same ending—an impasse that opens old wounds and leaves them exhausted and angry." I would add that this is all too often the case between parents and kids and between siblings as well. These arguments Hendrix and Hunt call "core scenes." The lines of these arguments get to be so predictable that it's as if everyone is following a script. I'll leave it to you to read Hendrix and Hunt to get help in identifying the underlying cause or causes of your core scene. For now, here is a fun way to change your scripts in a way that will reduce, if not eliminate, the destructive impact these scenes have.

How to Play:

1) Pair up and discuss what seems to be one of the most common big arguments or core scenes you have, in particular what triggers it, what then in general takes place, and how it usually ends. Be sure to paraphrase back and forth to reassure each other that you've really heard each other. Take notes.

2) Together write down the script of your core scene, line by line. If you disagree on the basic lines, paraphrase back and forth until you both can agree on something.

3) Spend a day or two thinking and writing about what you'd like each other to say or do to create a happier ending to your core scene. Write it down exactly. For example, one typical argument that partners have with each other or between parents and kids involves one person saying they will do something "later," and then never doing it. One player might write: "When I ask you to do something, be honest with me if you don't want to do it, and if you really are intending to do it, tell me specifically when you are willing to do it— don't just say later."

4) Using your notes from above, the two of you go over your core scene script, and discuss some different ways you can rewrite the script, taking into account each other's needs and wants. Brainstorm without judgment as many ideas as possible, even if they seem entirely wacky. If it seems too difficult to meet each other's needs, agree on something you think you can do. Any change at all is beneficial.

5) Together write the new script. Read it together out loud over and over as you would a play or scene from a movie, and make working revisions, so that it sounds conversational and at least halfway natural.

6) For this to work, you will want to remember your lines, so you need to memorize them. It will seem awkward at first. That's to be expected. Continue to practice until the lines are memorized, on the tip of your tongue for the next time the trigger event comes up. Practice your lines in front of a mirror.

Helpful Hints:

1) Alert yourself to those warning signs of the impending argument.

2) Don't worry about feeling awkward when you first start using your lines: sounding like a robot is a whole lot better than blowing your lines and ending up again in a huge fight.

3) If neither of you can agree on how to rewrite your lines, invite a sibling, friend, parent, or professional mediator to give you some advice.

Clown Nose Arbitration

Thank You:

Matt Weinstein, founder of PlayFair, Berkeley, California, or Bob Greyson, New Haven, Connecticut, two of our nation's most brilliant game creators and leaders.

Benefits

1) Quick way to settle an argument or to take the edge off an argument.

2) One way to avoid taking yourselves or an issue too seriously.

3) You'll get some more exercise, and maybe find other things you've lost around your home.

Equipment Needed:

A red clown nose for each person playing. They cost at most a dollar each. Each player should initial the inside of their clown nose with a marker (so you know whose nose you've got). Sorry about requiring special equipment, but, really, don't you think everyone should have at least one clown nose?!

How to Play:

Each of you hides your nose in a designated room. You can both use the same room

as long as you take turns, so you don't see where the other person has hidden their nose.

The next time two of you get into a big argument, either of you can shout out "Clown Nose! Clown Nose!" Then the other shouts "Go!" and whoever finds the other's nose first gets to be right and gets their way in the argument. Actually you both win by not taking the argument quite so seriously.

Bully Defense

Thank You:

George Lucas and my friend, Arthur Kanegis. (Arthur brought it to my attention.) Apparently when George was a kid, he was being bullied in high school. When George suggested the following idea, the bully ended up taking orders from him the rest of the school year, and the rest is history. George went on to make *Star Wars*, and become one of our most famous filmmakers.

Benefits

1) A great nonviolent way to handle a bully.

2) Develops your play or screenplay writing abilities.

3) Develops the bully's acting abilities.

4) Develops your directing ability.

How to Play:

Just dream up and write down (nothing elaborate, a page will do) a simple story or plot for a play or video (if you have access to a video camera). The script should have a strong male lead (assuming the bully is a male) and members of the opposite sex, just for insurance.

Then, preferably at a time he's not picking on you, say something like this: "Excuse me, but I'm going to be producing and directing my play (or video), and wondered if you would like to be the lead, since I need a guy who's tough-looking. There'll be some pretty girls in it too."

Be prepared for the bully to ask you more specifics, if they have any intelligence at all. They will probably get very enthused very quickly. That's when you start telling them what to do and where to go and when, like, "Okay, well, be sure to be at such-and-such a place at 4:00 for our first rehearsal." And get used to giving them orders from then on.

Forget about them ever bullying you again. In fact you've probably just found a bodyguard for the rest of your time in school.

Warning:

Bullies are a serious matter. Parents and other adult authorities should always be informed first and consulted with before carrying out this or any other plan.

We are in no way guaranteeing success. Just because it worked for George Lucas does not guarantee it will work for you.

Helpful Hints:

If you need some moral support, or just find writing easier with a partner, find someone to be your cowriter. Just be sure you decide ahead of time who the director is. This partner might also come in handy as a witness. If you can't think of anyone, ask your English teacher to suggest someone.

Be open to your bully friend actually having good ideas, and incorporating those ideas. Who knows, once you've discovered the hurt and fears under their anger, you might become good friends. In this connection, if you haven't seen Woody Allen's film, *Bullets over Broadway*, be sure to check it out. It's my favorite of all his films, and extremely funny.

Be prepared that the Bully might not be impressed with a play, but only if he's in front of a video camera.

Anger games seem to be the hardest to discover or invent. So if you have invented your own games to deal with Anger or Conflict, please let us know. You'll be delighted and so, perhaps will, millions of others. Please see the end of Chapter 20 for details on how to send in your ideas and how we'll reward your effort and ingenuity.

CHAPTER 19

Helping Others

When you liberate others, you liberate yourself.
—*Ram Dass*

• • • •

Never doubt that a small group of dedicated concerned
citizens can change the world. Indeed, it's the
only thing that ever has.
—*Margaret Mead*

The "How Can I Help" Game

Making Helping More Fun

There once was this inspiring minister whose sermons were incredibly insightful as to sources of suffering and apathy in America. And these sermons were extremely inspiring as to what we each needed to do to turn things around. For example, the minister urged people to get involved in some of the institutions in the local community that most needed help, like schools in the poor section of town. He told them of organizations that were helping the homeless and victims of abuse, and of the state and national organizations working on issues such as the corruption of the health care system, the democratic process, and industrial pollution.

This minister had an ardent admirer who'd come each Sabbath and who loved the sermons. After a couple months, the admirer went up to the minister and said:

"You know, I really love your sermons and your analysis and what you are asking me and my fellow worshippers to start doing. And I myself am very involved. But I know this congregation. They might come every Sabbath and listen. But they aren't changing. They still care only about themselves or their own family, their careers, getting richer and acquiring more things, and the trappings of success and prestige, wasting their time watching TV every night and all sorts of petty things, when they could be volunteering or writing letters. I don't see you changing them at all. So why do you keep doing this? Why do you keep trying to change them?"

The minister replied: "Do you think I keep doing this just to change them? I also keep doing this to keep them from changing me!"

While helping our communities and those less fortunate than ourselves is not as common as waking up or eating dinner, I'd like to think that for most of us, or at least those buying this book, it's at least a once-a-week event. Whatever the frequency, I'm sure you'll agree that whatever it lacks in frequency it more than makes up in terms of its importance, both to our own psychological and moral health, and its critical necessity to the health of our society.

Most people often feel that helping others is inherently not fun, just like doing chores. Hopefully, this chapter will do for "helping others," what our chapter on chore games did for chores.

Helping others is necessary for your very self-respect. Deep down, I think we all know that the only real respect one can have for oneself comes from what we've given to others, not for what we've acquired. One of the most unfortunate mistakes of most traditional religions today, as well as of the New Age movements of the past thirty years, is their understatement of the central place of service and standing up for the underdog to our personal happiness and to our own personal evolution.

The games that help others are perhaps the grandest or "highest" of all games, because they not only can bring happiness and satisfaction to our selves (one might say, to our souls—our deepest selves), but to others at the same time, and perhaps even improve society in the process. It's also a great way to make new friends with, by definition, the least self-centered people around.

I realize that helping others is not often considered fun, in the sense that most of the other games in the book are fun. But these games provide a much deeper and more lasting feeling, that might be better described as joy.

If you have kids, doing these activities together is the most powerful way to teach values. As the famous writer and civil rights leader James Baldwin once said, "Children rarely do what you say, but always do what you do." And if you find activities that you can all do together, such actions can be powerfully bonding.

We can't wait until we are adults to start doing something about the things we care deeply about. Pollution, endangered species, the homeless, drug abuse, whales, the ozone, or rain forests—if there is some problem you're concerned with, find out what you can do and DO IT!

—*Kristin Johnson, Woodinville (Washington) High School, class of '92*

The "How Can I Help" Game

Thank you:

Moses, Isaiah, Jesus, Gandhi, Abraham Lincoln, Dorothy Day, John L. Lewis, Ida Tarbell, Martin Luther King, Cesar Chavez, and many others.

How to Play:

The object of this game is twofold: 1) to find something going on in the society around you that you have strong feelings about, something that either brings you to tears or makes you angry—something that you know is not right (see examples below); and 2) to find an organization doing something about that problem where you can help in some way.

First, think of a few causes you care the most about, that you really get angry or concerned about. Here are just a few of countless examples:

- the abuse of innocent children and animals;

- the torturing and killing of innocent peoples (until recently in Guatemala, continuing in Indonesia, Burma, many places in Africa, etc.);

- a health-care system that short-changes too many people too often;

- the greed-based practices of many large multinational corporations (eg. Mitsubishi's and McDonald's whole-sale destruction of our rainforests);

- the imprisonment of hundreds of

thousands of people year after year in our country for victimless crimes, in particular the possession of substances less harmful than tobacco, while the CEOs of the tobacco companies which have knowingly caused the deaths of millions, go scot-free;

- hardworking Americans losing their jobs because of Wall Street greed;

- putting toxic-waste incinerators in poor people's neighborhoods;

- lack of child-care options for low-income working people;

- the buying-off of our representatives by the rich and for the rich;

- lack of principle among our political leaders;

- continued extermination of whales, gorillas, chimpanzees, elephants, and other endangered species;

- the increasing focus on prison construction in many states at the expense of education and crime prevention;

- unwanted pregnancy and hence unwanted children.

Appendix C of this book contains a list of many of the organizations trying to respond to some of the problems mentioned above, as well as many others, along with their phone numbers and/or addresses. Many more organizations could be added. If you would like to suggest

some for our next edition, please write and let us know.

> It's one of the most beautiful compensations in life that no man can truly help another without helping himself.
>
> —*Ralph Waldo Emerson*

Next, call the organization most related to your concern and ask if they have a chapter in your hometown. You might first check your local listings to see if they have a local chapter in your city. Also, in the United States you can call toll-free information (1-800-555-1212) in case the national organization has a toll-free number.

You might also talk with people you know who might already be involved in this or related causes and ask them what organizations they could suggest.

If you have no friends involved in any causes that interest you, but you live in a large city, you might look up the public interest research group, or PIRG, for your state (Cal-PIRG in California, NY-PIRG in New York, or Mass-PIRG for Massachusetts). Alternatively, the League of Women Voters also has chapters in most major cities and might have a good directory of citizen organizations concerned with a wide variety of causes.

Here are some other good sources for lists of organizations:

- the reference librarian at your local library;

- the Internet (webactiv.com or neravt.com);

- tour local bookstore (ask for directories, local or national, of humanitarian organizations);

- the yellow pages under the relevant topic;

- your local zoo (if your concern deals with animals);

- your local police department (if your concern relates to crime, drugs, etc.);

- your city or county's Child and Family Services Department (if your concern deals with children and family issues);

- your local hospital, if your concern deals with drug and health issues;

- your local newspaper's city reporter;

- larger papers will have reporters who specialize in topics like business, the environment, or children and family. These people are extremely busy, so when you call, be as brief as you can and just ask them how to find a directory of organizations in your city dealing with your issue;

- your city might also have its own volunteer center or clearinghouse, where you can choose among many organizations according to your interests, abilities, and schedule. These organizations can usually suggest other organizations for you to contact that are more directly concerned with your concern. They are often staffed by volunteers or poorly paid workers. So be patient if they are not able to help you quickly.

> I couldn't make a better suggestion or a more important one I think, than to suggest that people do socially conscious things as families ... like feeding the homeless, helping out at a shelter, or going to a demonstration against some injustice here or abroad. It makes us more aware that we are part of a larger human family. And if you do socially conscious things, and sometimes difficult things, there is a certain energy that takes it to another level. I hesitate to call it a spiritual level, but that's exactly what it is.
>
> —*Martin Sheen*

Once you have found an organization that is doing something about the issue that concerns you, ask how you can help. If you are an adult and have a particular skill or want to develop a particular skill, let them know that. The chances are slim you'll get to work in the area you wish, since most organizations' work is either phone calling, door-to-door soliciting of support, stuffing envelopes, and office work. But you could get lucky, so it doesn't hurt to ask. For example, you might say, "I'm an attorney. Can I help you with any legal work you might need done?" Or, "I'm interested in changing careers and becoming a veterinarian. Is there any chance I could do any volunteer work with animals?"

Some good activities for the whole family might be:

- feeding the homeless. Many churches and other organizations actually have programs that allow children and parents to help out together. If they don't, maybe you and your kid could help start one. A good model in Los Angeles is Children Helping Poor and Homeless People (CHPHP), founded by Christine Schanes (310-840-4777);

- writing letters together to your representative, senators, and the president of the United States on whatever issue you can all agree on. If you have different issues, that's fine. The main thing is doing the writing together at the same time! If your family is still into watching television, you could

actually get these letters written during the commercial breaks;

- going through your neighborhood door-to-door to get a petition signed, or to solicit donations for a cause you all believe in, such as an upcoming election or initiative campaign, or simply to cut your city's parking tickets and tow charges in half!;

- going together to a demonstration about an issue you all believe in. These are usually advertised in a section in your city's alternative weekly newspaper, or regretably in only a few church or synagogue newsletters. If you have a Pacifica public radio station, they will have a community calendar twice a day. Some National Public Radio stations also have community calendars;

- volunteering at a nursing home;

- planting trees together in the city (many cities have groups that do this on a voluntary basis). Check your parks department or environment editor of your news-paper;

- helping to build homes for and with low-income people (through such organizations as Habitat for Humanity);

- volunteering together at an animal rescue shelter;

- baking things together for a benefit project;

- selling tickets together for a benefit;

- cleaning up a local park or seashore area together. Often environmental groups have specific weekends, but you could just go out on your own.

- volunteering to help a labor union that's on strike.

Helpful Hints:

Try to figure out what you really want to learn more about, or what skill you would like to further develop, and pick an organization that you think might best help you develop that skill. For example, if you want to become proficient as a singer, guitarist, or piano player, volunteering to perform for nursing homes is excellent practice.

Be prepared to do some networking to find a group that you really enjoy working with. If it isn't fun and satisfying to you on some level, you won't stay committed for long. And be realistic about the time commitment: can you give one weekend a month, four times a year, one hour a week?

> Love is something; if you give it away, you end up getting more.
>
> —*Malvina Reynolds*
> *(songwriter)*

Making Helping More Fun

Benefits

1) Makes working in any of the above even more fun.

2) By making it more fun for everyone, you have better volunteer and employee retention, and you attract more volunteers.

People that get involved with humanitarian organizations tend to be overly serious, with some wonderful exceptions, (like Wavy Gravy or Ben Cohen of *Ben and Jerry's*). They all could do with some fun and most of them know it.

How to Play:

1) For volunteer work that involves going door-to-door, or staffing a table at a public event, or stuffing envelopes at an office, you can be doing almost any of the car-ride games from Chapter 7, and even many of the dinner games from Chapter 9.

2) If you are volunteering regularly in an office, see if you can get the office manager to read Chapter 12 "Office Games", and to okay some limited trial efforts of the games in your office. (Note: If you are thinking of doing this, please let me know as soon as you can. See Ch. 20 for how to contact us.)

If you were going to die soon and had only one phone call you could make who would you call and what would you say and why are you waiting.

—*Stephen Levine*

• • • •

The most essential thing in life is to establish an unafraid heartfelt connection with others.

—*Sogyal Rimpoche*
author of The Tibetan Book of Living and Dying

Helpful Hints:

1) These humanitarian organizations tend to attract people who are not usually fond of competitive games. So I suggest starting out with non-competitive games.

2) Be sure to not begin a game until you and the other volunteers have mastered the volunteer job tasks sufficiently well so that your game will not cause you to make any major mistakes with your primary job. Be conservative and only try very simple games that take little or no concentration.

More Fun Ideas

1) Offer to lead a "Play Shop" at the next volunteer retreat. Facilitate games you like from this book or from the books mentioned in the Bibliography and Resource Guide.

2) Have Fun(d)raising dinners. Since all of these organizations often have fundraising events, offer to make them more fun, and therefore more appealing by offering to lead some games there. You can teach attendees a dinner game or two just before they eat. This can be done most easily at house parties—fundraising events held at private houses.

"It's simply a matter of fighting for the weak againt the strong. Something the best people have always done."

—*Harriet Beecher Stowe*
author, abolitionist

Please make up your own Helping Games, or games that make helping more fun, and then send them to me, so that we can share them with other people and help make the world a better place (See Chapter 20 for Details).

What's Your New Game?:
Make Up Your Own Games
and Share Them with the World

We're right on the edge of discovering millions of new ways
of being together, millions of new dances we can do
together minute by minute.

—*Anne Herbert*

My goal in writing this book is to help others. I want to encourage my readers to live their lives more playfully and to help their families do the same. I want you to create your own games and share them with the world via our Web site and, I hope, a TV series. I want to help those less fortunate than me by contributing my profits to causes like child abuse prevention, decent health care for all, the elimination of cancer-causing toxins from our environment, the strengthening of our democracy, and the preservation of our rain forests.

With these goals in mind, I am asking your help to spread as much playfulness around as possible. I need your own game inventions—new and free ways to make the ordinary situations of everyday life extraordinary. (See next page for addresses.)

4) You get lots of recognition (on our Web site, in our newsletter, and possibly on a national TV show).

5) You get appreciated by the hundreds of thousands who hopefully will see your idea, try it, love it, and want to thank you for it.

6) You gain the supreme satisfaction of knowing your imagination is helping thousands, or maybe millions, of kids, parents, and families to live a much happier life.

7) You gain the supreme satisfaction of knowing your contribution may help us in turn improve the world (since all post tax profits of the SimpleFun™ Company go to organizations working to help kids, the environment, those less fortunate than ourselves, and to increase democracy).

The Game of Games: Creating Your Own Games and Giving Them to the World

Benefits

1) Develops the imagination. Remember from chapter 5, the imagination is like a muscle.

2) Eliminates loneliness. You can't feel lonely and creative at the same time.

3) Creates additional sources of income (if you become a regular source of ideas for us, we'll start paying you!).

> We make a living by what we get, we make a life by what we give.
>
> —*Aaron Copeland*

How to Play:

First, create new games and activities of your own. Your games can simply be your own variations to the games and activities in this book, or games that are entirely of your own making. On the pages that follow, I'll give you some helpful hints to perhaps make it easier to invent your own games. A good test of your game is whether other people want to try it when you show it to them.

Whether you invent new variations to our games or invent whole new games of your own, whatever you dream up should meet the following rules or criteria if you wish to send them into us:

- They must not already be a commonly known game.

- They must cost little or no money (free if possible, five dollars maximum, unless they are for use in a corporate environment)

- They should be able to fit into any common situation of everyday life. By the way, our next books might be on ways to make married life, office life, and the mall more fun, so we're especially looking forward to any ideas you have in these areas.

- They should take little or no preparation.

- They should be able to be done by as few as two people.

Your name, address, and phone should be on the same paper or email describing the game. You can also send a photo of yourself, if you like, and if we're able, we'll show it.

Send in your games or new variations of our games to us by mail, email or at our Web site, where you can read about what

others are inventing and sending in every day. Our mailing address is:

SimpleFun
P.O. Box 55518
Sherman Oaks, CA 91413

Or contact us through our Website:
www.SIMPLEFUN.COM
or our email:
Easyfun@flash.net
or Bestfun@aol.com

Once I receive your game, I or members of my "Fun team" will try it out. If the response is positive, I'll put your game on our Web site, and you'll receive the following:

- A public thank-you, and hopefully your picture, if you send us one.

- A free copy of our newsletter, containing latest and best new games.

- A monetary reward, to be announced on the Website, SimpleFun.com

- A free copy of our next book.

- When we get our show off the ground, you'll be acknowledged on national TV and be fairly compensated, depending on our budget. In fact, if your game is amusing to watch, send us a videotape of people doing it. If we use your tape in our show, your compensation will be much larger. The more good videos we get, the better our chances of getting on the air.

> Keep on the lookout for novel and interesting ideas that others have used successfully. Your ideas has to be original only in its adaptation to the problem you're currently working on.
>
> —*Thomas Edison*

Helpful Hints:

Don't feel you have to create something that's original in every respect to be original. Virtually all inventions are combinations of things already invented or being used. They are often, as Mr. Edison says, adaptations of existing things (in our case, rules, actions, props, complete games) to new situations or contexts.

Before you start trying to invent a new way to have fun, don't forget to think of any games you or other members of your family or a friend might already have invented or discovered. That game or games might be the very best ideas to send in. Parents and kids accidentally discover or invent new and free ways to have fun all the time. Your family is probably no different. You only need to write them down and send them in.

Now if you want to go the next step and purposefully invent your own games, it won't always be easy. So I'd just like to mention a few of my thoughts on this, having dealt with this challenge for much of the past several years. I think these tips will make your work easier, and hopefully more fun. You must be playful at it—be willing to play around with many elements in potentially an infinite number of combinations. As is true in any art there is a medium. For painting, the medium is color and line, for music it's sound and silence. For play it's all of these elements and many more—really all the elements of life itself.

Fooling Around

It's entirely possible for you to create a wonderful game or activity without any method or systematic plan of attack. Here's one such story: Let's say you wish to invent a fun thing to do at dinner. The elements here are numerous: There are utensils, many food items, the personalities of the people there, background music perhaps, the furniture, etc. In most cases, if you were to just start in trial-and-error fashion to dream up fun ideas, you'd either be paralyzed by the number of possible combinations, or you'd come up with ideas that will be either boring or too difficult. And if you recall what was said in Chapter 3 about play, the key is to come up with something where there can be a nice *balance between ability and challenge.*

It helps a great deal to give yourself some limits. It seems almost a paradox that we need limits or boundaries in order to become more free and creative. For example, you decide that the game must involve dinner rolls, forks, and hands. Then start fooling around with the rolls and forks: stab the rolls, massage them, knock them around, fiddle this way and that, try to balance them, etc. Then a song comes on the radio—and you have it! You discover that if you take two forks stuck into two rolls, they resemble legs and feet, and you've created the legs of a puppet that dances. You discover that it's a lot of fun to move your dinner roll feet in rhythm to music. And everyone at the table is cracking up. In fact your son has just made his own dancing roll feet and is dancing with you!

As you see, this is usually a process of trial and error. The more patient and the more aware you are and the more you can look at anything and see it as many other things, the more likely it is you'll come up with something that will be fun.

Most theories or approaches to creating new games come at it from one of three approaches—*game adapting, game combining, and game component*—all of them somewhat more systematic than the above. I am going to just give you just one or two examples using each of these approaches, and you get to experiment for yourself to see which method best suits you.

Game Adaptation

What you decide to keep and what to elim-
inate depends on what aspects or features of the game(s) you like and don't like. It's all pretty intuitive. You might be someone who likes competition a lot and you also like Emotional Salad, the dramatic mealtime game in Chapter 9. So you try to add an element or two to make it more competitive. To do this you eventually realize that you will need to invent a scoring system, something that defines "winner" or "points." So maybe you decide to have someone be the judge. And the judge keeps score, giving a point to each side for correctly changing to the emotion being announced without missing a beat or otherwise flubbing.

Or say you want to invent a new leaving-home game. You start with the Dress Race game in Chapter 8, and you decide to adapt it by changing or adding a prop, like a balloon. If you introduce another prop, you need a new rule that governs what is done with the prop. So you decide they must try to keep the ball in the air while dressing. Sounds interesting, but you don't have to contemplate the game too long to realize that the challenge level might be too difficult and it will cause anxiety and stress, not fun. So you decide to add a new rule instead: before someone can be at the door ready to leave, he must accomplish one of the chores not yet done for the week (that is listed on a chore chart somewhere in the house). Another adaptation you intuitively think of is to involve music. Each player gets a turn to choose the music that all must dress to.

Game Combining

This approach simply combines the elements you most like from two or more different games to create a hybrid game. Again, hours or days of trial and error might be necessary, unless you just have a talent for this sort of thing.

Let's start with the Dress Race game again. One of your other favorite games is the Hinky Pinky word game from Chapter 7. So what happens if you play Hinky Pinky while doing the Dress Race? Essentially you have two games going on simultaneously.

You might just play around with two of your favorite games, or first decide on the context, and then see what games that context might suggest. Let's try the first strategy.

Pick two favorite games and no context, like Knock Your Socks Off and Thumb-Hat Wrestling. You could do both simultaneously, therefore only having one hand free to pull the other person's socks off. You realize immediately that it might be hard to keep the thumb-hat on in this full-body fighting situation. So you allow the hat to fall off, and add a few other rules to keep fairness in the game and to keep it from getting too frustrating. For example, in the course of trying it out, you discover that it's extremely difficult to get even one sock off. So you decide to create a new rule, requiring that the sock already be pulled off enough so that the heel is showing.... I'm not saying you have a good game yet. My purpose here is to just show you the process.

By the way, while thinking about how to combine Thumb-Hat Wrestling with Knock Your Socks Off, I suddenly thought of two-handed Thumb-Hat Wrestling, which is simply an adaptation of the original. So sometimes working in one method, you'll get a brainstorm that doesn't necessarily follow from your current train of thought. It's critically important to stay open to flashes like these.

Another way to begin is to pick any two or three games arbitrarily from this book, pick two or three elements from them, and see if you can make up a new game. For example, on page 170 we find Kitchen Hockey and on page 174 we find Psychic Nonsense. So here are two new games I came up with based on elements from these two games:

While playing Kitchen Hockey, during each playoff (between face-offs) you take on an extra physical action and sound, which you constantly perform while playing.

While playing Psychic Nonsense, you incorporate kitchen utensils. A version of this, which you could do while eating, might be to just close your eyes and on the count of three do one of your three action-sound pairs, wherein the action involves the spoon, fork, or knife.

Game Components

The third and last approach is the most systematic one. If you're more left-brained or your right brain gets tired doing either of the above two methods, try this one. It is an aid to tapping your own creativity and applying it to game design. Again, if you work on this with another person, you'll generate ideas even faster. To tap your creativity in different ways, all you have to do is change the headings on the columns.

Our example on the next page gives six headings or categories. These categories go across the grid. All the ways you can think of exemplifying the category would go downward as many times as you wish. Our grid leaves seven examples per category, but you could make it ten by twenty or however many you wish and have the patience and space on your paper for. You can also anywhere you wish on the grid. This seven-by-six-square grid could theoretically yield 112,469 new combinations or games.

The definitions of the game categories on top of the grid are as follows:

1) *Life Situation:* in other words, the situations as I've split them up in my table of contents, or any other situation you choose. No doubt there are other common life situations which we have not yet touched on.

2) *Focus:* the main activity or task of the game upon which the players concentrate their attention (tagging, acting out emotions, pulling a sock off).

3) *Props:* any equipment needed, like balloons, thumb-hats, tape, or clothing.

4) *Obstacles,* including handicaps: what, if anything, obstructs the main activ-

ity (keeping your eyes closed, expressing yourself emotionally, having a time limit, doing it while standing on one foot).

5) *Goal:* the object of the game. How do you know when it's over? (you've got the other person's socks off, when dinner is over, when people get tired.)

6) *Rules:* that determine how one plays and achieves the goal.

Keep in mind that you can add additional categories, like energy level (contemplative, gentle, manic, frequently changing in pace), role of leader, or scoring system. By adding and changing the categories, you can generate additional games. I've filled in a few boxes in the grid to give you the general idea.

Creating games and new playful activities is an art, not a science. So I think it's helpful to think of inventing games as you would any other art. And whichever approach you use to invent your games, it helps to start with the question: how can I do whatever I'm doing differently? That question is the key to enlivening not only your own life, but all of your relationships.

Creative people run best on the high-octane fuels of play and freedom, on the pleasure that comes from being able to pose and answer the question, 'What if?'

—*John Kao*

Life Situations	Focus	Props	Obstacle	Goal	Rules
Waking up	Waking up happy	Balloons	Waking up	Being wide awake	Must pretend to be Capt. Kirk or Capt. Janeway
Chores	Cleaning your Room	All sorts of clothes	1) A very messy room 2) A time limit	Finishing the task by the time limit	Can only pick up items alphabetically
Shopping	Buying a surprise gift	Colored hats	1) Avoid gift being seen 2) Limited money to spend	To buy gift before timer runs out	Gift must cost less than 99 cents
TV watching	To share an important moment in your life	TV show	Avoiding distraction, and self censorship	To share highest number of personal moments	When you don't share personal moments, you must parrot your character's lines
Waiting	To tag someone or avoid being tagged	Songs (maybe written)	Must move on tippy toes (everyone)	When everyone is exhausted	You must chase other if you've been tagged
Office Meeting	etc...	None	etc...	etc...	When anyone says a particular word or phrase
Washing up	etc...	Water			
etc...					

240

Be sure to write down your ideas, no matter how stupid or silly they seem. Probably the stupider or sillier, the better. When you look at them again, next time you're alone, they might spark or combine into an even better idea. After all, the guys that came up with Teenage Mutant Ninja Turtles originally were just trying to come up with the stupidest spoofs they could think of. They never expected it to be taken seriously.

This may at times not be fun and feel very hard. It may even cause anxiety. You will sometimes not be in the flow. But remember, you're doing one of the most important things in life that any one can do: You're creating things that can provide more joy and creativity to potentially millions of others for many years into the future. Don't forget what I said in Chapter 4: The best things in life aren't things.

> Western man has purchased prosperity at the cost of a staggering impoverishment of the vital elements of life. These elements are festivity—the capacity for genuine revelry and joyous celebration—and fantasy—the faculty for envisioning radically alternative life situations.
>
> —*Harvey Cox*

More Helpful Hints:

- Don't expect to always be able to come up with a new game every time. Inspiration is like germination: It takes frequent watering (thinking) before you see something sprout.

- Playfulness, as we discussed in Chapter 3, is like a muscle. The more you practice, the stronger it becomes, the more inventive you become.

> The more mistakes you can make, the better.
>
> —*Shirley McClaine*

- Be sure to keep all your previous work and inventions in a folder, journal, or on your computer. It's usually easier to improvise off of an existing game than to invent a completely new game.

- Cultivate a receptive attitude, especially if you are brainstorming with other people, which is another good idea (two heads are better than one). Never judge if you are brainstorming, and never censor yourself.

- Last but not least, try out the game yourself with someone else. You almost always discover important problems you had not foreseen when you were just playing the game in your head.

I've always grown from my problems and challenges, from the things that don't work out. That's when I really learned.

—*Carol Burnett*

To order SimpleFun for Busy People
• Videos (with TV Karaoke™)
• Car Games audio
or
• Top 30 new best games
(see next page)

To order our bumper sticker;
"THIS DRIVER TELLS JOKES AT STOP SIGNS®"
send $7 to address on p235
(includes shipping and handling)

Appendices & Index

Rewards List

Privileges (for children)
later bedtime or curfew
day off from chores
getting some space/privacy
going out with a friend
more telephone time
sleeping in
getting one's own room
choosing one's own: wake-up time, chores, meal
cooking privileges

Family activities
EasyFun games
hiking, canoeing, camping trip
building something together: treehouse, backyard sculpture
painting something together: wall mural, inside or out
flying a kite
ice- or roller-skating
ice-cream outings
cooking meal together
going to a restaurant, movie, picnic
trip to the playground or play center
going to the beach
going to the museum or aquarium

One-to-one parent time
visiting parent's work
day at the mall
living-room camp-out
reading books
go for a quiet parent-and-child walk
playing cards or board game
going out to lunch
surprise day trip with parent
breakfast in bed

Sports equipment
balls of all sorts (basketball, baseball, football, soccer ball)
baseball mitt
hockey gear
swimming goggles
special sports shoes
ski poles/boots
ice skates
roller skates
golf equipment
skateboard or surfboard
playground equipment
gymnastic mat
cheerleading items
baton

boating gear

tennis or badminton equipment

horseshoes

sports bag

fishing rod

windsurfing equipment

Arts and crafts

coloring books

crayons, markers, paints, chalk, fabric
    paints

easel

clay

beads and string

sewing equipment and materials

Special classes

ceramics

swimming

dance

gymnastics

arts and crafts

music

sports (baseball, football, cheerleading
    camps)

sailing/boating

painting

horseback riding

drawing

calligraphy

cooking

tennis

martial arts

Toys

dolls and their accoutrements (clothes,
house, furniture)

stuffed animals

puppets

dress-up clothes

board games

building blocks

playhouse

outdoor toys

puzzles

jump rope

jacks

marbles

swimming pool toys

spending money at a toy store

Foods

sweet desserts

special treats (candy, cookies)

making favorite food

eating with hands

cooking with parent

Big Family Rewards

swimming pool

vacation

computer

tree house

Bodily delights

new clothes

visit to beauty salon or health spa

visit to hot tubs

massage
makeup
perfume or cologne
lotions and powders
blow dryer
jewelry

Social rewards
hugs and kisses
sleep-over
party
joining a club (Scouts, ski club)
having friend over for dinner
visiting a mentor in a craft or profession
meeting a locally revered or famous person
   (read the newspaper for ideas)

Special Items
a pet
books
backpack
new lunch box
computer game
telephone
records, tapes, or CDs
special plaque, ribbon, or trophy
money
gift certificate to favorite store

Discussion Topic List

Environmental issues

What concerns you the most about the condition of our planet and the environment in our hometown?

What do you think has caused this problem?

What do you think we could do to solve it as a family, in our schools and workplaces, or through our local, state, and federal governments?

Male/female differences

When you get lost, who wants to stop for directions and who wants to keep driving?

Do the boys and girls in our family get treated differently in terms of household chores, dating privileges, et cetera?

Teen/parent conflicts

Is it okay for the older kids to have parties at our house when the parents are out of town?

Should we get a family dog?

Population and hunger

What are some of the biggest problems facing the planet? Why?

What can be done about these problems? What can be done about hunger?

Homelessness

How big a problems is homelessness here in our town?

Why are there people homeless in America? Whose fault is it?

Abortion/sex education

If your friend is pregnant at age seventeen, but she just got accepted to a good college, should she have an abortion? Who should decide? What information would be good to know to make an intelligent decision?

Peer relationship conflict

Everyone smokes and drinks, what should you do?

What should you do if someone spreads a rumor about you?

Brother/sister conflicts

Why do you get stuck doing the dishes alone when your sibling leaves right after dinner?

Who gets in trouble if something is broken, and the parents don't know who did it?

Love relationship conflicts

What do you do if you want to break up with your boyfriend/girlfriend?

What do you do if your parents don't like them?

Television

What values do most TV shows propagate? Why? Who controls the media?

What does TV watching do to our brain? Our lives?

How much TV is okay to watch? How long should you watch TV in one sitting?

Special events at school

What are the most worthwhile things being offered at school now?

What special classes can you take?

Sports events

Why do you think so many people are obsessed with watching or talking about sports events, but don't even play them themselves?

Why do you think people talk about sports stars instead of real heroes (people who are truly courageous and risk their lives and careers to help others)?

Political events

What do you imagine Martin Luther King, Jr., would want us to do on his birthday?

If we could create a new national holiday celebrating someone's birthday or the day we put into law an important right (like women's right to vote, or the creation of the Environmental Protection Agency), whose birthday or which right should it be? Why?

Politicians

Who or what do you think controls many politicians? Why?

How could the system be changed?

Which politicians do you admire and why?

Racism

What do you think causes people to be racist? What can be done about it?

What's wrong about racism?

Religious prejudices

What do you think about such and such a religious group? Why?

Is our religion prejudiced against any group? Why?

Violence

What happens when violence is used to "settle" a conflict?

Is there ever a justification for violence? When?

What are some alternatives to violence (cite various hypothetical conflicts, and see who can come up with the most imaginative solutions)?

Bilingual education
Should we teach English-only to children in American schools?

Foreign affairs
Why do people have wars?

Why should we be concerned about the economy in Russia?

Capital punishment
Why do you think we should or should not keep the death penalty?

New laws
If you could make two new laws, what would they be?

How would you begin to make that law a reality?

Elections
What do you think we should do to have a more democratic system, so politicians aren't so controlled by big money?

What do you think of federal financing or requiring media to be free? (The airwaves are actually owned by the public and leased [for a song] to the big networks.)

Drugs and drug abuse
Which drugs are harmful? Which are addictive?

Why do people get addicted?

Should drugs be legalized? Which ones, if any?

Should use or possession of marijuana be a crime? cocaine? cigarette tobacco? Why or why not?

Crime
Why do most people think there's lots more crime, when statistically it's been basically the same for the past twenty years?

How should the CEOs of the tobacco companies be punished?

Why do CEOs who do grave harm rarely get punished or get punished much less than people who do tiny crimes in comparison?

Gang problems
What if one of your good friends wanted you to join a gang?

Why do kids join gangs?

What would be a better alternative?

Resource Guide for Helping Others

What follows is a partial list of national organizations involved in helping children, the environment, and many other worthy causes. For a much more exhaustive directory, including federal agencies, administrative and Congressional Office listings, check out the appendix in NO Kidding Around: America's Young Activists Are Changing Our World (call 800-KID-POWER to order this book, or email them at ACTIVISM@AOL.COM). If you have access to the Internet, I suggest a visit to the following Web sites: www.WEBACTIVE. COM or www.NERAVT.com/left/ Here you will find literally hundreds of organizations listed covering many other issues in addition to those I list below.

Advertising and Consumer Concerns

Consumers Union
101 Truman Avenue
Yonkers, NY 10703
(914) 378-2000

Public Citizen
P.O. Box 19404
Washington, DC 20036
(202) 833-3000

U.S. Public Interest Research Group (PIRG)
218 D Street SE
Washington, DC 20003
(202) 546-9707

AIDS and HIV

AIDS Action Council
2033 M Street NW #802
Washington, DC 20003
(202) 293-2886

Teens Teaching AIDS Prevention
3030 Walnut Street
Kansas City, MO 64108
(800) 234-TEEN; (816) 561-8784 in Missouri

Animal Rights (see also Wildlife)

American Society for the Prevention of Cruely to Animals
441 East 92nd Street
New York, NY 10128
(212) 876-7700; Fax (212) 348-3031

Animal Welfare Information Center
National Agricultural Library #F304
Beltsville, MD 20705
(301) 344-3704

Humane Society of the United States
2100 L Street NW
Washington, DC 20037
(202) 452-1100

People for the Ethical Treatment of
Animals
P.O. Box 42516
Washington, DC 20015
(301) 770-7444

Sea Shepherd Conservation Society
P.O. Box 628
Venice, CA 90294
(310) 301-7325 or (888) WHALE-22

Child Abuse
(Check your local Family & Children's
Services under city or county government
in your telephone directory)

National Committee for the Prevention of
Child Abuse
332 South Michigan
Chicago, IL 60604
(312) 663-3520

Clearinghouse on Child Abuse and Neglect
P.O. Box 1182
Washington, DC 20013
(703) 821-2086

*Campaign Finance Reform (see
Government Reform)*

Corporate Responsibility
Council on Economic Priorities
(212) 420-1133

(publishes *Shopping for a Better World*)

Public Citizen
P.O. Box 19404
Washington, DC 20036
(202) 833-300

The Nation Magazine
72 Fifth Avenue
New York, NY 10011
(212) 242-8400

MultiNational Monitor
P.O. Box 19367
Washington, DC 20036
(202) 387-8030

Government Accountability Project
1612 K Street NW
Washington, DC
(202) 408-0034

Defense Spending
Campaign for New Priorities

Center for Defense Information
(800) CDI-3334

Drugs and Alcohol
Drug Policy Foundation
4801 Massachusetts Avenue NW,
Room 400
Washington, DC 20016-2087
(202) 895-1634

Mothers Against Drunk Drivers (MADD)
511 East John Carpenter Freeway

Irving, TX 75062

(214) 744-6233

National Clearinghouse for Alcohol and
Drug Abuse Information

5600 Fishers Lane

Rockville, MD 20857

(800) 729-6686; (301) 468-2600 in
Maryland

Students Against Drunk Drivers (SADD)

Box 800

Marlboro, MA 01752

(508) 481-3568

Energy

Consumer Energy Council of America
Research Foundation

2000 L Street NW, Room 802

Washington, DC 20036

(202) 659-0404

Energy Conservation Coalition

Environmental Action

1525 New Hampshire Avenue

Washington, DC 20036

(202) 745-4874

Safe Energy Communications Council

1717 Masschusetts Avenue NW

Washington, DC 20036

(202) 483-8491

Environment

Environmental Defense Fund

1616 P Street NW, Room 150

Washington, DC 20036

(202) 387-3500

EPIC (Env. Protection Info Ctr.)
(specializes in saving remaining California
redwoods)

(707) 923-293; fax (707) 923-4210

Friends of the Earth

218 D Street SE

Washington, DC 20003

(202) 544-2600

Greenpeace USA

1436 U Street NW

Washington, DC 20009

(202) 462-1177

*Green Party Of America (see Government
Reform)*

Kids for Saving Earth

P.O. Box 47247

Plymouth, MN 55447

(612) 525-0002

League of Conservation Voters

(415) 896-5550 (listed starting with your
state's name)

National Audubon Society

1244 Nineteenth Street NW

Washington, DC 20036

(202) 832-3200

Rainforest Action Network

301 Broadway, Suite A

San Francisco, CA 94133

(415) 398-4404

Right to Know
218 D Street SE
Washington, DC 20003
(202) 546-9707

Sierra Club
85 Second Street, Second Floor
San Francisco, CA 94105-3441
(415) 977-5500

US Public Interest Research Group
(USPIRG)
218 D Street SE
Washington, DC 20003
(202) 546-9707

Youth for Environmental Sanity (YES)
706 Frederick Street
Santa Cruz, CA 95062
(408) 459-9344

Food

Center for Science in the Public Interest
1875 Connecticut Avenue NW
Washington, DC 20009
(202) 332-9110

Government Reform (Campaign Finance Reform)

Americans for Democratic Action
1625 K Street, Suite 210
Washington, DC 20006
(202) 785-5980

Center for Voting and Democracy
(301) 270-4616

Citizen Action
(800) 652-0827 or (888) 777-7135

Public Citizen
P.O. Box 19404
Washington, DC 20036
(202) 588-1000

Common Cause
2030 M Street NW
Washington, DC 20036
(202) 833-1200

Green Party Of America
(check your telephone book for local listings)
(607) 756-4211

League Of Women Voters
(202) 429-1965

National Voting Rights Center
(617) 867-0740

Health (including Food)

Citizen Action
(800) 652-0827 or (888) 777-7135

Physicians for Social Responsibility
(202) 898-0150

Center for Science in the Public Interest
(202) 332-9110

Physicians for a National Health Program
(310) 554-0380

Housing and Homelessness

ACORN (see *Legal Services*)

Catholic Worker Soup Kitchens
(check your telephone book for local listings)
(213) 267-8789

Community for Creative Non-Violence
425 Second Street NW
Washington, DC 20001
(202) 393-4409

National Alliance to End Homelessness
1518 K Street NW, #206
Washington, DC 20005
(202) 638-1526

National Network on the Homeless
1319 F Street NW, Room 401
Washington, DC 20004
(202) 783-7949

Hunger

Campaign to End Childhood Hunger
Food Research and Action Center
1875 Connecticut Avenue NW, #540
Washington, DC 20009
(202) 986-2525

Zero Population Growth
1400 Sixteenth Street NW, #320
Washington, DC 20036
(202) 332-2200

Human Rights

American Friends Service Committee
(800) 262-2372 or (800) 226-9816

Amnesty International
(800) AMNESTY

Jobs

AFL-CIO
815 Sixteenth Street NW
Washington, DC 20006
(202) 637-5000

Teamsters International
(check your telephone book for local listings)

Service Employees International
(check your telephone book for local listings)

American Friends Service Committee
(800) 262-2372 or (800) 226-9816

Legal Services for the Poor

National Lawyers Guild
(212) 627-2656

Legal Services and Legal Aid Society
(check your telephone book for local listings)

ACORN
(Association of Community Organizations
for Reform Now)
(718) 693-6700, ext. 4002

Prejudice and Racism

Anti-Defamation League of B'nai B'rith
823 United Nations Plaza
New York, NY 10017
(212) 490-2525; Fax (212) 867-0779

Congressional Black Caucus
H2-344 House Office Building Annex 2

Washington, DC 20515
(202) 226-7790

Congression Hispanic Caucus
H2-557 House Office Building Annex 2
Washington, DC 20515
(202) 226-3430

League of United Latin American Citizens
400 First Street NW, Suite 716
Washington, DC 20001
(202) 628-0717

League of United Latin American Citizens
(LULAC) Foundation
400 First Street NW, Suite 721
Washington, DC 20001
(202) 628-8516

Mexican-American Legal Defense and
Educational Fund (MALDEF)
634 Spring Street, 11th Floor
Los Angeles, CA 90014
(213) 629-2512

National Association for the Advancement
of Colored People
(NAACP)/Youth and College Division
4805 Mount Hope Drive
Baltimore, MD 21215-3297
(301) 358-8900

National Council of La Raza (NCLR)
Twenty F Street NW
Washington, DC 20001
(202) 628-9600

Rainbow-Push Coalition
1002 Wisconsin Ave NW
Washington, DC
(202) 333-5270

Oceans
Center for Marine Conservation
1725 DeSales Street NW, Room 500
Washington, DC 20036
(202) 429-5609; Fax (202) 872-0619

Save the Whales
P.O. Box 2000
Washington, DC 20007
(202) 337-2332

Ozone
Carbon Dioxide Campaign
Children's Earth Fund
40 West 20th Street
New York, NY 10011
(212) 727-4492; Fax (212) 727-1773

Peace and Nuclear Disarmament
American Friends Service Committee
(800) 262-2372 or (800) 226-9816

Center for Defense Information
(800) CDI-3334

Children of War
85 South Oxford Street
Brooklyn, NY 11217
(718) 858-6882; Fax (718) 237-3193

Educators for Social Responsibility
23 Garden Street

Cambridge, MA 02138
(617) 492-1764

Physicians for Social Responsibility
(202) 898-0150

Sane/Freeze (a.k.a Peace Action)
1819 Sane Street NW #640
Washington, DC 20006
(202) 862-9740 or (800) 228-1228

Senior Citizens

Gray Panthers
1424 Sixteenth Street NW, #602
Washington, DC 20036
(202) 387-3111

National Council of Senior Citizens
925 Fifteenth Street NW
Washington, DC 20005
(202) 347-8800

Sexism

American Assoc of University Women
2401 Virginia Avenue NW
Washington, DC 20037
(202) 785-7700; check your telephone book for local listings

Institute for Women's Policy Research
1400 Twentieth Street NW, #104
Washington, DC 20036
(202) 785-5100

National Organization for Women (NOW)
1000 Sixteenth Street NW, #700

Washington, DC 20036
(202) 331-0066

Suicide Prevention

(check your telephone book for local listings under Suicide or Crisis Hotline)

National Committee on Youth Suicide Prevention
65 Essex Road
Chestnut Hill, MA 02167
(617) 738-7800

Television and the Media

Accuracy in Media
1275 K Street NW, #1150
Washington, DC 20005
(202) 371-6710

Center for Investigative Reporting
530 Howard Street, Second Floor
San Francisco, CA 94105-3007
(415) 543-1200

Fairness and Accuracy in Reporting
130 West 25th Street
New York, NY 10001
(212) 633-6700

Teen Pregnancy

Adolescent Pregnancy Program
U.S. Department of Health and Human Services
200 Independence Avenue SW, #736E
Washington, DC 20201
(202) 245-7473

National Abortion Rights Action League
11101 Fourteenth Street NW, Fifth Floor
Washington, DC 20005
(202) 408-4600

National Right to Life Committee
419 Seventh Street NW, #500
Washington, DC 20004
(202) 626-8800

Planned Parenthood Federation of America
810 Seventh Street
New York, NY 10019
(212) 541-7800

Water

Clean Water Action
317 Pennslyvania Avenue
Washington, DC 20003
(202) 457-1286

Save Our Streams (SOS)
Izaak Walton League of America
1401 Wilson Boulevard, Level B
Arlington, VA 22209
(703) 528-1818

Wildlife

Defenders of Wildlife
1244 Nineteenth Street NW
Washington, DC 20036
(202) 659-9510

National Audubon Society
950 Third Avenue
New York, NY 10022
(212) 832-3200

Resource Guide for Play

I've read many other books and many research reports to write this book, but these are the sources that I think will be most applicable to your daily life. You can find a continuously updated collection of "New Games and Tips for Making the Ordinary Situations of Everyday Life Extraordinary" at our website at www.easy-fun.com

Becoming More Playful and More Creative

Blatner, Adam, and Allee Blatner. *The Art of Play: Helping Adults Reclaim Imagination and Spontaneity.* rev. ed. New York: Brunner/Mazel, 1997.

Cameron, Julia, and Mark Bryan. *The Artist's Way: A Spiritual Path to Higher Creativity.* New York: G.P. Putnam's Sons, 1992.

Csikszentmihalyi, Mihaly. *Finding Flow.* New York: Harper Collins, 1997.

Csikszentmihalyi, Mihaly. *Creativity.* New York: Harper Perennial, 1996.

DeKoven, Bernie. *The Well Played Game: A Player's Philosophy.* New York: Anchor Books, 1978.

Garcia, John David. *Creative Transformation: A Practical Guide for Maximizing Creativity.* Eugene, Ore.: Noetic Press, 1991.

Huizinga, Johan. *Homo Ludens: A Study of the Play Element in Culture.* Boston: Beacon Press, 1950.

Montagu, Ashley, *Growing Young.* Boston [?]: Bergin and Garvey, 1989.

Nachmanovitch, Stephen. *Free Play: The Power of Improvisation in Life and the Arts.* New York: The Putman Publishing Group, 1990.

Rasberry, Salli, and Padi Selwyn. *Living Your Life Out Loud.* New York: Pocket Books, 1995.

Weston, Denise C., and Mark S. Weston. *Playful Parenting,* New York; G.P. Putnam's Sons, 1993.

Play, Marriage and the Family

Hawkes, Steven. "Recreation and the Family," in *Family Research: A sixty-year review,. 1930- 1990.* Vol. 1. New York: Lexington Books/Macmillan, Inc, 1991.

Markman, Howard. *Fighting for Your Marriage*. San Francisco: Jossey Bass, 1994.

Orthner, Dennis, and Jay Manicini. "Benefits of Leisure for Family Bonding," in *Benefits of Leisure,*. State College, Penn.: Venture Publishing, 1991.

_____. "Leisure Impacts on Family Interaction and Cohesion," *Journal of Leisure Research* 22, no. 2 (1990): 125.

Shafer, C.E. *Therapeutic Powers of Play*. Northvale, New Jersey: Jason Aronson, 1994.

Smith, Diane. "Investigating Playfulness in Family Process." Department of Family Sciences, Brigham Young University, 1996. [(801) 378-3016.]

Noncompetitive Games Sources

Bernardi, Philip. *Improvisation Starters*. Cincinnati: Betterway Books, 1992.

Hall, William, and Paul Killam, eds. *Playbook*. San Francisco: Bay Area Theatresports, 1993; (415) 824-8220.

Michaelis, Bill. *Noncompetitive Activities and Play*. N.p.: self-published, 1994; (415) 338-7576.

Orlick, Terry. *The Second Cooperative Sports and Games Book*. N.p.: [Pantheon?], 1982.

Rohnke, Karl. *Silver Bullets: A Guide to Initiative Problems, Adventure Games and Trust Activities*. Dubuque, Iowa: Kendall/Hunt, 1984.

_____. *Cowtails and Cobras II,* Dubuque, Iowa: Kendall/Hunt, 1989.

Sher, Barbara. *Extraordinary Play with Ordinary Things*. Holbrook, Mass.: Bob Adams Inc., 1997.

Spolin, Viola. *Improvisation for the Theater*. Chicago: University of Chicago Press, l996.

Weinstein, Matt, and Joel Goodman. *Playfair*. San Luis Obispo, Calif.: Impact, 1980.

Eliminating TV Addiction

Bennett, Steve, and Ruth Bennett. *365 TV-Free Activities You can Do With Your Child*. Holbrook, Mass.: Bob Adams Inc., 1991.

Dermer, David Pearce. *Breaking Your Child's TV Addiction: A Guide for Parents*. Pullman, Wash.: Marquette Books, 1989.

Healey, Jane M. *Endangered Minds*. New York: Simon and Schuster, 1990.

Winn, Marie. *Unplugging the Plug-In Drug*. New York: Penguin Books, 1987.

Play, Corporate Life and Productivity

Hemsath, Dave, and Leslie Yerkes. *301 Ways to Have Fun at Work.* San Francisco: Berrett-Koehler, 1997.

Play and Medical Benefits

Abadie, M.J. *Healing Mind Body Spirit.* Hollbrook, Mass.: Adams Publishing, 1997.

Benson, Herbert, M.D. *Timeless Healing: The Power and Biology of Belief.* N.p.: Fireside, 1996.

Pert, Candace B. *Molecules of Emotions: Why You Feel the Way You Feel.* New York: Simon and Schuster, 1997.

Shealy, Norman, M.D. *Miracles Do Happen: A Physician's Experience with Alternative Medicine,* Rockport, MA: Element, 1996.

Siegel, Bernard, M.D. *Love, Medicine, and Miracles.* New York: Harper Perennial, 1990.

Simonton, O. Carl and others. *Getting Well Again.* New York: Bantam, 1980.

Sinatra, Stephen, M.D. *Optimum Health.* New York: Bantam, 1996.

Compassion, Social Change, Play and Conflict Resolution

Cannan, Crescy. *Social Action with Children and Families.* New York: Routledge, 1997.

Cloke, Ken, and Joan Goldsmith, *Thank God It's Monday.* New York: Irwin, 1997.

Random Acts of Kindness. Berkeley, Calif.: Conari Press, 1993.

Dass, Ram, and Mirabai Bush. *Compassion in Action: Setting Out of the Path of Service.* New York: Bell Tower, 1992.

Dass, Ram, and Paul Gorman. *How Can I Help?* New York: Alfred A. Knopf, Inc., 1985.

Eyer, Linda, and Richard Eyer. *Teaching Your Children Values.* New York: Simon and Schuster, 1993.

Kreidler, William J., and Furlong, Lisa. *Adventures in Peacemaking.* Cambridge, Mass.: ESR, 1996.

Lasko, Wendy. *No Kidding Around.* Washington, D.C.: Information USA, Inc., 1992. [(available by calling (800) Kid Power)]

Lewis, Barbara. *Kid's Guide To Social Action.* Minneapolis: Free Spirit Publishing, 1990.

Tavris, Carol. *Anger:The Misunderstood Emotion.* New York: Simon and Schuster Trade, 1989.

Miscellaneous

Canter, Lee. *Parent Resource Guide.* Los Angeles: Lee Canter and Associates Inc., 1985.

_____. *Homework without Tears.* Los Angeles: Lee Canter and Associates Inc., 1987.

_____. *Winning the Chores Wars.* Los Angeles: Lee Canter and Associates Inc., 1994.

Index

(By game title and game category—artistic, dramatic, mental, and physical)

After each game I have noted the name of the ordinary situation under which the game is described in the book. Please Note that "Car" activities will usually work for walking and biking, and that most car activities can be done during dinner and visa versa. If the game falls into more than one modality, for example physcial as well as mental, I also try to note that.

Acknowledgements

This is my thank you to the following for their help over the years in making this book a reality.

To Pinky Zalkin, one of the most wonderful women in the world, for being essential to the book and TV series conception in 1986.

To Justina Klimkevich for having enough faith in me and this idea to have dedicated herself to do the desktop version of the book within my minuscule budget, and under an incredible deadline.

To genius game inventors Bernie DeKoven, Karl Rohnke, and Fred Schildmeyer for their suggestions of many wonderful games, and to Bob Gregson, another great game inventor for his consulting on my own game development.

To John Bradshaw for his foreword; to Jules Minton, Dave Bortman, Joseph Conarkov, Sam Williams, and dozens of other TV professionals who helped me over the years to produce and shop the TV version of Simple Fun FunOnTheRun! TM ; Patrick Wells and Dr. Manuel Jaffee of Minneapolis, for their wonderful generosity and belief in me; to Ed Asner, Jack Lemmon, Martin Sheen, Casey Kasem, Spike Lee, Christine Lavin and the many other celebrities who donated their interviews for this book and subsequent TV show; to Scot Grossman for his photographic genius and generosity; to Terry Hunt for his grant; to Lori Grace and Bonnie Karin for their loans; to Carolyn Permentier for her editorial help on one of the sections and help in testing out some of the games; to too many families to mention in Minneapolis (especially the Cambanes's, Kleinfelters, and Salones), and in Marin County, California, for allowing me to test many of these games; to my attornies Tom Gherardi and Eric Elias (Tom is the sharpest attorney and most wonderful one I know); to Mary Jane Ryan, my editor at Conari, for her faith, patience with my perfectionism, and perspicacity, to Will Glennon, Conari's co-publisher with Mary Jane, to his fairness; to Laura Marceau, the most patient and helpful production manager an author could hope for; to Brenda Knight and Sharon Donovan, Conari's sales and promotions directors, respectively; and to Suzanne Albertson for her hard work on making the book look good; to Karen Gilbert, Irene Ehrlich, and Karen Ehlirch for their editorial assistance in the book's later drafts; and to Kinko's (Westwood-Los Angeles, Sherman Oaks, Minneapolis and Astor Place, NY) and Copymat (Hollywood) for their generosity in xeroxing and computer services.

And finally, and most importantly, to my wife, Karen Ehrlich, for being absolutely essential to the book's nourishment and for my sustenance, which enabled me to finish the book. She took on the immense physical and emotional stress of not only the book's final stages, but that of the home videos and TV show pilot as well, all the while keeping her fulltime job without ever a complaint. She continues to be the sunshine of my life, almost always being willing to play and try something new. She is the best wife a man could ever hope to have.